The
Good
Eater

the true story of
one man's struggle with
binge eating disorder

RON SAXEN

New Harbinger Publications, Inc.

Publisher's Note

This publication is designed to provide accurate and authoritative information in regard to the subject matter covered. It is sold with the understanding that the publisher is not engaged in rendering psychological, financial, legal, or other professional services. If expert assistance or counseling is needed, the services of a competent professional should be sought.

Distributed in Canada by Raincoast Books

Copyright © 2007 by   Ron Saxen
                       New Harbinger Publications, Inc.
                       5674 Shattuck Avenue
                       Oakland, CA 94609
                       www.newharbinger.com

Cover image: Rubberball/Jupiter Images

Author photo on inside flap at right: Courtesy of Donna Olson

Interior photos: page 2 top & bottom: Courtesy of Frank Saxen; page 3 bottom: Courtesy of Frank Saxen; page 4 bottom: Sacramento Union Magazine, September 9, 1984. Reprinted by permission of the Special Collections Department, University of California Library, Davis; page 5: *Sports Fitness and Training*, Pantheon Books, a division of Random House, 1987; page 6 top: Courtesy of Donna Olson; page 7 ©2002 Crystal Cruises, Inc. Ships' Registry: The Bahamas; page 8: Courtesy of Jeff Sosnick

Cover design by Amy Shoup; Text design by Michele Waters-Kermes; Acquired by Melissa Kirk; Edited by Amy Johnson

Library of Congress Cataloging-in-Publication Data

Saxen, Ron.
   The good eater : the true story of one man's struggle with binge eating disorder / Ron Saxen.
      p. cm.
   ISBN-13: 978-1-57224-485-6
   ISBN-10: 1-57224-485-2
   1. Saxen, Ron. 2. Compulsive eaters—United States—Biography. 3. Models (Persons)—United States—Biography. I. Title.
RC552.C65S39 2007
362.196'85260092—dc22
[B]
                                 2006039642

09   08   07

10 9 8 7 6 5 4 3 2 1   First printing

Contents

1982–1985
The Insanity

1985–1996
The Road to Recovery

2002–2005

Acknowledgments

I would like to thank first of all Leslie Sosnick, the love of my life and the person truly responsible for giving me a story worth telling. I thank and promise a kidney to my sister Robin for her continuous encouragement and endless hours of editing when my writing truly sucked. Thanks also go to Penny Kramer for picking up where Robin left off; to Jeanne Ramsey for being my first willing reader that wasn't Leslie; to my agent, Sharlene Martin, for being a tireless advocate; to my editor, Melissa Kirk, for taking a chance and showing me a better way; to Heather Mitchener for remaining calm when I wasn't; to Amy Johnson for her finesse in the final polishing; to Jessica Kaye for her timely advice; to my brothers Rick and Robert for being there for me during my childhood; and to my father for having the guts to embrace the past so there can be a future.

1984

CHAPTER 1

Magic

"Please take a seat. I'll let them know you're here."

I look at the receptionist. Is she thinking, "He's cute," or "I can't believe this guy really thinks he's got what it takes to be a model"? I bet *she's* a model—she's gorgeous, a short-haired brunette with flawless makeup and a perfect smile.

I take my seat. It all feels wrong—bad. Nine months ago I weighed 267 pounds, 85 more than I do now. I was rotund and flabby, no one you'd want to imagine without the protective shield of his clothes—a joke for the pretty people, the jocks I longed to be and cheerleaders I longed to be with. I was the one at the dinner table eyeballing my fourths before most had finished their firsts, the one who ate three pounds of chocolate in sixth grade under the cover of darkness, the one who still thinks a good time consists of three Big Macs, a large order of fries, and a chocolate shake followed by four Hostess fruit pies and a half-gallon of Häagen-Dazs ice cream slathered with a pound of M&M's and a pint of hot fudge sauce—hardly a model.

Hunks and hunkettes with gleaming white teeth and perfect cheekbones stare down from the walls, judging me. A giant photo of a blonde bombshell hangs over the receptionist's desk, the kind of knockout who scares the hell out of me. Come to think of it, all the photos—men and women—scare the hell out of me. What am I doing here? Who am I kidding?

"Ron Saxen?"

I look up into the benign smile of a tall, thin woman with long, flowing hair. The lines around her eyes reveal age without denying beauty. She is flawlessly put together and smells like the perfume counter at Macy's. I surreptitiously wipe my sweaty palms on my pants.

"Yes, I'm Ron."

She stretches out one elegant hand. "My name is Sharon. Did you have a hard time finding us?"

My hand still partially moist, I shake hers. "No."

Great, a whopping one-word sentence. I'm known as a funny guy, and the best I can do is *no*. This is not going well.

As I follow her down the hallway, she says, "Andrew tells us we should take a look at you."

Perfect. She's doing this as a favor to Andrew—this is now a favor to a favor to a favor. As a favor, this cute girl I worked with introduced me to her neighbor who did some modeling. He then did her a favor by seeing me and recommending me to his agent, probably so the cute girl would go out with him. Once his agent says no to me, the circle of favors will finally be closed.

We enter an office. An older woman, who must have been a model at some point, looks up from her large desk. "Hello, I'm Barbara."

I sheepishly grab her hand, "Hi."

My voice does the puberty thing. It's not puberty, it's nerves—I'm twenty-one and so far I've demonstrated that I know a whole two words.

"Um, here's my portfolio. I finished it two weeks ago."

"Great! Let's take a look. Have a seat."

I spent three weeks posing for more than 500 photos. The cameraman was a wedding photographer looking to branch out; I was an experiment. *I* think the pictures look professional, but who am I to judge? While the photos were being shot, I was so hungry, I almost passed out.

It's weird to watch two ex-models scrutinizing photos of me while I sit right there, not thirty-six inches away. Maybe I should do some selling: "Am I cute or what?" Or maybe, "What's it gonna take to get you interested in this nice, previously-fat model?" No. I study the framed magazine covers that adorn the walls, check out the large bronze statues that sit on the table behind her desk. I bet each one is worth more than my entire estate...

I look at Barbara and Sharon. They aren't showing much in the way of emotion as they consider my worth. This can't be a good sign.

Three minutes later, they close my portfolio. Sharon stands up and smiles. "Ron, Barbara and I would like to speak alone. Will you please take a seat in the waiting room? We'll call you back when we're ready."

I know what this means: we're done. Well, that didn't take long. That's okay, I wasn't expecting much anyway. "Okay... of course... sure."

The receptionist looks up as I enter the lobby, and I smile uneasily as I return to the relative safety of my black leather chair. I bet they're doing a background check on me right now. "Sorry Ron, we've checked around and it's always been our policy not to let undercover fatties like you into the club. Why don't you go back to the all-you-can-eat buffet you came from? Security!"

It still amazed me that I'd even gotten this far. I'd been at the low end of one of my many yo-yo diets (260 to 225, 260 to 225, 260 to 225) when a customer at the coffee shop where I worked studied me for a second, then asked, "Are you a model?"

I remember wondering whether she was trying to be funny. Was this the punch line to a joke I'd missed the setup to? Or maybe she was just trying to score points with the Big Guy—"Come on, St. Peter, you've got to let me in. Remember when I was nice to that fat guy?"

But over the next few weeks, I got the modeling comment several more times. What had made my current diet different from past ones was that this time I'd gotten all the way down to 205. Finally, for kicks, I went to a bookstore and found a book on male models.

Most of the guys in it were still 20 to 30 pounds lighter than I was. I decided to go for it.

Damn, I'm hungry. It's one thirty and all I've had today is three cups of black coffee and a banana. At least I was able to get my workout done before this meeting. I'd like to see one of these pretty people run five miles, bike thirty miles, swim twenty-five Olympic-pool-sized laps, and then lift weights—all without putting any food in their stomach before three in the afternoon.

Until recently, I didn't know a body could be pushed this hard. The trick seems to be to listen with a different ear. When your body cries out in hunger, if you listen carefully, you can hear the chisel carving fat off your statue. If faintness overwhelms you, it's simply evidence that the tools can work no faster.

At three in the afternoon, when I'm ready to eat my first meal, I walk with conscious virtue into Skinny Haven, a restaurant that lists the calorie count of every item it serves. My usual, a Skinny Haven Banana Split, is beautifully chaste in its mere 335 calories. Sometimes, when I arrive at my job at six (I wait tables), I've kept my food intake for the day to under 500 calories. I still can't believe I'm down to 179 pounds. I haven't seen that number since I was thirteen.

Here comes Sharon.

"Ron, we're ready for you."

My heart feels like it's going to come out of my chest at any moment. The emotional overload has dulled my senses. This is so strange. I have no idea how to act. Everything seems backwards— the job requirements are based on values my parents taught me were sinful, like what's on the outside matters more than what's inside. According to my old religion, that's the sin of vanity. And a sin, if unrepented, would lead to my being burned to death and forgotten by all. I feel so uncomfortable. Why am I putting myself through this?

But I know the answer. I'm here because I want this one act, becoming a model, to do two things: to erase my embarrassing history of weakness and insanity and to force women to accept me as worthy—it's been almost three years now without a single date. I want magic—magic powerful enough to destroy the excruciating, ugly film of my life that perpetually plays in my head, magic that will kill the fat, ugly wrong Ron and anoint me as perfect.

"Ron, Sharon and I have made a decision."

For months, I've been starving myself, working out like a dog, and dreaming about a modeling career. I'm fried. I just want this to be over.

"Now, it's not our policy to sign someone off the street, someone with no experience, someone we've only met with for a few minutes."

This doesn't sound good.

"However, we'd like to offer you a one-year contract with our agency. We have the paperwork right here."

They stare at me, enjoying the surprise on my face. I don't know what to think. I never expected this to happen, I never thought magic could truly exist. How is it that nine months ago I was fat and ugly and now I'm one of the prettiest of the pretty people? I guess I always was who I am today—I just needed to master the art of punishment and starvation to make it visible.

"If you want to take it to a lawyer, you can."

I'm still dazed. "No, no, it's not a problem."

"Good. There's a fashion show in San Francisco in two weeks. You're in it. We also have a very important fashion show in seven weeks. It's one of the hottest shows, it's a big deal—and it's yours."

✳ ✳ ✳ ✳ ✳

That was 1984, and the final event that would set the wheels of a terrifying eating disorder into motion. Little did I know then that the magic I so desperately looked for was still twenty years away.

1968–1981

The Early Years

CHAPTER 2

The Great Adventure

The wrong Ron started out as a solution to a problem: keeping Dad's anger at bay. My first memory is of standing in my bedroom with my brother Robert when I was five years old, listening to my six-year-old brother Rick scream as my dad disciplined him. Being wrong Ron—eating fast and eating whether I was hungry or not—seemed to be the only way available to me to placate him.

It wasn't until I was fourteen that I started to get a feel for what was wrong with my family and who I was becoming.

* * * * *

Every year the Saxen family made a summer pilgrimage to our Promised Land: Ute, Iowa. My parents were both from there, and they'd go on and on about how wonderful it was: a wholesome town with clean air, no traffic, friendly people, and neighbors who'd pitch in to help harvest your crops if you were ailing—and yet, we didn't live there. Was I the only one who saw the flaw in this logic?

Every summer, as we reached Donner Pass, 7,208 feet above sea level, I drank in the granite mountains that encircle the clear, blue Donner Lake far below. It was a vista to beat all hell. We passed it twice every summer; each time I wondered why a bunch of pioneers who got stranded one winter and ate each other by spring got huge landscape features named after them. Why Donner Pass but not Mount Lee Harvey Oswald or Lake Hitler?

Ute was 1,830 miles from our home outside the tiny farm town of Knightsen, California. By the time I was ten I knew how to get to Iowa without a map. Made me feel smart. Some kids would have hated being stuck in a car with two older brothers and two younger sisters for two solid days. Not me. I looked forward to the trip every year. As we drove, I'd imagine the great explorers seeing the land for the first time, how curious they must have been, wondering what was over the next hill and around the next bend. I even liked going to places we'd visited many times already. But this summer, our trip was different.

First, we were dropping my oldest brother Rick off for the Saxen version of a Mormon mission. Long ago, my dad had spent a summer painting bridges in Yellowstone Park. It had been a crucial life experience for him, something that had made a man out of him. Now, at eighteen, it was Rick's turn. So, instead of driving straight to Iowa, we were headed north to West Yellowstone, where we'd drop Rick off. In two weeks we'd come back to check on him and make sure he was okay. If he was thriving, he could stay, if not, we'd pick him up. I was hoping he didn't starve—or get eaten. I didn't want to come back and find out the town was named after him.

Rick's opportunity proved that our life at home could finally end. I just needed to survive a few more years, and then—freedom from our long boot camp. And boot camp it was: Just like Richard Gere in *An Officer and a Gentleman*, we had to have our beds made without a wrinkle, our shoes shined, and our hair combed. Even dinner had at least fifty rules: napkin on the left, a complete set of silverware displayed from left to right, water at the two-o'clock position, salad dressings lined up by height. Raise your fork straight up and then straight into your mouth. Elbows off the table. Ask to be excused loudly and clearly: "Sir, may I please be excused from the table?" If you weren't loud enough he'd ignore you. If you asked improperly—or asked properly but he'd forgotten that you had—the penalty could be a whipping you'd never forget.

Rick's freedom had taken on even more meaning three weeks before our trip, when we'd accidentally broken our silence to our friend Scott about life inside Cell Block Saxen.

* * * * *

"My parents don't do that! No kids I know live that way." My brothers and I just looked at each other silently. Scott drove the point home: "No way. If my dad did that shit, I'd be gone."

We'd told him about Robert's latest whipping. Mom had found an expensive lock-blade knife in his underwear drawer.

"So, where did you get the knife?" Dad asked, already angry.

Rick and I sat in the family room, listening, knowing we could be next. When Dad lost it, no one was safe.

"I bought it."

"You bought it? Where'd you get the money to buy it, Robert?"

"It's money I saved."

"Bullshit. You're lying to me. You either stole the knife or you stole the money. Which is it, Robert?"

Robert was screwed. Rick and I knew he was telling the truth. The only problem was he got the money selling illegal fireworks—not exactly an answer he wanted to tell Dad.

"I'm going to ask you one more time, Robert."

The chance to be spared had passed. We heard Robert scream as all 225 pounds of my father rained burning leather on his naked skin. In all my years, Dad's punishments were by far the worst pain I've ever had or imagined. On television, no one yells when they're punched. But when a mutinous sailor is strapped to the mast and whipped, he screams in agony. That's accurate. I know, too, why Captain Bligh tied his men up before whipping them. When a body is whipped it tends to writhe uncontrollably.

Dad told us we shouldn't complain about our whippings because in the Bible Jesus was whipped—but He was whipped with a cat-o'-nine-tails which had nine straps with metal tips to gouge out chunks of flesh. I can't speak for my brothers, but I know I never felt lucky that I was just whipped with a simple belt. When it was over, my butt was often flaming red in patches; when the end of the leather snapped around my hips, I'd get welts on my side. Once in a while, Dad would miss, and the imprint of his belt, holes and all, would appear on my back. Backs don't seem to handle blows as well as butts.

The only difference about this particular whipping—the whipping we told Scott about—was that it was severe enough that Robert had to risk ridicule by refusing to shower after gym in order to hide his bruises.

When Scott told us we were different it was like a dam bursting. We'd held our lives inside for so long. Poor Scott—there was just one of him and three of us unloading.

For my testimony I offered up an incident from three years earlier: Twice a month, the whole family piled into our station wagon and drove from our small town in the Northern California delta to the closest big town—Antioch—to get groceries. Rick, Robert, and I would wait in the car while Mom and Dad shopped.

"I'll be watching you guys from the store," Dad said. "Any fooling around and you'll be sorry."

Since we were parked far from the store and the supermarket's windows were covered with signs, I couldn't figure out how he planned to watch us, but to be safe, we took turns as lookouts while entertaining ourselves playing I Spy.

"I see Ben."

"That's easy. The Ben Franklin five-and-ten across the parking lot."

"I see Moses."

"Don't cheat. There's no Moses. Pick something real or lose your turn."

"Okay, I see a hose."

Rick saw Mom and Dad first. They were headed our way, weaving two overloaded carts through the mass of parked cars. Dad opened the back.

"I saw what you kids were doing. What did I tell you?"

We looked at each other, stunned.

"You boys think I don't know what you're doing? I told you..."

I scanned my brain. What had we done?

The groceries were loaded, Dad was in the car, and I still had no idea what we'd done, when Dad hit Robert. Not much of a blow—it was more startling than anything.

"Don't you flinch when I'm punishing you."

A backhanded fist headed my way. Oh no, I shouldn't have ducked—now he'd be pissed. But it's hard not to flinch when you see a blow coming. He reached back again—

"Frank, stop."

Mom grabbed Dad's arm. That had never happened before. Robert and I stared at each other. Mom had never protected us or even crossed Dad before. Did she realize we hadn't done anything? That this punishment was completely unjustified?

"Frank, there's people watching... I think they saw you."

"So what, they're my kids."

"What if they call the police?"

"What are you talking about? I can discipline my children however I see fit."

"You're right, Frank, it just looks bad."

"I don't care how it looks."

Still, Dad quickly turned around and started the car and we left.

Driving home from the store I kept thinking, why would someone call the police? Was Dad breaking the law? In the end, I decided it must be one of those things that was different about our family and our church. However, listening to Scott, it all started to make sense.

* * * * *

Puking out our lives to Scott was like getting a big old fat syringe of morphine—awesome until it wore off and the horrible pain returned twice as strong now that we knew our life wasn't normal.

The truth didn't set us free. It just made us feel unlucky. We didn't want to think that our lives were different, that we were different. When Dad said, "You think I'm harder on you than other parents? You're wrong," we wanted to believe him. Who wants to know you're different when you can't do anything about it?

They say you shouldn't shoot the messenger; if I could've given Scott some advice, I'd have told him, "Don't tell someone he's naked unless you're prepared to give him some clothes." I'd have preferred to hear, "Rick, Robert, Ron, just to let you know, compared to the rest of the world, you've been doing hard time. But don't worry about it—here are three get-out-of-jail-free cards and keys to your new house in Disneyland. Mickey says hi."

* * * * *

The city of Reno and the vast Nevada desert lay before us. I tried to imagine the fun that happened behind the walls of the casinos, fun I couldn't have until I was twenty-one—a forever away. Somewhere around here, maybe in the mass of buildings or outside of town, was a place called Mustang Ranch. Rick had told us about it again and again. At Mustang Ranch beautiful prostitutes came out in scanty lingerie and lined up for your choosing. Rick said if you were a virgin they had special girls who would take you by the hand and lead you through the process. That's what I wanted.

Reno's slogan, their sales pitch, amused me: "Welcome to Reno, the Biggest Little City in the World." My family didn't fall for it, didn't stop. My family knew a thing or two about selling. When it came to selling, we all knew Dad was awesome—he never let us forget it and he had the assets to back it up. He'd sold Fuller Brushes, Kirby Vacuum Cleaners, and Allstate insurance before he opened up his own insurance brokerage firm, the biggest and best around.

Even during his nine years in the Navy he'd always had something cooking. He cut sailors' hair for a dollar, and started car rental businesses in Guam, Alaska, and the Philippines. He even worked on crab boats in Alaska while serving his country in a top-secret communications position. One of his favorite sayings was, "Everything in this world is sold by someone."

To mold us into selling machines, Dad gave us no allowance. Instead, he'd tell us, "There's always money to be made, you've just got to go get it." So we did, not always legally. We sold candy bars, peanuts, chocolates, pens, seeds, fireworks, and even stuff we made ourselves.

When I was twelve and Robert was thirteen, we found a way to make the Knightsen Elementary School candy sale a little more profitable—for us anyway. Our success provided me with tons of surplus chocolate bars—and ended up reinforcing the lesson that food was a medicine I could use to ease my anxiety.

* * * * *

The Knightsen Elementary School candy sale raised money for school sports; prizes were awarded to whoever sold the most candy. The Saxen boys took first place four years running. There was no way anyone could touch us—we treated it like a job and crushed anyone who dared to challenge us.

Although we usually took the bus, during candy sale season we got curbside service—pickup and delivery to a neighboring town. Mom had barely pulled away after dropping us at our usual place—the railroad tracks near the A&W root beer stand—when Robert started explaining his scheme:

He first reminded me that, all by ourselves, during this contest we'd sell about 2,000 candy bars at fifty cents apiece. That meant the school got 500 dollars, the candy company got 500 dollars—and we got 20 dollars as a prize for selling the most.

"Does that sound fair to you?"

I shook my head no.

"If we stop selling right now, we'll still win the contest."

"So?"

"So? So, I say from now on we raise the price to a dollar and keep the extra fifty cents for ourselves."

"We can't do that, we'll get busted."

"Don't be such a wuss. Who's gonna know? We won't sell in Knightsen—the town's been beat to death anyway. We'll just make sure to go to houses we haven't hit before."

"But a *dollar* for a candy bar?" It was 1974; a regular candy bar cost ten cents, a large one fifteen.

"It's for charity, people expect to pay more."

When it came to plots and schemes, Robert was always a champion. I think it was because he was so smart; he was only thirteen months older than I was, but his mind always worked at a much higher level than mine. If there was an angle, Robert would find it. By the end of the day we'd sold fifty-two candy bars between us: thirteen dollars for the school, thirteen for the candy company, and *twenty-six* dollars for me and Robert.

Two days later, I lay awake in bed, petrified. Mom kept a notepad filled with my transgressions—that day these included not taking the garbage out on time and whining about missing *Hogan's Heroes*; she'd give it to Dad when he got home. Although Dad usually didn't get home until after ten, if he got mad enough, he'd wake me up for a whipping, no matter what time it was.

A few years previously, I'd tried praying to God as I lay waiting, dreading Dad's return—I'd even pinch and hit myself, hoping God would see that I'd been disciplining myself and consider using His power to stop Dad from punishing me. It hadn't worked.

This particular night, as my feet and hands became sweaty with fear—I had to keep pulling back the sheets to let them dry—I suddenly realized that my closet was filled with boxes of Ghirardelli five-ounce chocolate bars, chocolate bars that I now even had the money for. I got out of bed.

The smell and taste of the creamy chocolate, the warm feeling in my stomach—I felt better immediately. The only problem was that my relief lasted only as long as a chocolate bar did. I returned to the closet again and again. When I finally stopped I'd eaten nine candy bars—almost three pounds of chocolate.

This massive amount of chocolate in my belly successfully put me to sleep and out of my misery. I woke up the next morning to discover I'd survived the evening without being whipped. Later I buried the chocolate-bar wrappers deep in the trash can outside. I knew eating nine candy bars was wrong, but they'd brought such sweet relief... I invested every penny of my share of the profits in more chocolate.

Robert and I never did get busted for skimming off the top, but there was hell to pay when Robert couldn't explain why he had a better Polaroid camera than Dad.

I thanked God for candy.

* * * * *

We drove past Reno and struck out into the Nevada desert on good old Interstate 80, the one that went from coast to coast, sea to shining sea. The next 400 miles were all sagebrush, the only breaks being the towns and the road signs that went with them. I don't know if people really read signs in cities, but I can guarantee you they do in deserts. One year Robert and I decided to count all the signs between California and Iowa. Taking shifts—one person napped while the other stood watch—we came up with a total of 3,819, not counting traffic signs or mile markers.

In recent years our family had switched to one of the new nine-passenger station wagons. Mom and Dad sat in the front, Rick and my two sisters—Rebecca who was nine, and Robin who was almost seven—in the middle, and Robert and I in the back. Since we faced backwards, Robert and I were always the last to see anything. The upside was we could have fun with the other cars—waving, making faces, putting our fingers in our nose, and doing the rabbit-ears thing—all without Dad seeing.

"Is anyone hungry?" went out to the entire station wagon.

I'd had a big breakfast and I'd been snacking. But coming from my dad, that question was like the London air raid sirens going off.

No one said anything. I couldn't lie and say I was hungry—that would be a sin. Come on Rick, Robert. Couldn't count on Rebecca, she was as finicky as they came. If you gave her a cup of water she'd wrinkle her nose and say, "Yuck, this is too watered down."

Silence. Then I figured out how to answer:

"Dad, I can eat."

For a moment my words just hung there.

"So, you can eat, huh? Ron, you know what, we believe that you can."

Even from my backwards spot I could tell Mom and Dad were both smiling. Robert nodded to me—he got it.

"All right, since Ron can eat, we'll stop and get burgers in Winnemucca. We'll be there in about fifteen minutes."

I was humiliated by the smiles. In my family, food was forever linked to me. In a word-association test if my family was given "food" they'd say "Ron." It wasn't just the comfort binges, it wasn't just the attempts to appease Dad, I had a voracious appetite. The three together became impossible to control. Food brought me too much pleasure.

* * * * *

"Rick, why don't you say the blessing."

It was Tuesday, our last dinner at home before we left for our road trip. Just Mom and us kids sat at the table; during the week Dad left for work before we got up in the morning and came home after we'd gone to bed—fine by us.

My mouth watered while Rick thanked God for Mom's cooking and reminded us not to forget all those starving people in India. For a moment I felt guilty then shrugged it off. Maybe God didn't feed them because they were in the wrong church or they'd done something to piss Him off.

"In God's name, amen."

I loved amen. It was so positive—prayers' end and a starter pistol shot all rolled into one. For firsts we were allowed two pieces of chicken and a full plate of everything else: a mound of mashed potatoes, green beans, salad, Mom's homemade bread—when it was fresh, it was as good as cake—and a flood of gravy.

Rick and Robert chatted about school and their day. They always did; it worked well for me: I always got first dibs on seconds. Not to mention the time it typically took Rick to make his food look pretty—I was always waiting for him to sign it. As usual I was ready for seconds while Rick hadn't even started chewing yet.

"Mom, may I have seconds, please?"

"Yes, you may."

I was the only chunky one in the family, but Mom didn't seem to mind. I always figured it was because on the farm in Iowa, people always ate big.

For seconds I was only allowed one piece of chicken—but I knew how to work the system:

"Mom, since nobody likes the back or the neck, can I have them without it counting as my piece?"

"Does anybody want the back or neck?"

Heads shook.

"Go ahead, Ron."

Now the neck and the back didn't have much meat on them, but they did have the thick, greasy, batter-fried coating. Two necks, two backs, and a wing—perfect.

I ate fast—it was uncomfortable to eat any other way. For me it was always full speed ahead until the plate was clean. Why slow down before the task was done?

"Mom?"

"Yes, Ron?"

"Can I have thirds?"

"Has everyone who wants seconds had seconds?"

I wasn't getting thirds because I was hungry, and it wasn't because Dad was about to come home and kick my ass—thirds were about the simple pleasure of eating, a pleasure I'd learned to crave. When I ate candy in the middle of the night worrying about a possible midnight spanking, it did more than ease my pain, it also gave me pleasure—and pleasure was good any time I could get it.

It was my job to clear the table, a job I'd had for six years, and one I didn't want to give up. This was the part that took a little finesse. See, I would've loved to have eaten fourths, but Mom didn't permit it—legislation passed specifically for me.

"Mom, would you like me to bring your Bible and the church magazine into the family room?"

"I'll get them myself. You finish clearing the table."

That took care of Mom—one down, one to go. Robert had already started soaking the glasses in the sink.

"Come on Ron, quit screwing around. Put the leftovers away."

"Give me a second. Go ahead and start washing."

With Mom in the family room, and Robert rinsing the glasses, I turned to the food still on the table. Who needed a spoon? Caveman-style I dug into the creamy mashed potatoes with my hand.

"What are you doing, Ron?"

Swallowing as quickly as I could, "Nothing."

"Yeah, right."

With my back to Robert, I headed to the safety of the bathroom—to clean my fingers, drink a little water, and check for a potato mustache.

Dinner was over.

* * * * *

"What do you want, Ron?"

"I'll take a double cheeseburger, large fries, and a chocolate shake."

That was my usual order at the burger places in Winnemucca—the biggest of everything plus a chocolate shake. We took the food to our favorite park. In past years Mom had brought fried chicken and potato salad from home. Now we bought burgers, but we still went to the exact same park in Winnemucca. Just as my family associated Ron with food, I associated Winnemucca with lunch.

We sat at a picnic table under a shade tree. Even though the thermostat at the Fosters Freeze had read 97 degrees, the shade and a stiff breeze made it pleasant enough. As usual, I finished while everyone else was still eating.

I can still remember the first time my father challenged me to an eating contest.

"Ron, do you think you're a fast eater?"

"Yes, sir."

The whole family sat around the big Formica table in the dining room. At five, I was about to learn my first and best way to keep Dad happy.

"Do you want to race? I bet you can't beat me. Want to race?"

"Yes, sir."

"Okay, get your fork ready. No fair putting anything on your fork yet. On your mark, get set—go!"

I quickly finished my meat. Meat was the slowest thing to eat. Mashed potatoes were good, no chewing required. Then just the beans and the rest of my bread. The trick was to not chew too much, to just keep swallowing. A couple of mouthfuls more...

"Done, Dad, I'm done!"

"Good job, Ron. You beat me. You beat your brothers too. See, Donna? Your son cleaned his entire plate. Robert's still picking at his food, Rick's not halfway finished, but Ron's done."

"I won! I'm finished. I'm first. I'm fast, huh Dad? Huh, Mom?"

"Yes, Ron, you're faster than everybody."

At home, anything I could do to please my parents and maintain the fragile peace was a good thing. My parents assigned me "Devour anything that isn't nailed down!" and I took it. But I admit it—I loved the drug they hooked me on.

Mom always told me how happy she was with my eating. Said I was the best eater of the five kids and the only child to always finish his food. But it wasn't just my parents—all my life I heard other parents say, too, "You're such a good eater Ron, have more Ron, I made extra just for you, I wish my kids ate like Ron."

But at the same time, I knew I was different, and it bothered me. Why else would Mom say as I got older, "The way you inhale your food, do you even taste it?" I tried eating normally, like everybody else, but it was so awkward—it was painfully slow. The food screamed at me, "Hurry up and eat me, you moron! What are you waiting for? You better hurry up or you won't get first dibs on seconds..."

I knew there must be something wrong with me.

* * * * *

Instead of crossing the salt flats to Salt Lake City as we usually did, we turned north onto Highway 93 at Wells and headed toward our new destination: Jackpot, Nevada.

Why did I look forward to our two-week vacations so much? Normally I dreaded spending any time in Dad's presence. He wasn't home much, but when he was the chances of pain skyrocketed. You didn't have to do anything wrong to be punished. But on the vacations, Dad rarely disciplined us.

In part, this was because Dad loved road trips—so much so that on a road trip his personality would completely change. When a good song came onto the radio he'd sing along. To entertain us, he'd tell us about a movie we hadn't seen. He'd go from beginning to end without leaving out a single detail—sometimes the spoken version lasted longer than the movie itself. He loved spotting deer and antelope around us and we always had a contest for who saw the first and who saw the most animals. His happiness probably also came from returning down memory lane to a simpler time in his life, when he didn't have the pressures of running a business and taking care of a family of seven—something he complained about from time to time. I think he also liked seeing old friends, not only because they *were* old friends, but because he left Iowa a skinny young kid with little money and came back a successful businessman.

On road trips there was also another, obvious deterrent to disciplining us—witnesses. Dad rarely disciplined us outside of our own home—probably because there aren't very many places where shrill screams and the sound of leather hitting a child's skin are tolerated. The walls of the hotels we stayed in were too thin, as were those of Grandpa and Grandma's house in Iowa. He could've pulled off in the desert and done it there, but, even then, he might have been seen. Who knows, maybe for him knowing that whipping us was off-limits for a few weeks was relaxing. I always wondered if being on vacation was what it was like to be in a normal family. To this day my favorite thing to do in all the world is a road trip—I've never had my fill. Sometimes I think I could get in a car and never stop driving.

In Jackpot, we all waited in the wagon while Dad saw what kind of rate he could get for rooms with his superior selling skills. Jackpot reminded me a lot of Wendover, also a border town. Both towns—Wendover is on the Nevada/Utah border, Jackpot the Idaho/Nevada border—are last/first stops for fun in Nevada and located where no ordinary town would want to be: in the middle of nowhere.

Instead of "The Silver State" on Nevada's license plates, I always thought it should be "The Sinning State." And I meant that in a good way—if you were hankering for sin, it was important to know where to go. Nevada seemed like a special fort for parents, a secret place like I had in the bushes behind the orchard—a place where I could go to look at dirty magazines and cuss up a blue streak in peace.

"We're staying here. We can either unpack, or go to dinner first. Is anybody hungry? And Ron—we know you can eat."

* * * * *

In another few hours we would be arriving in West Yellowstone, the beginning of Rick's big adventure. Over the years, when our lives were particularly unbearable, we boys would dream of escaping to Wyoming to live off the land, just like old Liver Eating Johnson in the Robert Redford movie *Jeremiah Johnson*. Now Rick was going to get to do it for real.

The road to West Yellowstone took us by the Snake River Canyon. Every time we crossed over it I strained to see the place where Evel Knievel jumped it in his X-1 Skycycle. I'd been so nervous for him. The canyon was so wide—where did someone get the courage to do something like that?

"Rick?"

"Yes, Mom?"

"Did you pack your Bible?"

"Yes, ma'am."

"Just because there's no World Wide Church of God up here, doesn't mean you can seek your own pleasure on Saturday. I expect you to read the Bible and observe God's day from sunset to sunset."

"Yes, ma'am."

The World Wide Church of God had been our church for almost ten years at this point. According to Mom and Dad, we were the Chosen Ones. To the rest of the world—our friends and extended family members—we were just strange. It was odd: Dad was the boss in our house, but it was Mom who had signed us up with the church.

* * * * *

The first we kids knew of it was when two men in black suits rang our doorbell. I was five years old. The two men looked like Sergeant Friday and Officer Gannon from *Dragnet*. Since Dad was at work, the men went into the kitchen to speak to Mom alone.

"What are they doing, Rick?"

"How should I know? Why don't you look?"

"I can't—Mom told us to stay in the family room."

"Just ask for a glass of water."

It seemed like a good idea.

"Mom?"

"I thought I told you to stay in the family room."

"I just want a glass of water."

All of our cereal boxes were out on the table; the men seemed to be reading them. Rick's cowboy holster with the silver pistols lay with the boxes.

I reported back to my brothers. Rick was immediately concerned about his pistols.

Almost an hour later we heard, "You've got the list of all the things you need to do, Mrs. Saxen. We look forward to seeing you on Saturday."

The door shut. I knew something important had changed.

Mom called us into the kitchen. The kitchen table was strewn with toys and cereal boxes. We all listened eagerly. Mom said we'd been doing bad things for years—playing with the wrong toys, eating the wrong foods, watching the wrong TV, and not going to church. But now we'd joined the right church.

I didn't understand how eating Fruit Loops, Cheerios, and Raisin Bran made us bad people, but obviously Mom did. She told us, "The world's going to end in four years and all the bad people will be burned to death. We're lucky—we found out just in time."

An hour later, our garbage can was overflowing with cereal boxes and plastic guns.

As the years passed and I began to understand the church Mom had brought us into, I added another person to the list of people who made my life miserable: God.

* * * * *

West Yellowstone seemed as magical in reality as it did in our dreams of escape. Clean, pine-scented mountain air wafted from the surrounding green forests and slipped around A-frame buildings that begged for snow—I loved snow.

We drove briefly around town, to give Rick a tour, then found him a motel. Before we left to continue on to Iowa, Dad gave Rick his instructions:

"First thing you need to do is find a job. Just like in selling, the best thing to do is knock on doors. Hit every restaurant in town. Then you need to find a cheaper place to live. Now somewhere around here they've got those two-person, one-room cabins that are basically two cots and a fridge. They're not the best, but they're cheap. We'll be back in two weeks."

And just like that, Dad removed Rick's chains, releasing him to his great adventure. As we drove away and Rick disappeared into the distance I knew that one day, when I was eighteen, I too would be set free. Unfortunately, the mental chains of childhood proved much more durable than the physical, lasting well beyond age eighteen.

CHAPTER 3

Hello, Satan

There's no excuse for the boredom that is the 435-mile, straight-as-an-arrow, flat-as-a-pancake road running through central Nebraska's endless cornfields. Would it have hurt them to put a bend in the road or get an earthmover in to push up some dirt? Or if they were too lazy for that, the least they could have done is throw up some signs—the price of a bushel of corn, pig facts, *anything* for crying out loud. I'm sure the suicide rate in central Nebraska is artificially low just because there's nothing to jump off.

On the other side of that hell was Grandpa and Grandma Cooper's house in Ute, Iowa, population 472 and my own personal Garden of Eden. Here, in addition to the vacation from Dad's discipline, was a Grandpa who tried to defend me and a lunch regularly as large as dinner. But like any Garden of Eden, this one too had its snakes...

* * * * *

Somewhere during the last twenty miles before Ute, the scenery changed to wonderful. Flatness became hills, endless fields of corn became rivers and trees—this was a place with character. We passed Carl Dall's pond, our favorite place to fish. Some days the catch was so strong that at night, after I'd closed my eyes to sleep I could still see my red bobber diving under the water.

As we drove through the two blocks that made up downtown Ute, I checked to make sure that the little store with the creaky wooden floor where I did my candy shopping was still in business. We passed the laundromat—hopefully it still had its hot chocolate machine, at only ten cents a cup. I always got three servings. We passed the park. And then there was the happiest place I knew: Grandpa and Grandma's house.

Robert and I climbed out the back of the station wagon. Even if I closed my eyes I'd know exactly where I was—here was the cool of the tall shade trees, the smell of cut wood coming from Uncle Wade and Grandpa's wood shop, the rustling of leaves in a gentle breeze, the squeaks of the porch screen door... Grandpa and Grandma's.

Grandpa, Grandma, and Uncle Wade—who lived with them—were old. Mom always said she was an afterthought, born twenty-seven years after Uncle Wade. Grandpa was born in 1892, Grandma in 1896. We called her Little Grandma because she was: she was four foot ten inches, a woman who was short all her life and shrank further with age. Next to Grandpa, who was over six feet tall, Grandma looked like a child.

Grandpa walked with a noticeable limp. Years of farming and hard labor had taken a toll on his body. He'd broken both collar-bones, both legs, one hip, and one arm; at the age of four, he'd lost an eye after a pair of scissors was accidentally left within reach of his little hands. Grandpa was the only person who ever came to my defense. Grandpa didn't go to church—said it was nothing more than a gathering of hypocrites. So when Mom announced I had to leave the TV room because Batman was against our religion, Grandpa lit into her:

"This church of yours says my grandson can't watch this show with his grandfather?" he said. "I thought I raised you better than that!"

In the end Grandpa lost, though—it's hard to argue with some-one who has God on her side. But I appreciated the effort.

One thing I loved about Iowa was lunch: lunch was a huge meal, just like dinner. Of course in Iowa they called lunch dinner and dinner supper, but whatever they were called, it meant *two* opportunities to pig out. As I slid my suitcase under the bed in the guestroom, I could already smell the roast beef, sweet potatoes, and apple pies cooking in the kitchen. My first pig-out was just minutes away.

* * * * *

In Iowa I would be forever remembered as the cookie baron. Whenever I could get Little Grandma alone I would ask for a cookie. When she agreed I would then say, "Can I have two please?" continuing to raise the amount until either I got to seven or so or got busted by Mom. If I managed to get away with seven I'd eat four and squirrel the other three away in my suitcase—my emergency stress kit. If there turned out to be no need to medicate, I'd pick a night to have a cookie party and wolf down the dozen or so cookies I'd hoarded.

* * * * *

While I reloaded my plate from the overflowing dining room table, the adults mapped out our time in Iowa. There'd be dinners at Uncle Vernon and Aunt Leona's just down the street, a visit to Uncle Dick and Aunt Norma's in Omaha, and then one big get-together at Grandpa and Grandma's. What was important to me and Robert was the fishing; it looked like we'd have three or four days of it. Unfortunately the following day was Saturday, God's day, which meant we had to drive two hours to church in Sioux Falls, South Dakota. No matter what the distance, it was our obligation to go to the closest World Wide Church of God, even if it was 120 miles away.

For me, church sucked the color out of the day. God's day was black and white. On God's day there was no sunshine, there were no birds singing, no gentle breeze in the trees—no beauty. Time and progress stopped; nothing was accomplished. Apparently God wanted it that way.

The minister in Sioux Falls, Mr. Waterhill, used to be our minister in California. He had two daughters who were Rick's age; they were hot. A few years back, when we went over their house for dinner, the prettier one told me a dirty joke. I didn't get it, but pretended I did. She didn't buy it. Three years later, sitting in a quiet classroom, the joke flashed into my brain and I suddenly got it—and embarrassed myself a second time trying to choke back my laughter. She got me twice.

Two things made our church stand out from other churches. First, we were hard core: members had to pay the church 20 percent of their gross wages for tithing and church functions, go to church every Saturday, and obey all the rules or they were out. There was no middle ground. I respected that. Second, we had a lot of rules most churches didn't. I learned early on what was in store for my friends who didn't follow those rules.

* * * * *

"Since your friends at school aren't in our church," Mom explained, "they'll have to go through the Tribulation. When the end of the world comes in 1984, one-third of them will die from famine and pestilence, and one-third from war." But there was a ray of hope. "After that," she said, "God will resurrect them and give them one more chance. If they don't accept the church then, they'll be burned to a cinder."

Horrified, I said, "So, Danny, Brett, Greg, and Wesley will all die?"

"Most likely."

"And Mrs. Bun, my third grade teacher?" Mrs. Bun was a teacher I liked a lot.

"Yes."

At school I found myself looking at my classmates in a detached way. I alone knew their fate. I alone knew the horror that lay in their future. I watched my friends laughing and playing dodgeball, completely unaware they were doomed, and envisioned their emaciated naked corpses piled up like in the pictures I'd seen of Auschwitz.

"Mom? Why doesn't everyone just join our church?"

"Because God hasn't opened their minds yet."

"Why doesn't He open everyone's mind right now then?"

"God decides when the time is right."

Many of our church's rules and actual practices didn't seem to fit together right to me. A few years later, when I asked Mom why our church owned two Gulfstream jets, she said, "So Mr. Armstrong can preach the Gospel as a witness unto all nations."

"I thought you couldn't join the church until God opened your mind."

"Right."

"So, what good does it do for Mr. Armstrong to fly around in a jet witnessing people if their minds aren't open?"

"Well... um... Let me see. You know, it's kind of complicated." A few seconds later: "Uh... God says that there are many things we don't understand. We'll know eventually. Our minds can't comprehend everything right now."

I had a hunch Mr. Armstrong had jets because we gave him the money to buy them. Maybe it was a sin for someone so important to fly commercial?

* * * * *

As usual, we arrived at the church in Sioux Falls an hour early. Going to our church—whether in South Dakota or in California—was a four-hour ordeal. Our church held the record for length of overall service. We had one hour before the service itself for fellowship—hanging out and rapping with each other; showing up at the last second and leaving immediately afterward was frowned upon—followed by a service that was two hours long or longer, winding up with another hour of fellowship afterward. As a result I'd perfected the art of daydreaming my way through church—a habit which could get me into trouble if I didn't watch it. Of course, Robert was the first to catch on to my time passing technique.

* * * * *

"How'd you like the sermon, Ron?"

Robert was messing with me.

"It was good. How'd you like it?"

"You're so full of shit. You weren't even listening."

"I was too."

"How come for two hours you've only got one page of notes? And when the minister cited scripture I didn't see you turning any pages."

"I'm trying something new. I find that I don't get as much out of it if I have to take notes and turn pages."

I was lying of course. I'd been imagining my own book of Exodus in which Moses confronted the pharaoh with a John Wayne swagger:

"Now you listen to me, Pilgrim, let my people go. No? Fine. High noon at the Pyramid of Giza, my army against yours."

Right when the Egyptians were standing their tallest, looking invincible in their chariots and body armor, the Israelites pulled out Thompson sub-machine guns from under their togas—made the parting of the Red Sea unnecessary, but Moses did it anyway for entertainment.

Battle stories were good, but I couldn't do much with the plague stories. God killing all the first born sons in Egypt—how was that fair?

"But Mom, those kids had nothing to do with what was going on. Some of them may have been really good kids."

"Well, they were a bad nation, and God needed to punish them. God has His reasons."

It made me glad I wasn't the first born—and sorry for my oldest brother Rick. If God could kill innocent children once to make a point, He could do it again. Apparently God worked a lot like Dad: you didn't have to be guilty to be punished.

God and Dad became a team in my mind—both irrational, both with rules that were hard to follow, and both with a thirst for harsh punishment. Dad was punishment in the present and God was punishment in the future. To me, God seemed worse because He had no respect for privacy—like the KGB, only worse. Not only could He see everything you did when you were alone, He even knew your thoughts.

* * * * *

The Sioux Falls congregation was large, 500 people, and it met in the city's Veterans' Hall. Maybe that was another reason Saturdays seemed so drab—our congregations always held services in huge barn-like veterans' halls that were colorless, lifeless, and old. When I asked Mom why we didn't have our own churches like everybody else, she said it would be a waste of money since the world was coming to an end soon anyway.

Spending Saturday at a strange church sucked. We didn't know anybody so we just stood around looking stupid. True, this also meant that the girls there didn't know how uncool I was, but I knew trying to talk to them would be a disaster—I was better off just keeping my mouth shut.

We found six seats toward the front. The chairs had a little padding—a rare butt plus. And so far it was cool—another plus as a hot and steamy hall could make the service feel ten times as long. The routine was three songs and then the opening prayer, followed by a thirty-minute sermonette. If the minister had a sense of humor, or was at least a little alive, it made a world of difference. If not, I'd be forced to put on my own mental movie. I decided today's feature for me—and for eavesdropping God—would be "Noah and His Yellow Submarine."

"Brethren of Sioux Falls, the Bible tells us the Devil is a worthy opponent. Just look at Halloween, Satan's day. It attacks the young by plying them with candy and leading them to believe that witches and warlocks are harmless."

Our family had that lesson down. Every year like clockwork, we brought our notes to school to excuse us from Halloween parties. We also skipped pagan activities like drawing witches and bunnies and decorating the class Christmas tree, as well as Christmas and Easter pageants.

In fourth grade I got a Halloween surprise.

* * * * *

"You boys wait outside the classroom until your mothers come to pick you up," Mrs. Shelly said, patting me and Tony on our shoulders.

From where we stood I could see lots of kids in costume—there was a Superman, an Indian, a witch. And even though the teacher offered—and I wanted them—there were no cupcakes for me. They were Halloween cupcakes and that made them—

Wait a minute—why was Tony out here with me?

"How come your mom's picking you up, Tony?"

"Because Halloween is against our religion."

I knew Tony wasn't in our church. "What religion?"

"We're Jehovah's Witnesses."

Tony said his church didn't do Christmas or Easter either, and they went to church on Saturdays just like we did.

"Are you guys the ones that go walking around knocking on doors on Saturdays?"

"Yes," he said, looking away.

"Yeah, one time your church people came to our door and my dad started telling them about our church. Then he gave them some of our material."

At that point Mom walked around the corner. As I left Tony standing by himself, I realized it felt good to have an ally. Tony understood why I was forced to do the things I did; Tony didn't see me as totally strange.

When I got into the car, I told Mom about Tony's church. She said while our churches were the same in lots of ways, they weren't exactly the same.

"Does that mean Tony still has to go through the Tribulation?"

"Yes."

God sure was difficult. He should just give everyone a rule book to make it easy to worship Him. I felt sorry for Tony. He was close, but not close enough. Maybe I'd offer Tony some of my candy bars—seemed like he was going to need them.

* * * * *

"Remember, next week is our annual Sioux Falls summer picnic and potluck, so be sure and sign up!"

Announcements were my favorite part of church. They weren't the Bible, and if you got someone funny who liked to talk, the twenty minutes could go by pretty fast.

"Now this is the last week for you to put in for your choice of sites for this year's Feast of Tabernacles..."

The Feast of Tabernacles was Hanukkah and Christmas all rolled into one. Every fall we'd go to one of the seventy-five feast sites around the world for a combination retreat and revival. Of course we had to go to church every day—sometimes twice a day—for eight days in a row (not only hard on the butt, but also a real workout for my imagination), but we were also required to blow 10 percent of our family's gross income during Feast week. Whatever we didn't spend we had to give to the church—what an incentive to party!

* * * * *

Just like our Iowa vacations, our Feast trips seemed to put Dad in a great mood—for all of the same reasons I'm sure. The only difference was that instead of showing off to his old friends and relatives he got to show off to church people, often treating other families to dinner. We'd eat at the best restaurants and sometimes Dad would even kick down some booze. One night in our hotel room, Dad gave me a brass monkey and a whiskey sour—I didn't much care for the drinks, but I got a little tipsy. It made me feel like an adult.

Oh yeah, our church said you could drink alcohol. They cited scripture proving it was okay, but myself, I think they had other reasons for allowing it. Our church was so hard-assed—no Christmas, no Easter, no Halloween, no birthdays, no smoking, no marrying outside the church, no divorces, no makeup, no seeking your own pleasure between Friday night sunset and Saturday night sunset, no gambling, in addition to taking 20 percent of wages before taxes— that I think they just had to throw us a bone. Booze was a good one.

Every once in a while, one of the two big guys, Herbert W. Armstrong and his son Garner Ted Armstrong, came to our Feast site. Herbert was a well-fed, burly old guy with a round head and slicked-back white hair. Garner Ted also sported slicked-back hair, though his was salt-and-pepper gray; he had a medium build and a square jaw. Mom said he was good-looking. I'd stare in awe at both of them—if our church was right, they were the closest thing to God on earth I'd ever see. While I listened to the announcements in Sioux Falls, I thought about Garner Ted's recent appearance on a country music variety show.

* * * * *

It was a Saturday night, quarter to seven—luckily just after sunset; the family room was buzzing with anticipation. Our guy, the second in command of the truth, was about to be on *Hee Haw*, one of our favorite shows. I was nervous for him. What was God's plan with all of this?

Garner Ted talked a bit and sang a song. He got on *Hee Haw* because he was friends with Buck Owens, the show's star. I wondered why Buck didn't join our church—Garner Ted must have told him about the Tribulation.

"Mom, when is Mr. Armstrong going to tell all the people that they're sinning and they're in the wrong church?"

"This may not be the right time for him to talk about it."

"Why not?"

"Mr. Armstrong knows what he's doing. He'll do what God wants him to."

The show ended. Garner Ted never witnessed the TV viewers. It was strange—you'd think he would have wanted to let the world know it was all coming to an end soon.

* * * * *

There were still another twenty-five minutes of Mr. Waterhill's sermon to wait through. Mr. Waterhill had a tendency to go long.

"Now let's all turn to the Book of Proverbs..."

Robert and I looked at each other with raised eyebrows. We hated Proverbs. We'd had our first experience with this mean-spirited book one Saturday when I was seven.

* * * * *

We'd just gotten home from church when we were told to march into the family room. Dad was going to read to us from the Bible.

"Today I'm going to read to you boys from Proverbs. Are you paying attention?"

All together, "Yes, sir."

"Proverbs, chapter 4, verse 1: 'Hear, ye children, the instruction of a father, and attend to know understanding.' Do you boys hear that? The Bible says to hear the instruction of your father. God wrote that for a reason. When you boys sin against me and disobey your father, you're also disobeying God."

"Verse 10: 'Hear, O my son, and receive my sayings and the years of the life shall be many.' Who knows what that means?"

All I could do was stare at him and hope Rick or Robert knew the answer.

"Well? Someone say something. You either know the answer or you don't."

Rick said, "Sir, I don't know the answer at this time."

"Were you even listening?"

"Yes, sir."

"I doubt it. Basically, it says that if you disobey your father—like not taking out the garbage when it's full, Robert—you will die soon because God has no use for you. According to the Bible, if a child constantly disobeys his parents, it's better if he just dies."

Oh no. It was just a matter of time now. I wished I was outside playing in the sun; I wished it was Monday.

"Donna, has Robert been taking out the garbage on time?"

"Well, it's hit or miss."

"Now do you boys understand why we spank you? We do it because we love you. If we didn't love you, then we would let you do whatever you want. But the Bible says that someone like that will die young. I'm not going to stop reading Proverbs to discipline you, Robert—I'll do it when we're done. It's for your own good."

My brothers and I wanted to know what complete asshole wrote Proverbs. It was like, "Okay parents, if you're running out of ideas for why to beat the shit out of your kids because the Ten Commandments are too broad, here you go." It was probably originally called the Book of Beatings until the publisher got cold feet and did a little editing.

* * * * *

Fifteen minutes to twelve. Let's start wrapping it up now, Mr. Waterhill. Grandma's got a late dinner waiting for us—letting a mouthwatering table full of food get cold, now that's a *real* sin.

"You see brethren, Satan is waiting for you to slip up, to take your eye off the Lord and His teachings so that he may enter your hearts and minds. You must be wary, for Satan knows his days are numbered. He will do all he can to possess you."

This idea used to scare the hell out of me, used to keep me awake at night, until I did a little experiment in second grade.

* * * * *

Robert and I shared a room. We slept in bunk beds; I was on top because Robert was afraid of heights.

"Lights out. You boys stop talking in there and go to sleep."

"Yes, ma'am." No more stalling. It was time. I'd thought about it a lot, and I figured I could do it. Mom said that God wouldn't talk to humans anymore or do cool things with us like He did with Moses in the Bible—no more parting of the Red Sea, no more making food come down from heaven. He definitely didn't stop whippings, no matter how hard I begged.

If God wouldn't get involved, that left only Satan. According to Mom, if we didn't keep our hearts and minds on God, the Devil would take us over. I knew it was risky, but I decided to pretend that I wanted to follow Lucifer to get his power on my side. I figured I could still secretly be a good person and he wouldn't know. I could then protect myself from Dad—and protect Robert and Rick, too. I could even take care of the bullies at school. I swore I'd only use my powers to do good.

I was trying to barter one hell for another. Compared to my father and God, Satan seemed like a much better person—at least he was fair and easy to understand. And if in the end neither side held a future for me, why not go with the entity that could give me power now, when I needed it?

I figured Satan was probably pretty informal—I didn't have to get down on my knees to him like I did with God. Since it was so dark I just kept my eyes open and whispered:

"Satan that is in hell, I'm ready to switch from God to you. I know God has been very mean to you. You guys got into a fight and He beat you. Because you lost, you got sent to live in hell. That's not fair. Maybe you want to change and be good. I think God should forgive you. I would like to work with you if you give me some powers. And maybe, if you want to go back to heaven, I can talk to God for you, but only if you want me to—I'll work for you. Amen. I'm sorry, I don't know what to say at the end of talking to you. If it's wrong to say amen, I'm sorry."

Satan and I never did hook up. I tried every sales trick in the book to join his club, but he just wasn't interested—even though I'd been taught that Satan was always waiting to pounce, just like in *The Exorcist*. In the end though he did bring me some peace: he taught me everyone in the church was either lying or misinformed.

* * * * *

My head was bowed but my eyes were open as the deacon led us in our closing prayer. At this point, although I had my suspicions about the church, I still believed the chances were good—maybe sixty/forty—that the church was right. And if it was, I was pretty clearly doomed to die a fiery death.

Mom told me thinking a sin was the same as doing it—which meant I was really Charles Manson and a sexual deviant all rolled into one. I'd committed the thought crime of fornication with all the good-looking girls at church and school—and a few of their mothers —not to mention the ladies in the Sears catalogue's underwear section. I'd also dreamed of hurting or killing all those who hurt me.

Mom said God would not only burn sinners like me to death, He'd make everyone who knew us forget we ever existed.

There was no hope for me. How could I never get angry, never think dirty thoughts? The answer was simple: I couldn't. I couldn't bear this vision of what was going to happen to me. I looked for relief, and so far I'd found only one thing that made me feel better about the future: food. My only hope lay in the forty part of that sixty/forty split—the 40 percent chance that God was really a much better person than church led me to believe.

Driving home, fighting to push thoughts of the Tribulation and a fiery death out of my head, I found myself wondering what kind of feast was waiting for me at Grandma's.

* * * * *

This year, for the first time in Iowa, Dad dropped me and Robert off to fish by ourselves, a miraculous blessing. Years later, over beer, Robert and I theorized our good fortune had more to do with Dad's desire to do some tomcatting around than him suddenly deciding we'd earned the right to be on our own.

With our tackle in tow, Robert and I took turns holding down the top wire of the barbed-wire fence as we made our way to our favorite spot of Carl Dall's pond. It was ten in the morning and the temperature was on the rise—thank God our spot was in the shade! The grass was lush, knee-high, and alive with grasshoppers—back-up bait if we needed it. The pond was surrounded by tall trees on one side and tall corn on the other. The end closest to the spillway was choked with algae and lily pads; dead, bleached-white trees poked up out of the water, hungry for tackle.

Today we were out for revenge. Today we were out to get the mean bastard who'd stolen a whole day's catch the last time we were here—a king-sized snapping turtle. You should have seen our faces when we saw that turtle carrying our stringer with thirty-five crappies and a dozen blue gills out to sea. Snapping turtles are no joke. Swimming in turtle-infested waters can cost you your fingers, your toes, your pecker.

When we told the bait shop guy about the turtle thief, he'd put us in touch with a turtle salesman. Turned out turtle soup was a delicacy—he'd pay us twenty-five cents a pound. Revenge was sweet. Getting paid for it made it even sweeter.

Following the salesman's instructions, Robert and I caught about a dozen fish: bait. Then we put a blue gill on the end of a large hook attached to a strong piece of rope. It didn't take long before the algae and lily pads of the pond were moving up and down as something sizeable swam toward the bait lurking beneath the shade-darkened waters. Everything was going like clockwork.

Thirty seconds later the rope straightened.

"Turtle on!"

"Pull, Robert, pull!"

When the turtle was six feet from the bank we could see him—oh my God, he was massive. He was dark green with feet as big as your hands and toenails angrily digging into the mud. He was pissed.

Robert and I were on fire. The only problem was, we hadn't figured what to do with a turtle once we caught one, let alone such a large one. Since at three feet long and two feet wide he was twice the size of any container we had, the only solution we could come up with was tying him to some large exposed tree roots near the bank. We grabbed him by the tail and dragged him, snapping and hissing, over to a tree.

In the next half hour, we caught only one more turtle, nowhere near as big as the first, the granddaddy of them all. For the rest of the day we just fished and looked at our captives, proud in our triumph. Later, the turtle salesman tried to recruit us to catch more. Unfortunately we were going home the following day—our days as turtle bounty hunters were over.

It was the best fishing trip Robert and I had ever had. By ourselves we could relax and just have fun. Fishing with Dad, we always had to be vigilant. If Dad suddenly decided you'd been casting too much, losing too much tackle in the trees, or wasting too many expensive minnows because you weren't baiting your hook properly, you could get yelled at—or worse.

Worse being what had happened to me three years earlier.

* * * * *

Dad, Rick, Robert, and I were fishing at O. P. Bennett's, a pond where my dad had fished as a kid. We'd caught about thirty bass by this point, but had gone almost an hour without a bite.

"Dad, is it okay if I walk to the end and fish by the spillway?"

"Sure."

I didn't expect to catch anything over there. It just felt good to move around and stare at different water. However, no more than three minutes later I had my first bite—and it felt big. It flopped out onto the bank. It was dark—a catfish. Bummer. The church said we couldn't eat a fish unless it had both scales and gills. Catfish had gills but no scales, making them unclean.

"What'd you catch, Ron?"

"Catfish."

"Well, we can't eat it, and if you throw it back, it'll probably die. Go ahead and put it on the stringer. We'll give it to Uncle Vernon."

I had another fish on my line. It felt big, too—another catfish. They must have been hanging out near the spillway. But so what if these fish were against the Bible—this was fun. Chalk up two for Uncle Vernon. I felt another bite on my line—

"What the hell are you doing?"

Dad was walking fast in my direction—and he was taking his belt off.

"Don't think I don't know what you're up to."

I stared at him in shock.

"You're catching catfish on purpose."

"I'm sorry, I didn't mean to…"

"Don't lie to me. Those are unclean fish, against God's law."

The belt was suddenly right there, on me.

* * * * *

The whipping I got that day at O. P. Bennett's pond proved to me that our life was wrong. It was a stupid, indefensible act the three of us boys would never forget. Years later we would even joke about it: "Ron's so good he can command only certain types of fish to bite his hook."

It was an important realization. Sometimes you doubt yourself, sometimes you don't want to believe your childhood was different, that you're getting the shaft. You say to yourself, "Well, I was bad sometimes, and it's not wrong to discipline children when they're bad, and the whippings weren't always that severe, and..." And, and, and.

Life has a way of confusing you and clouding your mind. The truth is, as much as I feared him, there were also things about my dad that I liked. He was funny—to this day I think my sense of humor came from wanting to be as funny as he was. He was hardworking. He was successful—more so than any father I knew, and I liked that he provided for us so well: we always had nicer cars and a nicer house than anyone else I knew. He could kick any other father's ass—he used to box Golden Gloves. I respected all of that. But for the three of us boys, that day at O.P. Bennett's pond summed up our childhood—additional evidence that proved to us that the suffering we were enduring wasn't right.

The knowledge I gained that day—the realization that not everything my parents did and said was right—would eventually help me recover, leading me to question my parents' definition of me as lazy and unlikely to ever amount to anything. Unfortunately, much suffering and many years would pass before recovery came.

CHAPTER 4

Polaroid

I was always sad when our time in Iowa was over, but that particular year I looked forward to the drive home for two reasons. First, we would be swinging by West Yellowstone to see how Rick was handling his newfound freedom. And second, our new northern route would take us within spitting distance of Mount Rushmore.

We left Sioux Falls, South Dakota—a town rendered colorless by its association with the church—and headed west on I-90.

If judged by scenery alone, South Dakota might actually top central Nebraska as the boredom capital of the world. But unlike our lazy friend to the south, South Dakota had a gimmick: Wall Drug. By the hundredth mile marker, Robert and I had counted more than 374 signs for Wall Drug and the place was still two hundred miles away. The signs were funny—at least to a fourteen-year-old. "Come to Wall Drug, the first glass of water is on us," and "Visit our Coffee Shop—Pet Dinosaurs Eat for Free" had me and Robert laughing for miles.

After a while, Robert took over sign-counting duty so I could nap. But my mind wouldn't let me sleep; I found myself thinking over and over again about how my relatives in Iowa had reacted to my size.

* * * * *

Every time I saw an aunt, uncle, or cousin for the first time, I'd get a quick double take, then a tactful, "Boy, you've really filled out," or "You're going to be one big man when you grow up!" A few even blurted out, "Wow, you've put on weight!" before quickly changing the subject.

What shocked me most were the Polaroids Aunt Norma took. In the shot with all the cousins, I was the one with the fattest cheeks and the biggest belly. I'd always known I ate more and ate faster than anyone else at the dinner table, but now I had to admit it went beyond that.

For one thing, how many people had an eating buddy? I did.

* * * * *

Johnny was my age, his family in our church. Every summer, I'd spend a week at his house in the Napa Valley. I loved going to Johnny's—no discipline, new scenery, and his parents served foods I didn't get at home, like tacos, burritos, and pizza. (Dad didn't like spicy food and Mom was a strictly meat-and-potatoes cook.)

More important, when it came to eating, like me, Johnny thought outside the box:

"Do we have enough money for all that?" I asked, looking at the mound of candy and junk food he'd piled on the 7-11 counter.

"Oh yeah. Mom gave me extra money because you're here."

I drooled in anticipation as we rode our spider bikes to our usual hangout, a baseball dugout that provided shade and protection from adult eyes. Our fort, our rules.

"I've got a surprise."

"What?"

"Feast your eyes: the December issue."

The dugout's wooden bench, soda-stained concrete floor, and smell of fresh cut grass welcomed us back. Cars whizzed by on the road behind us as we unpacked our next hour's entertainment: two thirty-two-ounce wild cherry Slurpees, a one-pound bag of peanut

M&M's, a one-pound bag of plain M&M's, four Hostess fruit pies, and the December issue of *Playboy*—our idea of a balanced meal.

An hour later, with sugar coursing through our veins and money to burn, we stopped off at the local grocery store to browse for more forbidden treats. We were in the baked goods aisle when I had a sudden epiphany: the best part of a cake is the frosting.

Back at Johnny's, we set up camp in a two-man pup tent in the backyard. Luckily for us, Johnny's house had a sliding glass door leading directly to the kitchen. Once Johnny's parents were asleep, we snuck into the kitchen, found a small cake pan, and filled it with two sixteen-ounce cans of Betty Crocker chocolate frosting. When it was packed in and perfectly level, we ran a knife under hot water and pried the molded contents onto a plate. Voila!: a perfect cakeless cake.

"Johnny, our creation needs a name."

"Pure sugar?"

"No, no. Although, a dusting of powdered sugar on top would be a nice touch…"

"How about—"

"No, no, I've got it. Let's call it a 'frosting.'"

At Johnny's I didn't pig out to escape something bad that was about to happen to me, I pigged out to enjoy the by-product of my anxiety medicine: pure gratification. Like Vicodin, pigging out worked for both pain and pleasure. Without knowing it, I was planting the seeds of something called a pleasure binge.

* * * * *

A loud laugh jolted me awake.

"Ron, wake up!"

"I wasn't asleep. What?"

"Look—Wall Drug has dinosaur statues, too! They've got to be three to four stories tall—how cool is that?"

Man, I had to hand it to these guys—what salesmen! I had no idea what Wall Drug was, but I definitely wanted to stop and check it out.

* * * * *

My visits with Johnny always ended on a Saturday, when Johnny's family met mine at church. As they turned me over to Mom and Dad, my body and mind would immediately switch to red alert. Just transferring my suitcase from their car to ours increased my anxiety and blocked out the sun.

If I got lucky, at the end of the church service, Dad would announce that on our way home we would be stopping at Smorgabob's—an all-you-can-eat buffet—and I would enjoy a temporary reprieve.

At Smorgabob's, from the moment I saw the eucalyptus trees and the park outside to the moment my plate was firmly in my grasp, I felt like I was moving in slow motion.

I'd be eight people from my plate and it was all I could do not to yell, "Hey dumbshits! Don't you know they *want* you to fill your plate with salad and Jell-O? Fine, be stupid, but don't be so slow about it."

At last it would be my turn. I'd give myself a courtesy scoop of salad in case Mom was watching, then quickly make my way around the buffet rookies. What if the place ran out of fried chicken? It never did, though. I'd get not only my three pieces of chicken, but also enchiladas, roast beef, a mound of mashed potatoes, and a gravy bath for all.

We usually sat in the back room with three other church families. Although at Smorgabob's I was always allowed to eat as much as I wanted, the nice thing about being at the kids' table was I didn't even have to ask to be excused—I could just devour everything as fast as I damn well pleased and get up for more without being noticed.

I'd fill my plate three times, then go back for a half plate of fourths. I would have filled it all the way, but I had to save room for dessert. Dessert probably cost Smorgabob's the most—they gave you the tiniest plates possible for your cake and pie; the dinkiest bowls for your ice cream. One of the advantages of being at the kids' table was that I could use a dinner plate for dessert, with no adult intervention. Who said I had to play their game? In the end, I'd eat two full dinner plates of dessert, plus two little bowls of ice cream—in addition to my four other plates of food.

I know my parents realized how much I was eating but they didn't seem to care. They probably looked at it as, "Hey, we paid our $5.99—let's get our money's worth. The more Ron eats here the less we have to feed him at home."

For me, gorging myself until I popped made sense. It was the most I could get of a good thing. Food was not only an excellent way to cope with stress, it was pure pleasure, too. Stopping before you absolutely had to was just plain stupid.

I have to admit: the early Smorgabob days were the best eating days of my life—massive pig-outs with no guilt. Until you go on your first diet, discover girls, or see your weight in a negative way, there's absolutely no repercussion to any eating action—the Smorgabob's days were my good ol' days. Food was the best thing in my life, and what's better than all you can handle of the best?

Although even the good ol' days had their moments of fear—I remember one Saturday when Mom, reading from church books, announced, "When we're swept into heaven, we won't feel pain, thirst, or hunger."

I panicked. My reason for living was under attack. I took a deep breath, let it out, and—as calmly as I could—said, "Mom, even though you don't get hungry, there's still food in heaven, and you can eat it if you want, right?"

A little puzzled, she said, "I guess so. I don't see why not."

A religious crisis was averted.

* * * * *

What bothered me most during our drive to Yellowstone was what I'd found myself doing recently at home when no one was around to see. Three weeks before we'd left for Iowa I was left home alone—an event that, until recently, had had no meaning for me. Now it excited me.

My sisters were visiting a friend from church, Rick was at work, Robert was hanging out with Scott, and Mom was going out shopping for three hours. As she gathered her purse to go, I felt my pulse quicken.

I couldn't think of a more perfect thing than an afternoon of TV and food. I could either eat a hamburger or eggs—or go totally crazy and eat both. My choices worked on the safety-in-numbers principle: on our mini-farm, we had our own cows and chickens. With 500 pounds of beef in the freezer and six dozen eggs gathered every day, what was a few pounds of hamburger or a flat of eggs here or there? Still, I figured both would be too much; I chose the eggs.

I pulled out Mom's large black skillet, a big mixing bowl, two blocks of cheese, a jug of milk, and butter. How many eggs should there be in my Rockin' Ronnie Omelet? I cracked six jumbo eggs, then wondered what nine would look like. Hell, if I was going for nine, I might as well round it up to a dozen. Now we were talking—a new record. I added some milk for fluffiness and it was beatin' time. I didn't want to get busted, so instead of taking my cheese all from one block, I went with a quarter-pound of cheddar and a quarter-pound of pepper jack.

I enjoyed watching my eggy beast cook. This bad boy was way too big to turn. Too bad—would've been cool to see a perfectly folded two-pounder on a plate... I had to harvest it in sections.

Watching *Gilligan's Island*, I drowned my platter of eggs with their thick, creamy gobs of melted cheese in an additional half-bottle of thousand-island dressing, then scarfed it all down. Mom wouldn't be home for another two hours—was there still time to defrost a two-pound package of hamburger?

Without knowing it, with these fast, solitary feasts, I was creating another weapon, one I would spend the next few decades using against myself: the opportunity binge. Even well into my early thirties, if left alone at anyone's house—and I mean *anyone's*—the moment I heard the door shut I'd be opening the refrigerator and cupboards, devouring as many Nestle chocolate morsels and scoops of Skippy peanut butter as I could and still keep my thefts unnoticed. Sometimes I'd just say fuck it and pig out as much as I wanted, leaving the blame to fall on kids or babysitters.

* * * * *

Remembering my huge, solitary feasts—it wasn't just the once, I found myself doing it more and more often—I squirmed uncomfortably in the car seat and promised myself I would never do *that* again.

* * * * *

The sign said, "Mount Rushmore, eleven miles." I'd been looking forward to seeing it for months. No matter what happened, it had to be better than Wall Drug. What a rip-off! 1,187 signs and—nothing. Well, not exactly nothing. Maybe there was stuff there that adults liked, but I was definitely expecting something more than a few gift shops and a restaurant—after all of those creative signs I wanted a theme park, at least a few rides. Still, I admired their salesmanship, and thanked them for the boredom-busting signs—Nebraska, take note.

Unlike Wall Drug, Mount Rushmore delivered. Each carved face was as big as a seven-story building—talk about a hobby getting out of hand! The cynic in me wondered if the huge faces were truly there to honor great men or if they were just a better Wall Drug sign—a trick to get you to stop and buy a cup of coffee and a sandwich. The hills around Mount Rushmore were beautiful enough, but you definitely paid your dues in boredom to get there.

We didn't stop for long—we still had a few hundred miles to go before pitching camp. Dad was aiming for dinner and lodging in Sheridan, Wyoming. The following day we'd see if Rick was eatin' well or eatin' people.

* * * * *

Sheridan's a small, dull town, with a couple of old-time western saloons, several gift shops stocked with Indian trinkets and animal pelts, and the mandatory western museum. The Big Horn Mountain Range, where Sheridan's located, however, had me jacked. As we approached the range, I psyched myself up, putting the word "mighty" in front of everything I described—e.g., "Robert, are you ready? We're about to enter the Mighty Big Horn Mountain Range."

To Robert's further annoyance, I also insisted on doing my Rod Serling *Twilight Zone* imitation: "Robert, we are about to enter a place that time's forgotten... a place untouched by man... a little place I like to call, 'The Mighty Big Horn Mountain Range.'"

Dad got us up and out of the hotel early that morning—we had a lot of ground to cover and the earlier you're on the road the better chance you have of seeing wildlife.

An hour outside of Sheridan the scenery changed from alfalfa fields and sage to lush meadows bordered by pine trees, all watched over by snowcapped mountains of granite. According to Dad, Cloud Peak, which was 13,000 feet tall, usually kept its snow all year round.

"Elk!"

Oh my God—at least ten elk were grazing not far from the road. Dad pulled onto the shoulder, got out the Polaroid. When it comes to hunting, elk are at the top of the list. While a big deer may weigh 240 pounds, a bull elk can weigh 600 pounds or more.

We were a hunting family. Every year Dad hunted pheasants, doves, and deer, going deer hunting in both California and Wyoming. Sometimes, in Wyoming, he'd get tags to shoot two deer and two antelope; although he always put in for an elk permit, he had yet to be chosen.

It was a recent thing that Robert and I were allowed to hunt. Five years ago, we'd shot our slingshots at each other after being told not to; as punishment, we were severely beaten and forbidden to get a BB gun or a real gun until Dad decided it was okay. But just because we'd been forbidden guns, didn't mean we didn't fool around with them. After Grandpa Saxen died, Dad inherited all his guns and ammunition—boxes and boxes of ammunition—too much to count, and too much to keep track of.

At first I just took a few of the guns out and played with them without bullets. Once I got bored with that, I started firing them. I fired Dad's shotguns, his deer rifles, and his one and only pistol. One time I even strapped on his holster, grabbed a shotgun, and went walking around the surrounding fields and orchards looking for trouble. No animals presented themselves to be shot that day, so I drew down on a large mound of dirt and nailed it. On other days I shot pheasants, doves, quail, hawks, seagulls, jackrabbits, and squirrels.

Two months earlier, fooling around with guns had almost changed my life forever.

* * * * *

It started when my friend Eddie and his brother were joking around and watching TV at my house with me and Robert. Suddenly I got a great idea. I went to my parents' room, opened the walk-in closet where Dad kept his guns, and pulled out his Winchester—a lever action rifle just like the one John Wayne used in *True Grit* to shoot Robert Duvall.

I heard the guys laughing. Sneaking around the corner, I pulled the lever out and back, so it made that clack-clack sound you hear in movies that shows the hero means business. I pulled back the trigger.

Without Eddie knowing, I snuck around the corner and put the barrel within one inch of his temple on the left side of his head. I figured when I squeezed the trigger he'd hear the sound, look left, and see the barrel staring him in the face—so cool!

My finger was starting to squeeze the trigger when Robert said, "Hey, Ron, what're you doing?"

Eddie turned toward me. The surprise was ruined; I dropped the barrel toward the floor.

"Hey, Saxen, nice gun! What is it?"

"It's a .30-30."

"Your dad's?"

"Yeah."

"Cool."

I walked over to the sliding glass door, opened it, pointed the barrel toward the grass, and pulled the trigger.

The ear-ringing explosion reverberated throughout the house. Everyone stopped talking. A second later everyone was laughing; Eddie and his brother got up from the couch to check out the gun—could they have a turn?

I felt numb and sick at the same time. I'd almost blown my friend's head apart! Even though my stomach felt queasy, I did the only thing I could think of to make myself feel better—I poured myself a whole mixing bowl full of Cocoa Pebbles, dumped five heaping tablespoons of sugar on top of it, and gorged in the kitchen while everyone else laughed and fooled around with the gun.

To this day Eddie doesn't know.

* * * * *

After we crossed the Mighty Big Horn Mountain Range, we stopped off at Mighty Cody, Wyoming, for a quick visit to Grandpa Saxen's gravesite. He was a big man who drank 7&7s, smoked, and played the accordion and organ; his favorite cuss word was goddamn. I'd just found out why he'd always made us sit quietly whenever Lawrence Welk was on television: apparently Grandpa had been Lawrence Welk's first accordion player. When Welk decided to take his act to Hollywood, Grandpa told him he was crazy. He, Grandpa, had a successful auto repair garage in Ute—he wasn't about to leave it to go on a wild-goose chase.

Dad rarely talked about his father with affection. Apparently Grandpa had had no problem kicking the shit out of him— supposedly much worse than Dad did to us. Thus, according to him, we had nothing to whine about. This confused me: telling us he'd had it worse implied that he knew he was treating us badly, too—just not as badly.

The only person my dad spoke fondly of was his grandmother on his mother's side. He was sent to live with her when he was sixteen, after his parents moved to California. A few years ago, after my aunt's boyfriend roughed Dad's grandmother up, Dad called him and said, "I'm catching the next plane to Iowa. Just so you know, if you're there when I arrive, I will kill you." I believed him.

We left Grandpa to his own devices and headed on toward Yellowstone National Park, one of my favorite places in the world. The day after we'd arrived in Iowa, Rick had called and given us the address of the cheap cabin he'd found. We entered the park in the east and drove all the way through, past deer, elk, antelope, moose, and buffalo, to Rick in the west.

I figured it must be great to live totally on your own and do whatever you wanted. If it were me, I'd explore, hike, fish, hunt, eat lots of store-bought food, and watch whatever I wanted on TV—I'd stay up late and watch Johnny Carson every night. But mostly I wondered what it would feel like to live free and unafraid. Maybe when we were old enough, the three of us boys could live in West Yellowstone together and protect each other.

We pulled into a gravel parking lot surrounded by four or five little red buildings. Rick's was number three. His door had a faded black "3" stenciled on it; we parked in front of it. The six of us piled out of the station wagon. Dad walked up to the door, knocked. A few seconds went by. Nothing. Dad knocked again—still nothing.

"Maybe he's at work," Mom said.

Dad was about to knock yet again when the door opened. Rick definitely looked the worse for wear. His hair was a mess, his eyes bleary and unfocused, his chin dark with the beginnings of a beard.

"Sorry, I was asleep—late night."

Immediately Mom said, "Late night doing what, may I ask?"

"Donna, he just woke up, give him a break."

Rick's cabin consisted of one square room with a fridge, two cots, and a bare concrete floor, just like Dad had described. Décor had been kept simple: four walls, a roof, and a *Charlie's Angels* poster: Farrah Fawcett—nice art.

"I've got a roommate but he's at work. His name is Tim. He's nice."

We sat on the cots while Dad and Mom proceeded to question Rick. Strangely enough, Mom was the bad cop, Dad the good. It seemed Dad just wanted Rick to live; Mom wanted Rick to live right.

Rick had found himself a job. He'd started out washing dishes but had already worked his way up to assistant cook. He'd explored Yellowstone and done something called "hot poddin" at a place in the park called Firehole—I think this meant he'd soaked in the hot springs.

"Well, everyone say good-bye to your brother, we need to be getting on the road. I want to be in Pocatello by nightfall."

We all got up from the cots. Robin, only six years old, walked over to the mini-fridge opened it. All eyes turned to the contents of the fridge.

Mom's eyes opened wide. "What in God's creation is that, Rick?"

Rick didn't say a word.

Dad snapped, "What do you think it is, Donna? Haven't you ever seen beer before?"

"Whose beer is that, Rick?"

"Never mind, Donna. Let's get going so Rick can go back to sleep."

It was the strangest thing—Mom was really pissed about the beer; in the car she kept going on and on about it—but Dad just laughed.

When Mom wouldn't shut up, Dad finally put his foot down.

"Listen, Donna, you need to get over it. He's eighteen. No one learns a hangover is bad until they get one. He needs to grow up, figure it out. When I was his age, I was married, had a kid, and been drunk more times than I can count. Let it rest."

"But—"

"I don't want to hear any more about it."

I'd never seen Dad come to Rick's defense—or any of our defenses—like that. It was cool.

For about seventy-five miles Mom was real quiet. Then, out of the blue, "You boys have got a lot of work to do when you get home. The manure is building up in front of the feed trough. I want it shoveled and piled at the far end of the garden. The nests need changing and the roosts need scraping. And I want you to weed the garden. Just start at one end and keep going 'til you're finished. Also, the fruit trees are definitely going to need irrigating. But before you do anything else, I want the lawn mowed."

I suspect Mom didn't appreciate Dad telling her to get over it—particularly in front of us kids. This seemed to be her way of saying, "Rick may get to do what he wants, but don't forget—I still control the rest of you."

When we three brothers reflect on our past, sometimes Mom seems a victim, sometimes a villain. If we're feeling generous we attribute her behavior to being in the same boat as us: just trying to survive, turning on us to get Dad off her back. Other times we remember her anger and her use of Dad as a weapon to get back at us if she felt we'd crossed some line.

"And I think the boys' hair is getting a little long. It should be cut when we get home."

Boy, Mom would not let up. This one was aimed at us *and* Dad—work for him, fear for us. Robert and I had good reason to be nervous of haircuts: one Sunday three years ago, when Dad wasn't in the best of moods, Robert had walked into a hair-related trap.

* * * * *

"Robert, get your hair out of your eyes."

"Yes, sir."

Sitting in our bedroom, Rick and I heard Dad loud and clear. Our eyes met. Robert was busted.

"What have I told you boys about your hair?"

"Keep it out of our eyes, sir."

"That's right. Apparently you thought I was talking to hear myself talk."

"No, sir."

"I recall telling you that if I caught any one of you with messy hair I would cut all three of you boys' hair off—now didn't I?"

"Yes, sir."

"Ronald, Rick, get out here."

The three of us stood to attention in front of Dad.

"I told you boys what I was going to do, didn't I?"

All together, "Yes, sir."

"If I don't keep my promise, what kind of example does that set?"

"Not a good example, sir?"

Robert always tried to be humble when answering Dad back. It never worked—Dad saw right through it.

"After dinner I'm cutting all your hair off."

We were all silent while we ate dinner that night. For the first time since I'd had the flu I hardly cared what was on my plate. Don't get me wrong—I still cleaned my plate and had seconds, but there wasn't much joy in it. I didn't even know what I'd eaten.

When the dishes were almost done Dad opened the hall closet where he kept his haircutting kit, the same kit he'd used in the Navy.

"Robert, you started it, you're first."

I couldn't believe it was really going to happen. The teasing we'd face... Tracy, Tina, and Vicky—they'd all think we were ugly, so not cool. We were screwed.

As Dad lubricated the scissors and hair clippers, the familiar smell of oil floated through the house. It was a smell that always made me sweat—I was always afraid he'd cut too much. He safety-pinned a smock—an old sheet really—around Robert, making Robert look like Casper the Ghost with a head. There was the sound of hungry shears and then Robert's thick black hair began hitting the floor in huge gobs. By the end, although Robert still had a little bit of hair, he looked more bald than anything, his white scalp standing out from his tanned face.

There was no way out. We went from having cool length hair one day to being ready for boot camp the next. Which would've been okay, except we weren't at boot camp—we were at everyone-has-hair-except-you camp.

School was a bitch of course—though not as bad as I'd expected. Some of the kids must have felt sorry for us. In the end, the only teasing that made me cry came from my father. I don't know whether he felt sorry for what he'd done, wanted to break the ice, or just couldn't pass up the opportunity for a joke, but that first morning, after I woke up with an itchy sandpaper scalp, he greeted me with, "Good morning. Wait! Who's that? Now don't tell me. I know... you must be Yul Brynner." Of course I started crying.

Dad knew just how to stop my tears: "If you don't stop crying I'll give you something to cry about."

What the haircut drove home to me was that my personal self had no boundaries. I wasn't safe and I couldn't rely on anything. Whippings were one thing, but this was another. This was more personal, this was something I couldn't hide from friends. It was then that I realized that everything about me was at the pleasure and mercy of my parents.

＊ ＊ ＊ ＊ ＊

Leaving West Yellowstone, I felt happy for Rick. And although he was supposed to come back at the end of the summer and start working for Dad, I couldn't help wishing him the good fortune of never coming home.

CHAPTER 5

The F Word

As the basketball team made the four-hour drive to the San Luis Obispo basketball tournament (the biggest tournament of eighth grade), Coach Whitmore entertained us by predicting who we would all be when we grew up:

"Brent, you're six foot two inches now, but by the time you finish college you'll be six foot ten and fighting to make it in the NBA. Your wife will also be six foot ten and play basketball better than you. Your kids will be over eight feet tall."

Coach Whitmore was cool. He'd played in college with some guys that went on to play professionally; he was big and strong and wore a gold necklace that dangled on his dark hairy chest—a chest frequently visible; the top two buttons of his shirt were usually left undone. There was a rumor he was sleeping with the new eighth grade teacher, Miss Hackett. She was hot and sometimes wore a miniskirt.

"Saxen, if your church ever lets you play on Friday nights, you'll get into football and go on to play in the pros as a 300-pound offensive lineman. If that doesn't happen, you'll open a chain of restaurants and literally be huge as a famous chef. You'll always have plenty to eat."

Everyone laughed. I fought to clear the unhappy look from my red-hot face. Thank God the light was beginning to dim. I forced a smile, silently bobbing my head to indicate that I, too, thought it was funny.

"Now Phil, you'll..."

Two years later, Coach's prediction was still tattooed in my mind. I knew what Coach was saying. When I thought about the kids in my eighth grade class, I could tell which ones were going to be fat. Not just the ones who already were fat, but the ones with the full cheeks and the soft bodies. I was one of those guys—I'd had it demonstrated to me very clearly a year and a half previously.

* * * * *

At first, the sore between my legs wasn't all that big; it would come and go, hurting just a little. But it grew into two four-inch-by-six-inch, solid, raised, red patches that burned like fire. I tried to walk as little as possible, but I didn't complain, even when I was in extreme pain—it was too embarrassing.

I knew my sores and my weight had to be linked to each other. When I looked at my family of seven I was the only fat one—I was different; different things happened to people like me. I was ashamed. And although food was the enemy in all of this, I still needed it for comfort, needed it to help me cope with this, too.

"Mom, I might need to go to the doctor. I've got this rash and it's real bad."

I was dying, in extreme pain. I couldn't live like this anymore.

"Let me see."

It was too late now to do anything but drop my drawers in front of Mom. I hadn't done that since the last time Mom had tried to spank me. When we were little, Mom had whacked us with a stick over our clothes. As we got bigger she went to bare skin, eventually giving up and leaving the task entirely to Dad. I couldn't believe how stupid she was—a simple weapon change was all she needed. She used a light, flat piece of wood. And while, sure, it was easy to swing and made one hell of a pop, it was too blunt. A thicker, narrower stick plus a better windup, and she might still have been in business.

Maybe she got tired of being the bad guy—or maybe, unlike my father, she realized that if we ever lost it while she was beating us, we were big enough to kick her ass.

"You've got baby rash. All you need is some Desitin, just like on a baby's bottom."

Mom giggled. I didn't care. I started to laugh, too. Growing up in my family taught me that laughter really was the best medicine— laughter and cleaning my plate. Trying to keep my family laughing, so bad things wouldn't happen, was my comedy training ground— although years later I would discover that even audiences without belts ready to whip you could be excruciatingly painful.

I lay in bed with my legs spread, my crotch covered in a thick film of cool white cream that smelled like medicine. My spirits lifted. Still, no one else in the family had baby-rash-cream lathered between their legs. Coach Whitmore was right: I was different—fat.

*   *   *   *   *

A month after I started my baby rash treatment all was well between my legs. Well, not really. A few months previously something had happened in the bathtub that felt really good at the time, but left me feeling scared, dirty, and dark—like a deviant sinner. Just thinking about it made me uneasy. A month later, I did it again. Then two weeks later, then a week. I wanted to stop, but it felt so good. I couldn't stop thinking about it. Even sitting in class I just kept thinking and thinking about it. Like eating, it was a source of great pleasure and relief, one that both delighted and disgusted me.

Time for lunch. At our school cafeteria you could get a chocolate shake for sixty-five cents. I had enough money for two, one with lunch and one after. I sucked on my second one as I walked into the sunshine—which always felt good when you were full of milk shake. A couple of the cool guys were throwing a Nerf ball in the quad just outside the cafeteria. The ball went over Alberto's head, came my way. I caught it—a one-handed catch.

"What the fuck are you doing, Saxen? I had it until your fat ass got in the way. You fat motherfucker."

I stared at him, my face hot.

"What the fuck are you looking at? Fat ass."

The other kids laughed. I was bigger than Alberto, I could have kicked his ass, but I didn't. I didn't like fighting. I just turned and walked away in the direction of my locker, numb. I'd known I was overweight. But no one had ever said it to my face like that—and in front of so many people, all the cool guys, all the cool girls. I wasn't just big-built or chunky anymore, I was fat, a fat ass, a fatso.

The incident dominated my day. I was silent on the bus ride home.

"How was school, Ron?"

My mom and two sisters were home, Robert still at school working on the yearbook, Rick at Dad's insurance brokerage.

"Fine."

I was christened a fat ass today.

"I need to pick up a few things at the grocery store. You're in charge of your sisters. They're watching *Sesame Street*."

Mom left. All I could think about was what had happened. I badly wanted the pain to just vanish. I needed something to make me feel good… I didn't want to do it—it was a sin. But with the bathroom door shut, the fan on, and my sisters engrossed in their show, I'd never be discovered. Just one more time. I'd never do it again.

As I cleaned up after myself, my brief moment of euphoria slipped away, replaced by shame. I was disgusting, outside and in. I could feel again, and I didn't want to.

I walked through the family room; my sisters didn't even look up. Mom wouldn't be home for at least another thirty minutes. I put last night's roast on the kitchen counter, slapped a huge chunk between two pieces of Mom's bread, and smothered it in A.1. Sauce. I took half-a-dozen cookies from the stack on the counter, pushing a few cookies to the center, fluffing them up a little so it didn't look like the mountain had lost too much altitude.

Fifteen minutes left. My sisters were still engrossed in Big Bird. I filled a small mixing bowl with Lucky Charms, smothered them in sugar.

When Mom got home, I was on the couch, watching TV with my sisters. The bowl of Mom's delicious canned peaches with a half-cup of Skippy crunchy peanut butter floating in it was a sight Mom was used to and fine with. I'd do my best to eat it slowly. When it was gone, reality would be back.

For me, shame was another powerful, devastating trigger to eat. Masturbating made me feel worthless in the Lord's eyes. And if I'd already doomed myself to a fiery death at the hand of God, why not pig out?

* * * * *

Dances were tough. I'd spend the whole night staring, dreaming, and drooling. I figured if I could just dance once, with a cool girl, my life would be made. But who was I fooling? I was fat and ugly. I was never going to ask anybody to dance.

I only went to church dances—I couldn't go to dances at school because they were on Friday nights after sunset: God's time. Even if they hadn't been, I don't think I would've been allowed to go. Apparently regular kids danced sinfully, doing something called "The Bump." Regular kids played the wrong music. Regular kids were not the Chosen Ones. We Chosen Ones weren't allowed to date outside the church—having a girlfriend outside the church was considered an "unequal yoke." And when it came to marriage, we had to marry church members who were the right color. Blacks weren't allowed to marry whites and Latinos couldn't marry Asians. Even then I knew that was stupid. What was wrong with being of mixed race? And what did they think they could do about it?—"I'm sorry son, your eyes just aren't round enough. You'll need to keep your chopsticks off whitey and the sisters—and remember, God loves you."

One Saturday, Rick drove the three of us to a church dance. We spent the whole ride talking trash: who was hot, who we'd like to do (realistically that was anyone who'd let us). I wore my new rust-colored leisure suit with cordovan slip-on dress shoes.

Inside, one of those cool disco balls hung from the ceiling, but only a few kids were dancing. It was dark, which was good—meant I'd be able to hide my red face if I were lucky enough to have verbal intercourse with a female. I hardly knew any of the songs they were playing. In our house we weren't allowed to listen to rock and roll. The only approved music at home was country music. Ronnie Milsap was my favorite—because of his voice, the Ron in his name, and the fact that he was blind. He seemed like an underdog, something I could identify with.

The church's hot girls were all there: Tina, Vicky, and Susan. This was my third church dance and I'd still not gotten the courage up to ask anyone to dance—if they said no, they'd be saying I was too ugly to dance with. Too fat, a lardo, a pig. I couldn't bear that. It was better to have hope than to know the truth.

As usual I didn't dance. Why couldn't I just ask someone? I just wanted to touch a girl so bad—or at least talk to one. Why did I keep putting myself through this? Raging hormones fucking suck. I'm positive my GPA suffered in high school from all the nights I stayed awake until two in the morning fantasizing about girls. If there's a blue pill to get you excited, there should be a pink one to get you unexcited. Until then, easier access to Valium or lowering the drinking age to twelve would be helpful.

As we drove home through the dark, I needed something good—something to make me forget, something to help me cope with my shortcomings. "Rick, can we stop at the 7-11 for some candy bars on the way home? I'm buying."

* * * * *

A few months after that dance, Robert and I concocted a brilliant hormonally driven plan. (Robert wasn't any better than I was with girls. I think his bad luck with ladies came from being on the short side and less than cool.) The first step of Operation Tina was to acquire a piece of fine jewelry worthy of such a beauty. It couldn't be cheap—it had to be awesome. Unfortunately, at most, our funds would only cover a down payment on cheap, not awesome. But we had a plan. One afternoon we got Mom to drop us off at an outdoor mall in Antioch.

I stayed outside while Robert cased the two jewelry stores in the mall. I couldn't believe we were going to do it. My palms were sweaty, my heart pounding.

"Okay, the one on the corner it is. There's only one guy working. If it goes bad, just run like hell. I'll meet you where Mom's supposed to pick us up in thirty minutes."

I was so freaked out—if Dad found out, we'd be so dead, jail really *would* be protective custody. But at the same time, I wasn't ready to give up my dream of Tina.

Blackstone Jewelers was typical: glass cases displayed stuff for passersby; a "50% off" placard sat on the sidewalk in front of the store. Robert told me to give him five minutes before I walked in. "Don't worry about me," he said. "Just do your part."

It was time. I took a deep breath, wiped my hands on my pants, forced a smile, and started moving. I crossed the threshold, entered the air-conditioned store. Out of the corner of my eye I saw a man in a suit waiting on Robert.

Eyes forward, look relaxed. Going to the far corner of the store, I pretended to be interested in the watches, just like Robert had said. I dipped my head slightly to the left, looked: the well-dressed man and Robert were locked in conversation, five or six rings on a cloth on the glass counter between them. A couple more seconds. I cleared my throat.

"Excuse me, sir?"

"Yes?"

"I'm looking to get a watch today. Can I try one of these on?"

He looked at Robert, then looked my way and said, "Can you give me—"

Before he could finish his sentence, Robert said, "Go ahead, it's fine, I'm not in a hurry."

I didn't look at Robert at all as the salesman headed my way. Like a child who doesn't want to see his measles shot coming, I turned my back and looked down at the jewelry case.

"Which one are you interested in, son?"

The salesman was wearing a pinstripe three-piece suit; his fingers were full of jewelry. I couldn't bear to look at his face.

"The one with the gold and silver band."

The seconds were ticking away slowly. I couldn't look.

"You've made a great choice. It's a Timex, best bang for your buck in the store. Try it on."

"Thank you, I will."

He handed me the watch. I kept my head down as I looked at it.

"Now when it comes to winding it, you need to remember to—" His voice broke off. Robert was leaving. "Excuse me, son, where are you going? Do you have a question?"

With a backwards glance at me, the salesman headed in the direction of the rings. My heart pounded. I'd agreed to this because I'd figured I had the easy part, the safe part. But how safe was my part if I was the one left stranded in the store? No, I needed to calm down. Everyone said that Robert and I didn't look alike. He looked like Mom's side and I looked like Dad's. He was skinny, I was not. He had black hair, I had blond.

"Excuse me, sir, I love the watch, but I'm going to have to wait until I can afford it."

The salesman looked up at me, saw the watch on the counter, and said, "Thanks for ahh... coming in. Thanks. Come see us again," and immediately went back to the cloth full of rings, a puzzled look on his face.

Outside in the hot sun, I headed in the opposite direction of Robert, trying not to walk too fast or be too obvious. It seemed like an eternity before I could slip into the large department store at the end of the mall. Only then did I dare look back. Nothing.

During the next month Robert and I sent four secret admirer letters to Tina. It made lying awake at night fantasizing about her all the sweeter—she had something of mine, my handwritten letters, in her house, in her bedroom, maybe even in her underwear drawer. We saved the stolen ring for the big finale. Finally we mailed it off, too—making sure we sent it early enough in the week that it would arrive before church on Saturday.

When we walked into church the area where the kids hung out was buzzing. Tina looked beside herself with happiness. All of her friends were around her, smiling, giggling, looking around—I loved it. Robert and I had created this. We were part of her life.

Church started. I caught Tina looking my way. Why would she do that? Oh my God, she knew. Wait—maybe she didn't. I never thought about her finding out. If she had, what should I say to her? Shit! I needed to stop looking in her direction.

At last church ended. I retreated to the parking lot to talk to Johnny. I couldn't hold up my end of the conversation—I kept getting distracted, kept glancing at the double doors leading from the church.

"Ron, look who's coming."

It was Tina. I was going to die. Maybe she was just getting something from her car? For a brief moment, panic switched to lust as the sun lit up her dress like an X-ray, clearly defining her underwear; I could even make out the pattern. And then a proximity alarm went off, and my brain sped back up to my skull.

What the hell was I supposed to do now?

"Hello, Ron. You're the one who sent me the letters and the ring, huh?"

I didn't know what to say. I just stared at her. She was so beautiful. I shook my head ever so slightly, still silent. I just kept staring, afraid, drinking in her skin, her lips. I could see a tiny piece of her bra.

"Whatever. Thanks for the ring."

She turned around and walked back the way she came. Even though I was still reeling, my hormones had enough presence of mind to enjoy another sun-aided view.

Goddammit! I'd gotten what I wanted and done absolutely nothing about it. I'd never thought about that happening. The fantasy was over now, and I was back where I started: fat, ugly, uncool, and now a fucking fool to boot.

My kingdom for a pink pill—or at least a half-gallon of ice cream.

* * * * *

I couldn't hide from my weight problem any longer. I was tired of being fat and ugly. I decided to join the high school junior varsity basketball team, hoping the exercise would help me lose weight. I was second-string, both because I wasn't that good and because I could only play in half of the games. Those on Tuesdays were fine, but Friday games started after sunset, our Sabbath.

It was time to pick out uniforms.

"Saxen, we've only got one extra-large uniform, so you'll have to be number twenty-seven."

I pulled the top on. Man, it was tight. It was a struggle just getting it over my head. I yanked hard on the top and the bottom of the jersey, trying to stretch it out, and eventually got it on. But I couldn't get the extra-large shorts up past my thighs.

Humiliated I said, "Coach, the shorts don't fit. Can I get a bigger size?"

"They don't fit? That's as big as we got, Saxen. Are you sure they don't fit?" He considered the problem. "Tell you what, Saxen, take home both pairs of extra-large trunks and have your mother make one big pair."

My face was on fire—I was sure the flames were visible to the other players in the room. No one said anything. I grabbed my number twenty-seven top and my two pairs of extra-large shorts and headed for the door; as I did, someone said:

"Hey Saxen, maybe you should take 'em to a tent maker."

* * * * *

Our first game. I'd tried the shorts on earlier that day. All things considered, Mom had done a pretty good job. On the bus ride to the game a couple of the guys gave me a hard time about the fashion show I was about to put on:

"So, Saxen, is that one pair of shorts for each cheek?"

"Coach said since you're wearing two uniforms we'll have to introduce you twice."

I smiled, gave them the bird. There was no way I was giving them the satisfaction of knowing how I felt.

Game time, the moment of truth: I pulled the shorts up past my thighs and over my ass.

"Let's have a look, Saxen."

There was nothing I could do, no way I could get out of the teasing I knew I was going to get. I figured I might as well turn my backside their way and get it over with.

"Holy shit, Saxen. Are those seams going to hold? One fart and it's over."

"Did you hear that, guys? Sounds like someone's moaning. Oh no, it's just the threads in Saxen's shorts screaming for help."

I was saved by the coach. "Okay guys, get on the court and start your warm-up drills."

As I warmed up I imagined the other team, the cheerleaders, and the crowd giggling and pointing. I knew they were looking at me and my shorts. The waist felt good, but the legs were pinching my thighs.

What Mom had done was open up the seam in the back of my shorts and add a six-inch panel. So, instead of one seam in the back, I now had two—a little crooked, but not bad. Definitely different though. Why did I have to be different? It wasn't fair.

* * * * *

One Saturday something very strange happened: Dad didn't go to church with us. He stayed home sick. It had never happened before, not once. In fact, my dad often went on about how he was never sick, how he hadn't missed a day of work in fifteen years. "It's all about having a strong mind," he said. "If you think positive, your mind won't let you be sick."

Although not a minister or anything, Dad was a big force at church. He was responsible for setting up the sound system and would sometimes lead the opening prayer. He was also the funniest guy in church—and probably the richest.

After church had ended, the six of us made the fifty-three mile drive home—for the first time in a decade, without Dad. It was just after two o'clock when we pulled up the road to our house and Mom said, "Huh, your dad's car isn't here. He must have gone to the store."

We kids went to our rooms to drop off our notebooks and Bibles; Mom headed to the kitchen. Robert and I assumed our typical

Saturday positions: lying on our twin beds and watching out the window, waiting for the sun to set so we could play games and watch TV.

No more than five minutes after our heads hit our pillows, the loudest and most disturbing scream I've ever heard in my life pierced every inch of our large house. Robert and I looked at each other in shock. Before we could say anything, there was another scream.

"Rick, Robert, Ronald!" Then another scream, and another.

The screams were coming from the far side of the house. From the kitchen. From Mom. I was scared, though I didn't know what of. I was sixteen and whatever was going on, it had never happened before. As Robert and I ran down the hall I felt sick.

Ten feet from the kitchen I saw that Rick had arrived ahead of us. Another loud scream from Mom. She threw a plate of cookies across the room—something I'd never seen—crying all the while. The plate crashed against the wall. She grabbed a jar off the counter, her face cherry red and already swollen from her tears. The jar followed the plate, crashed against the wall. I felt terrible—scared and sick; I felt like I did when I was about to be whipped.

Mom grabbed a bunch of yellow sheets of paper from a legal pad and shook them at the three of us. Between gasping sobs, she said, "Your father's left us—he's abandoned us." Another wild scream. She tossed the pages at our feet. "Go ahead, read it yourself." More screams.

Our mom had always been in total control. Now she had clearly lost it. The room was spinning around me—it was like I wasn't there. I had to remember to keep breathing. All my senses were bruised, as if I were going into shock. Our family had no love, no emotion—and now this? We were ill-equipped for anything other than order, discipline, and fear.

Knowing we were way out of our league, Rick called a church family who lived less than a mile away. As Mom continued to disintegrate, my two little sisters and we three boys stood staring at her, motionless and unable to help, like a crowd gathered around a crime scene. Finally Mr. and Mrs. Bellows arrived, and we pulled back from the spectacle to let people trained in emotion step in.

* * * * *

I've been told the nine-page note began, "I don't want the kids reading this." Yeah, right. That's like saying, "I know I just totally fucked up your life, but would you mind doing me a favor?"

Our lives turned around so fast. One moment we were the most popular family around: wealthy, God-fearing, upstanding citizens; the next, our life was a tabloid headline: dirty and tailor-made for gossip.

I've heard that Dad also wrote that he was seeing another woman and couldn't stand living the lie any longer—apparently he'd been doing it for years. There was a lot more, but, the gist of it was that he was gone. He'd planned his departure carefully, down to the last detail. In the five hours we'd been gone, he'd moved out. His note instructed Mom not to try to get a hold of him. He'd be gone for a while. Although, of course, he couldn't hide forever—he had a successful business not more than fifteen miles from our house and Rick still worked for him.

The other big news in the note was the disposition of the family: Rick and Robert were ordered to leave. They had 120 days to pack their stuff and find someplace else to live. According to Dad's note, they were old enough to be on their own, and he didn't want them bothering Mom. Since I was only sixteen, I could stay. The note instructed Mom to "tell the boys that if they even think about stepping out of line I'll come back and kick their asses."

In the weeks and months that followed, it got a lot harder before it got better. It was nerve-wracking to be in public with Mom. Someone would innocently ask, "Where's Frank?" and Mom would burst into tears. We all felt like such losers. Ministers came over to our house; together, we'd all get on our knees and pray that God would bring our father back.

In the beginning, my reaction wasn't joy or relief at losing the person who'd brought me so much mental and physical pain, just sadness. I'd gone from having the funniest, toughest, most successful father of anyone I knew to having no father at all. My brothers and I even had a lunch meeting with him at a local café in Antioch to try to convince him to come home. It was very strange. He said he didn't expect us to understand. He basically repeated what he'd written in the note—he couldn't continue to live a lie.

For the first time since I could remember, my eating slowed. The neutralizing effect of shock treatment, perhaps. I felt like my brains were scrambled: I'd gone to church the third son of a dominant king and come home man of the house. It was a role change that increased my self-confidence and inspired me to make some changes—changes that would start out moderate but eventually spiral drastically out of control.

CHAPTER 6

Double Vision

I looked down at my blood-soaked shirt and I was proud. On the other side of the fence a dozen headless chickens bounced and twitched like jumping beans, their final movements as life left them.

When my dad lived at home we boys were relegated to the boring parts of butchering—bringing out tubs of near-boiling water to dunk the chickens in, thus ensuring their feathers came off effortlessly; burying their remains in the garden to sweeten our vegetables; and generally standing around waiting for the next barked-out order.

Today had been an awesome chicken-killing day. I'd finally gotten the head removal trick down and it rocked. I'd already known several ways to kill chickens: binding their feet and cutting their heads off with a hatchet, hitting them in the head with a stick and then the hatchet, and even the way Mom learned as a kid—sticking their heads under a broom handle and then pulling them up by their feet until the heads popped off—a skill you'll never learn at the best finishing schools. But today I had mastered the crème de la crème, the bare-handed single-motion pop-off. I'd never known anyone but my father to attempt this maneuver. And now, of course, me.

First you pick up the chicken and put your hand over its head. In less than three seconds the chicken's neck muscles will relax—the chicken thinks it's beddy-bye-time. Then, with the chicken tucked under your arm, you turn the head counterclockwise and pull up, all in one quick motion. Done right, the head pops right off—quick for the chicken, efficient for you. I felt sorry for the victims of my first attempts though—the practice runs weren't pretty.

The morning was crisp. As I sat on the bloodstained butchering chair, dunking the freshly killed chickens, the frost from my breath mixed with the steam from the pot of water between my legs. The odor of dirty feathers and blood released by the near-boiling water brought back memories.

* * * * *

Just six months previously my father had sat here with the three of us boys standing at attention beside him. I now sat here all alone. Listening to the noise of butchering and the shouting of crows from a nearby orchard, I thought about all I'd accomplished in the last 180 days: I'd fixed fences—before I'd only been allowed to hold Dad's box of nails; I'd driven a tractor—unthinkable during Dad's reign; and I'd dug up our septic tank and unclogged it, a dry-heave-inducing task. Dad used to complain about being overworked, but he never delegated. Turns out he didn't have to do it all—he wanted to.

I think deep down Dad must have had an inferiority complex or he was too competitive for his own good. Either way, it seemed he needed to be better than anyone, even his children. I suppose in some ways he passed his insecurity on—my knowledge of his superiority was so great that it was only later, when I had realized a certain level of financial means was I finally able to feel confident and relaxed while in the same room with him.

In the months that followed Dad's departure I often felt like I was the adult and Mom was the child. I understood. She'd been through a lot. But at times it was hard. I remember one such time, a Saturday night—Mom had invited a date over to our house.

* * * * *

Mr. Jennings was divorced and had two little kids. It was Mom's right to date and she certainly deserved to be happy, but I didn't care for Mr. Jennings. He was a manual laborer who probably owned only one tie—a clip-on. He was small enough that even I could probably kick his ass, and he wasn't that bright. Mom was slumming.

After dinner Mom and Mr. Jennings disappeared; they were nowhere to be seen. I walked down the hallway toward my room, and saw that the door to Mom's room was closed. It was Saturday, the sun hadn't gone down yet, my two sisters and Mr. Jennings's two kids were in the family room—and Mom had shut the door? I didn't want to think about it. It made me sick. Mr. Jennings was in the church, but they weren't married to each other: whatever they were doing in that room was against our religion. What did they think—with the door closed God couldn't see them?

I decided to eat some of the leftovers to take my mind off things.

"Hey, Ron? Where's the liquor cabinet at?"

I looked up from my plate. Mr. Jennings stood there, blurry-eyed and smiling. I shouldn't have to see this in my house! At dinner he and Mom had polished off a bottle of wine and started a second. He stumbled and caught himself on the counter. I could deck his ass right now and he wouldn't even know what hit him...

"Ron, man?"

I didn't say a word, just pointed and looked away. This was a first for Mom. What was she doing? Was she okay? She had to be—I wasn't about to go into that room.

He brushed by me on his way to the liquor cabinet. I was boiling.

He fished around and found himself a gallon jug of Vino Mio, wine we'd gotten from old man Firpo's, a little winery two miles from our house. In the last few years I'd made a point to work on my temper, something I was renowned for; but by this point I was seething.

The table where I was sitting was only a few feet from the counter. Without thinking, I scooted my chair over, making it just a little bit harder for him to pass by. I don't know why—I wasn't planning to do anything—I just did.

"Thanks, Ron. Me and your mother are having a little party."

He bumped the counter a little bit on his way to the Ron-created narrows.

"Whoops! Got to watch it there."

The urge was too great. I stuck my right leg out.

His smile still in place, Mr. Jennings awkwardly tried to catch himself—but with a jug of wine in his hand and a bottle of wine in his belly, he didn't have a chance in hell. He fell face forward, kissing the cabinet in front of him on his way down. The fat wine jug bounced off the counter and rolled across the floor, somehow staying in one piece. I quickly sprang to my feet, heart pounding from the adrenaline rush. The kids in the family room fell silent. What had I done?

"Are you all right?"

Like I gave a shit.

"I'm okay. I just hit my head a little. Got a hard head, it's cool. How's that wine?"

"It's fine."

Rubbing the back of his head, he got to his feet; he retrieved the bottle of wine and said, "Gotta be more careful."

I just stared at him, jaw clenched, blood racing. I couldn't believe I'd done that—I could've really hurt him. Even though he was drunk, I think he understood what had happened. For a moment his expression was dead serious. Then an intoxicated smile crept across his face and he turned and ambled back to Mom's room.

* * * * *

In the months that followed, every now and then Mom would have a little too much to drink and blurt out something shocking, like, "I should cut your dad's dick off and feed it to him." I didn't like hearing it, but figured Mom had earned the right to say it. Like the understanding parent I'd never had, I tried to show compassion, I tried to give her the room to do whatever she needed to do, to get it out of her system, to heal.

Once when she was having a particularly hard day, she broke down and asked me to hold her. She was dressed in her blue housedress; crying, she looked weak and vulnerable. I didn't want to do it. It felt weird.

"Can't you just give me a hug?"

I realized then that she'd never given me a hug, not in my entire life. Oh, maybe when I was small, too young to remember, but not when it counted, not when it would have meant something.

"Please."

I didn't have a choice. I had to.

"Sure."

I forced myself forward and lightly put my arms around her. It felt like a lie, but I don't think Mom cared.

* * * * *

I think I've always felt more emotion than the rest of my family. But having my dad leave and then living with three females allowed me to grow emotionally even more. The divorce worked out better for me than anyone else. The timing was perfect. I still didn't have a normal life, but I had a better life. I'd gone from one extreme to the other—one minute, imprisonment and total submission, the next, freedom with powers granted.

I made an important decision.

I was tired of putting Desitin on my thighs every time the redness started to rear its ugly head. Although the rash was mostly gone, my skin was stained dark in the offending area, a constant reminder of my fattest days, a sign that I was different.

I was also tired of being ugly. When you're fat you're branded as damaged goods. The world thinks you suck. I agreed—I did suck. I was weak.

But more than anything, I was tired of not having a girl. I would daydream, wet dream, masturbate in the shower. It was an empty stomach that wouldn't be filled until I talked to, danced with, touched, kissed a girl. Maybe if I could just check one or two of those items off my list of wants and dreams, I could stop being a deviant, disgusting sinner? But if masturbation was a sin, why in hell did God make it feel so good?

No matter. I was taking action. One of the biggest challenges that had stood in the way of my changing my weight was now gone—my father. To my mother I announced, "Mom, I'm going on a diet. I need you to buy a bunch of cans of tuna in water—not oil. Oil's got 485 calories in a can, and water's only got 225. I'll also be eating less bread, so you may not want to bake so much. No more peanut butter in canned fruit, so only buy peanut butter for you and the girls. And, as far as canned fruit goes, you might want to can less. I can't say the next time I'll eat any."

I felt bad about the fruit. Back when the family had more mouths to feed, Mom canned over 400 quarts of the stuff per year, and I ate the bulk of it. She was happy I loved her canning so much. Now I felt as if I was letting her down. But it had to be done.

"Good for you!" she said, "You'll feel better. The canned fruit's starting to get backed up anyway. I think it's okay to have my homemade bread, though—that's good for you. Maybe just cut out the butter. I'll pick up some tuna in water for you tomorrow. Is there anything else you need?"

That wasn't so tough. I was glad Mom was so supportive. She understood—she was always trying to lose weight herself. Throughout my childhood it seemed neither of my parents was ever satisfied with their weight—they were always either dieting or talking about going on a diet. But that wasn't going to be me. I would get the weight off and be perfect for the rest of my life.

"Some diet sodas would be great."

Starting tomorrow, I was going to run three miles every day.

* * * * *

What a great game—I scored twenty-seven points!

It was an away game, against the Sacramento World Wide Church of God's basketball team. That was one thing about our church, basketball was huge. We had leagues for both teenagers and adults. Church of God teams from all over the country competed to go to the national championships in Cincinnati, Ohio.

My diet and regular exercise had really paid off. I moved up and down the court a lot better and my knees didn't hurt as much.

As I walked out of the locker room in my slacks and dress shirt, I could hear music coming from a large room attached to the gym—the postgame dance. I wished I were still on the basketball court; there I was comfortable, there I was a winner. Every dance was just another reminder of my shortcomings, another chance to stand on the sidelines, to go home with nothing, to be left wanting.

They were playing Michael Jackson's "Off the Wall." I loved that song. (When Dad walked out the door, so did the rule that we could only listen to country music.) There were so many cute girls there, girls I saw now and then at away games and church services—girls who didn't know me. Oh God, it was a slow dance, when wallflowers always looked especially pathetic. I needed to get some punch, look for someone to talk to, do *something*—anything but stare hopelessly at the dance floor.

Cindy, one of the cheerleaders for Sacramento, was walking my way. She had a pretty face, a slender body, and delectable olive skin. I figured I better quit staring, she was getting close. Trying to act natural, I smiled and dipped my head. Just in case she didn't reciprocate, I looked away. Where was my friend the punch bowl?

"Hi, Ron."

Fuck! Here was my ultimate goal: a female standing less than eighteen inches away. I was absolutely freaked. Suddenly I was hot and sweaty again.

Since I had clearly forgotten my lines, she took over:

"Ron, you had a great game. Would you like to dance?"

Certain that I looked stupid and was about to sound even stupider, I smiled and said, "Sure."

I—*I*—was following a cheerleader onto the dance floor. It felt like a train wreck in slow motion. I'd never danced with a girl before, let alone a slow dance. I had no idea why she'd asked me. If she'd known me, I was pretty sure we wouldn't be out there. Her ignorance was my bliss.

Once on the dance floor, Cindy turned around, smiled, and put her arms on my shoulders. I put mine around her waist clasping my moist hands together—a little trick I picked up from the couple beside us. I couldn't believe I was actually touching the object of so

hing. They would be so impressed—unless I died before reach-
he finish line, that is. With only an eighth of a mile to go, I was
than ten yards from the second place guy. I don't think he even
y I was behind him.

I pulled even with him. He looked over at me, matched my
. Who was going to blink?

Blink!

With 100 yards to go, I was now in second place—and I could
Adidas on the ass in front of me. He didn't see me yet—and
he was looking back, matching my speed and then some. Fifty
s to go. One more hard burst—second place was mine.

* * * * *

d been a month since I'd run that race, but like the basketball
, I thought about it all the time—replayed the tape of it over
over again in my mind. Everyone was shocked. People even
me if I'd mind running the 440 since I'm so fast. Since I'm *so*
They said it, not me. I wanted to have a T-shirt made that said
FAST."

Time to stop daydreaming: the restaurant manager was ready to
my interview.

"So, Ron, I see your work experience has all been in farm
…"

The job was a seventeen-mile drive from home, but I didn't
much of a choice—there were no jobs in our little town or the
towns around us. At the end of the interview, like a fly walking
a spider's web, the manager asked me The Question:

"So, why should I hire you, son?"

"Because I'm a hard worker, today is my eighteenth birthday,
t will be great news for my mom who's lying in the hospital
ering from surgery. I'm visiting her when I leave here."

It was like shooting him with a stun gun. It was all true of
e. I started selling when I was nine—I know what I'm doing.
nly near fib was my birthday. It really *was* my birthday, but I
celebrated it because it was against our religion. Something
the Bible saying, "It's better to celebrate the day of one's death

many hours of late night fantasizing. Suddenly I panicked—what if I
got a boner?

"So, Cindy, you live in Sacramento?"

"Actually, I live in Placerville. It's about a forty-minute drive to
church. Where do you live?"

"I live in Knightsen, in the delta near Antioch."

I couldn't believe this was happening. I was seventeen and I'd
begun to think it never would. I wanted to leave right then and go
somewhere and scream, raise my arms in victory. Every second I
danced was a new second, a new record, uncharted territory.

The song ended. I'd made it through the dance without making
an ass of myself. I looked at her and smiled. Now what was I supposed to do?

"Well, thank you."

"Ah… you're welcome."

She smiled at me. I was so uncomfortable. I knew I was supposed to do something to make this scene continue, but I didn't
know what it was. I just wanted to find my friends and bask in my
glory.

She walked away, I was guessing a little dissatisfied. I couldn't
help it, I'd had no training. I headed in the direction of two of my
wallflower friends, a little bewildered but full of pride, my dancing
cherry now broken. I was still in shock about what had just happened. I couldn't wait to give them a blow by blow.

"Oh man, I had my hand—"

"Ron, would you like to dance?"

I turned. It was another cheerleader from the Sacramento
church. I didn't know her name. Before I could even dissect my first
contact with the alien species, I was walking back out onto the dance
floor into second contact. Wow!

I danced with Julie (she helpfully told me her name), then
Cindy again, and then Julie again after that—and then I couldn't handle any more success: I found Mom and told her I was tired and
ready to go.

On the ride home Mom said, "Ron, I saw you dancing with
those girls."

It wasn't something I really wanted to talk to Mom about, but what the hell, I needed to unload. Mom was happy for me. I was shocked when she told me that Tina, the girl Robert and I had sent the ring to, had told her that I'd grown into a good-looking guy. Tina had gotten married six months ago—I figured she was probably just being nice. But honestly, I didn't know what to make of the dance. I wondered what the girls from my own church thought about seeing me on the dance floor—I hoped they'd noticed.

More than a month later, I was still thinking about that magical night, hoping it would happen again—that was definitely part of what drove me to take part in the church track meet.

* * * * *

Sitting on the warm grass of the infield at Fresno State—the site of the church track meet—I prepared for the mile race by stretching and drinking my special coffee and honey cocktail.

Church-sponsored track teams were open to all of the teenagers in our 200,000-member congregation; teams all over the country competed to go to the nationals at our college in Big Sandy, Texas. In past years I'd only entered the shot put and discus throwing contests—the fat-guy events. This year I'd entered the one-mile race.

Each church can enter three people per event, and since our church only had two milers, there was an opening. The coach was surprised when I asked to enter the event and at first wouldn't let me sign up. He was determined to win and wanted only fast runners. I guess he couldn't get the picture of the old 247-pound Ron out of his mind, but in the end, he decided to give me a chance. Now that I weighed 55 pounds less and ran every day, I planned to show everyone—I fantasized about the girls being blown away by my speed, talking about me to their girlfriends, wanting me, coming on to me.

"On your mark, get set," and then: *Pop!* from the starter pistol.

The twelve of us took off. Most of the guys were just skinny, not real athletes, but there were also three or four real runners. One of the guys had previously run a 4:06 mile, just fourteen seconds off the world record.

I'd gone only 200 yards and I was already i[...] the fuck was I thinking? All the girls were watchi[...] that I pictured blouses being buttoned high and "[...] signs going up all around the track. And yet, I fel[...] moving fast, faster than they did when I ran at h[...] last place. Why had I thought I could compete wit[...] runners?

I was coming up on the quarter mile. I start[...] pack of four guys. If I could pass them at least m[...] hurt my image. I increased my pace just a lit[...] dejected anyway, they knew they were too far b[...] head, I was playing the Rolling Stones' "Start Me[...] rock-and-roll purchase.

I was at the half-mile mark. There was a pac[...] more than twenty yards ahead. If I pushed it, m[...] them. That way I'd beat seven of the twelve runne[...] pace. Holy shit, I was passing them. A quick g[...] prised tired faces. Maybe I was going too fast—[...] any harder. Fuck, I'd better not totally crap out[...]

I was halfway through my third lap now a[...] about fifteen yards ahead of me who looked to[...] some of these guys raced out of the gate way too[...] their wad trying to pull off a miracle: beat Mr[...] before the three-quarter mark, I passed another[...] place now—that is, I was if I could just hold o[...] coach, ran my way across the infield grass, carr[...]

"Ron, slow down. You're going too fast. [...] onto third place."

Wow! I couldn't believe he'd said that. We w[...] track meet and you only got points for first, secon[...] I didn't blow a gasket, I was points he'd never c[...] bonus. He was right though. I'd never run this[...]

I had only a quarter of a mile to go and I[...] light-headed. The two guys ahead of me were a[...] yards away. Mr. 4:06 was in first place, of course[...] guts no glory. As bad as I felt, I again quickened[...]

---

wate[...]
ing [...]
less [...]
knev[...]

pace[...]

read[...]
then[...]
yard[...]

It ha[...]
game[...]
and [...]
aske[...]
fast[...]
"SO[...]

start[...]

labo[...]

have[...]
little[...]
into [...]

and [...]
reco[...]

cour[...]
The [...]
neve[...]
abou[...]

than the day of one's birth"—which my parents cited as further proof that Christmas was pagan.

In fact, I hadn't celebrated a birthday since I was four. A few birthdays had even come and gone without anyone realizing it. "Mom, I just remembered—I turned fourteen three days ago."

"That's right, you did. Congratulations. Don't forget to take out the garbage."

Always thought it strange, God preferring funerals to birthday parties…

* * * * *

Mom had had gallbladder surgery three days previously. It was tough seeing her look so weak after she'd always seemed so strong.

"Hey Mom, how're you doing?"

She looked a lot better. The noisy hospital equipment had been disconnected and there were fewer tubes going into her, so it wasn't so strange. There was still that strange hospital smell though.

"Oh, fair-to-middlin'."

"Well, you look better."

"Doctor said I can go home tomorrow. Don't know if I want to leave all this good service—it's pretty nice getting waited on hand and foot."

"Oh by the way, I got the job."

I slipped it in subtly, for maximum effect.

"Ron! That's great!"

"Yep. Now I can cover all my expenses—car insurance gas, clothes—and maybe even help out with the groceries or anything else we might need."

Even though I was still a senior in high school, I'd committed to working full-time at the restaurant, thirty-five hours a week, Sunday through Thursday, 5:00 p.m. to midnight. I didn't mind. I was proud to do my part. The thought of being around all that food did cause me some pause. But, like most dieters, when I was in the zone I was bulletproof. That and the fact that my life seemed to be improving made me okay with it. Also, I figured being around all that food would be a good test—one that could prove I had changed, that I could be normal.

* * * * *

I loved working drive-thru. It was where all the studs worked. Working drive-thru I got my own little cubicle, my own little world. I also liked the pace—I loved going fast, the challenge of an all-out dinner blitz. I felt like Clint Eastwood standing in the middle of the street, bullets flying, people dying, and me just doing my job—another bloody day at the office.

One Thursday, during a momentary lull in the battle, I saw a blue Chevy SUV through the restaurant's distant windows. It looked strangely familiar. It entered the drive-thru; I caught a glimpse of a blonde at the wheel—oh my God!

"Andy, come here a second."

My heart was pounding, adrenaline pouring into my veins.

"What's up, Saxen?"

"You'll never guess whose order I just took."

"Big Foot?"

"Close. My dad's fucking new wife. The woman he left us for. The one I've never met."

"You want me to ring up her order?"

"Hell no. Give me the food. Come on, let's go around the corner. The manager's downstairs."

We peeled the hamburger patties from the home wrecker's sandwich and threw them on the floor. Then we stepped on them—not enough to mangle them, just enough to be sure the heels of our shoes kissed the meat. After we put everything back together, I decided to go one step further: I spit on a napkin and rubbed it against each of the top buns, then added a little more salt.

With the order rebagged, I turned the corner and there she was: the lady who'd fucked our family to pieces. Looking calm but feeling on fire, I slid the drive-thru window open. "Hi, that'll be $6.37."

Without saying a word she handed me a ten. She was a platinum blonde and not very good looking in my opinion. I didn't know what my dad saw in her. For some reason she never wanted to see us kids. The only time we ever went to Dad's house she'd hidden upstairs. Maybe she couldn't handle seeing the collateral damage, the bodies.

I handed her the bag of food, flashed a big phony smile, and said, "Thank you very much."

She didn't say a word, just drove away. Andy and I burst into laughter.

It would be a long time before I was able to see Dad's new wife as anything but the enemy. Although she herself wasn't ultimately the cause of my family's problems, she still represented to me the destruction of my world. But, the truth was, with Dad gone I was better off.

* * * * *

"Ron, read this."

"What?"

"Just read it. I'll watch drive-thru."

I leaned against the counter and started reading:

"Ron, I think you're so cute and funny. I want to go out with you but I'm tired of waiting for you to ask me. I've never asked a guy out before..."

I was in a total panic. This was ten times worse than my first dance—this wouldn't end when the music did. What was I supposed to do? My total experience with women added up to one Elton John song, one Billy Joel song, and two Michael Jackson songs. Before I went into total shock, Andy walked around the corner with Nicole, the hottest girl at the restaurant, and said, "Okay, I've done my part—start talking."

Nicole put her hands over her blushing face. "I'm so embarrassed. I don't usually do this. I'll understand if you don't want to go out with me."

Words could not describe how floored I was.

"No, it's great. I like you. It's cool."

She was a ten—I would've been happy with the south side of five. She was still smiling. I should ask her out on a date—that was what real people did, right?

"Would you like to go out this Saturday night?"

From the moment she said yes until after our first date, the world around me blurred into obscurity. I couldn't tell you what my teachers said, whether other cars shared the road with me, or whether the movies I watched ended with Clint Eastwood getting the bad guy. My anxiety was almost unbearable. I was so far out of my league. What the fuck was I talking about? I didn't even have a league. She was the student body vice president of her huge high school, the in-est of the in crowd, one of the pretty people, the ones that had always looked down on me and made me feel unworthy—the ones that still did at my school.

Every minute of our first date was like the scariest part of a horror flick. We went to Tiffany's, a disco dance place. We danced all night and kissed—big, wet, inexperienced kisses. We saw each other as often as possible and necked for hours in my old run-down Olds 98—plenty of room for rolling.

The farthest we went was rubbing our pelvises together with all our clothes on. I wasn't sure exactly what was happening, but she would start to breathe heavily, get very excited, and then stop, always very happy. I thought she might be having an orgasm, but I wasn't sure, and I wasn't about to ask. I wanted to do more, but I was too scared—and I didn't know what to do anyway.

* * * * *

"So, Saxen, you going to the senior prom?"

"Yes."

"You're lying. Who'd fucking go with you? Oh, I'm sorry. I did hear that your mother was shopping for a dress..."

Barry was one of the cool guys. I was eating lunch alone in the cafeteria; he was with four other jocks.

"No, I'm going."

"Sure you are. It'll be nice to meet your mom."

"No, I really am going."

"You do know you can't bring a farm animal, right? So, what's the blind girl's name?"

"Nicole Stevens. I'm sure you don't know her."

"Nicole Stevens... from Antioch?"

"That's right—exactly."

"You're so full of shit, Saxen."

"No, it's true. You know her?"

"Why in hell would Nicole Stevens go out with your sorry ass?"

"Because she's my girlfriend."

I got up and started to walk away.

"Keep dreaming, Saxen."

Throughout the next period I thought about our conversation. At Antioch, a much bigger high school than mine, I was the boyfriend of one of the most beautiful girls on campus. I was also friends with some of the cool guys and girls who went there. Meanwhile, at my own school, I was a loser. I felt like a double agent—two lives, two completely different sets of self-worth.

By the time the period ended I'd solved the mystery: in my high school I was tagged with Fat Guy. Yes, over the last couple of years the label had changed, but not that much: now I was Fat Guy Who Lost Weight. I still had the fat ass stink on me.

Needless to say, I reveled in going to my senior prom with Nicole on my arm. The guys in my high school were all shocked. I was so fucking proud. Not long after that, though, Nicole broke up with me. Maybe on one of her trips to the bathroom, one of the girls from my school told her the truth, who I really was: Fat Guy Who Lost Weight.

* * * * *

At this point things were finally looking up for me—I was free of Dad's domination, I'd lost some weight, scored some victories, and even got a girl. In many ways, I'd put fat ass Ron behind me. But despite my huge gains in self-confidence, I still suffered from feelings of low self-worth. And although I didn't know it at the time, by pushing my body so hard athletically to impress others, I'd laid the groundwork for even more destructive exercise patterns later.

CHAPTER 7

Burgers and Blood

College was a time of dramatic fluctuations for me. At times my eating was completely under control; binges weren't an issue at all—I simply didn't feel the urge or the need. And then there were other times, times I just couldn't stop eating, times I couldn't control my behavior, no matter what had just happened and how inappropriate eating might be...

* * * * *

Kim was my second girlfriend, the first girl I asked out after Nicole dumped me. It was almost 11:00 p.m. and we were parked outside her parents' house in an upscale housing tract in Modesto. We'd just returned from pizza and a movie. I took a deep breath.

"Kim, you know I'm starting college in a few weeks, and between college and working full-time, I'm not going to have time for a girlfriend. It wouldn't be... fair to you. I've got to get good grades."

I was scared of college, and desperately wanted to do well there—and I definitely hadn't done well during my last semester of high school while juggling school, a girlfriend, and a full-time job.

"You're breaking up with me?"

"It has nothing to do with you. I don't have time for anybody."

Without another word she got out of my 1968 burgundy Olds and walked toward her parents' house. Not much emotion on her part. Maybe she was keeping it inside—or maybe she was glad. I don't know. Either way, it had been easier than I'd expected. I was proud that I'd broken up with Kim in person and not over the phone or in a note like my old man.

To be honest, the fact that it didn't look like Kim was ever going to have sex with me definitely had something to do with the breakup. Doesn't say much for me I guess. Now I was zero for two—two girlfriends, zero sex. Not even nudity or a really good feel.

I'd tried to jump Kim's bones three times—three strikes and I was out. The first time I just started undoing her pants, the seasoned salesman's "assumed close." She smiled and said no. The second and third times involved alcohol. Both times I chose the dollar-ninety-nine Andre champagne, first the Brut and then the pink stuff. Both times, when I thought she was liquored up enough, I tried unsnapping the lock to the Promised Land, with the same result: "No," and "No." After the third strike I was desperately in need of a hormonectomy—or, at the very least, a handful of the pink pills.

* * * * *

The summer after I graduated from high school my mother, my two sisters, and I moved to Stockton so Mom could be closer to school. She was majoring in agri-business and starting next semester she and I would be attending the same school, San Joaquin Delta College. Even with the move I wound up working in fast food—but surprisingly, this time I worked with a guy from high school, someone who I'd always thought was a geek but turned out to be pretty cool—and my best friend.

* * * * *

I was sitting in the school lounge one day, studying, when Mark Roberts walked in. He was this brainy geek from my old high school—too smart for his own good. He had a thick unruly mop of blond hair, and although he wasn't particularly handsome, the lucky nerd was stacked with muscles. I looked down at my books, hoping he wouldn't notice me.

Shit, he saw me. Dammit, he was coming my way.

"Ron, is that you? How's it going?"

"Great, Mark. So, you're going to school here, too?"

Turns out he was—and he was looking for a job. Instead of keeping my big mouth shut I told him I could get him an interview where I worked. Of course he got hired. I could only hope he didn't make an ass of himself, start talking about Nietzsche, or get all Socratic: "So, why do you think you don't need fries with your hamburger?"

Six weeks later I couldn't believe how wrong I'd been about him. Sure, Mark was smart, loved history, and listened to classical music—shit, Dvořák and Wagner were his favorite musicians. But he was also incredibly funny. We hit it off big; he even moved in with me—when Mom transferred to Fresno State for her last two years of college, she let me and Mark rent her house for the price of the mortgage, $220 per month.

* * * * *

Although I worked forty hours a week while going to school full-time, I managed to get through my freshman year with a GPA of 3.83—but was pretty much a basket case. I was sticking to my no-girlfriend rule, which meant I'd be twenty in a few months and I was still a virgin. I'd obeyed God's no-sex-before-marriage rule, but not intentionally. At this point, it seemed like failing to get laid might well be a worse sin than sleeping around.

"But St. Peter, I never had premarital sex."

"Sorry, you're going to hell. The only thing we hate more than a sinner is someone who wants to sin and can't get the job done. You're pathetic. Next!"

One reason my life was a sex-free zone was that I'd gone from driving an Olds to driving a Schwinn—a real fucking chick magnet. Getting paid $3.75 an hour didn't bring in enough money to do much—especially not fix a car. So when the mechanic said a brake repair on my Olds would cost $400, I called my father and asked him for a loan—not a gift, just a loan. His response? "If I do it for you, I'll have to do it for all of you kids. You need to learn to solve your own problems."

I was beside myself. Dad was rich, made lots of money—he said so himself. And he'd told all of us kids he'd pay our way through college—he said he wanted to give us what his parents hadn't given him. All I needed to do was present him with a financial statement. Fine. Doing the math, I figured that what with working forty hours a week, all I needed was $80 a month more to be able to cover all of my expenses.

My dad made two payments and then informed me that since getting the whole $80 at one time might tempt me to waste it, he'd decided to break it up into two $40 payments. And oh, by the way, how come I didn't call? It was the least I could do.

Mad as hell, I called a confab of the Council of Elders—i.e., me and Mark. By this point Mark was my best friend. Turned out he was not only smart, he was wise beyond his years—beyond anybody's years. Like Socrates, he taught with questions.

"What's the real problem, Ron?"

I gathered my thoughts. "That I'm working my ass off and my dad ain't giving me shit—a lousy $80—*and* he's making me dance for it."

"What are your choices?"

"Well, I can stop taking his money and work more hours, pick up some extra shifts... I might have to reduce my class load though."

"Integrity isn't easy, Ron. It usually comes at a price. Can you afford your integrity?"

As always, Mark was brilliant.

Without hesitation, "Yes."

"Good, it's settled then. By the way, I didn't want to tell you until you made your own decision, but if you do ever get into a bind, either my parents or I will help you."

I could've—maybe I even should've—been a dick to my father. But I wasn't. I simply sent him a letter explaining that I'd taken another look at my budget and I didn't need the $80 from him after all.

* * * * *

Saturday, time for church. I'd been whining to Mark about needing the time to study.

"Why are you going to church, Ron?"

"Because I'm supposed to."

"Says who?"

"Well, the church does. And my mom will be pissed if she finds out I haven't gone."

"Okay, Ron, let's think about that. You've given me two reasons. Let's deal with the second one first. How old do you have to be before you can do whatever you want?"

"What do you mean? I can do whatever I want now."

"Excellent. That takes care of worrying about what your mother thinks. Now let's talk about the church."

Like Socrates, Mark asked great questions. To the best of my ability, I gave honest answers about the church teachings I'd learned. Previously, when I'd asked Mom or other church members about religion, I'd always end up cornering them. Then, instead of debating they tended to pull out the old religious Kryptonite: "Ron, we're not meant to understand that at this time." But that didn't work on Mark.

"Ron, do you think men are better than women?"

"Of course not—they're equal."

"But, according to your church, God says they're not. Does that sound like God to you?"

Women in our church weren't allowed to speak during service. Women couldn't be deacons or ministers or even lead prayers. Men had a spokesmen's club, but women didn't need one—they weren't supposed to talk. Once, the minister even said during a sermon, "Wives are like children. If they step out of line there's nothing wrong with bending them over your knee and spanking them like a disobedient child."

I looked at Mark and said firmly, "No."

"You said it's against your religion to celebrate birthdays?"

"Yes."

"Do you really believe that an entity—God, if you wish to call Him that—who is so powerful and great that He can create the vast universe, really gives a shit about you blowing out some candles?"

This went on for many hours and many beers—Mark didn't quit until I was saved. The weeks and months that followed weren't always easy—when you've gone to church every Saturday for fifteen years it's a hellishly hard habit to break. Then there was getting over God—not the good God, but my church's God. It was like going through rehab: it took me a while to get unscrewed, to get off the lies. Finally, though, I had only one big step left to take.

✳ ✳ ✳ ✳ ✳

During Easter break, Mom and my two sisters came to visit.

"Mom, let's take a walk."

I knew the church and I knew the rules. They said, "If you leave us you never were of us." As soon as you broke away, the church would have nothing to do with you. You were corrupt, doing the devil's work. If you had a girlfriend in the church, she'd dump you immediately if she knew what was good for her.

I didn't know how my mother was going to take my departure. Would she plead with me? I figured the best thing to do was to hit her with my decision right between the eyes so hard she couldn't get up and fight—and I wanted to do it away from the house so none of it spilled over onto my sisters.

We bundled up and walked out into the crisp spring air. After a little small talk I said, "Mom, the reason we're going for a walk is because I've got something to tell you. I don't want you to interrupt until I'm finished. Do you understand?"

She frowned. "Yes."

I didn't necessarily believe all the things I was about to say, but that wasn't the point. I needed a clean knockout.

I told Mom that the Bible was nothing more than the mythology of a people. Just as we looked back at the Greeks and laughed at their belief that lightning came from Zeus and rough seas were the wrath of Poseidon, one day people would look back and laugh at Noah's Ark, the parting of the Red Sea, and manna from heaven.

"It's because people always want to know where they came from and where they're going," I said. "It's human nature."

Just in case she still had the will to get back up, I added, "Leaving the church takes more guts than staying. Staying is buying into the fairy-tale ending, while leaving is living with uncertainty, future unknown."

I don't know whether I truly did knock her out or she was just too stunned to react, but she didn't get up off the canvas. Like most tough decisions, finally making this one felt both good and scary.

* * * * *

Things weren't going well.

That was an understatement. For the first time in my life the word suicide flashed through my mind. It wasn't that I was suicidal—I wasn't, not even momentarily—but I'd had a fleeting glimpse of how it could happen.

It was the middle of winter, cold and dark, outside the house and in. Regardless, I was so broke that most of the time I kept the electric heater and the lights turned off. I hadn't had a date in well over a year—an eternity at twenty. I was tired of pedaling my ten-speed to school through the winter rain, and physically exhausted from working while going to school full-time. I fell asleep at the drop of a hat—during class, while studying in the school lounge, or on my break at work. The only thing that kept me awake was moving and eating.

Oh, yeah, and although now six foot one, I'd gained 35 pounds, putting me at 240 or so. I was becoming ugly again. Worst of all, I was finding myself doing crazy things again—things regular people, good people, didn't do.

For example, one Saturday, as I was riding my bike home from work—I'd worked all day, a big sin just a few months ago—I saw my local Safeway up ahead, and knew I was about to do something I didn't want to. I didn't believe I was completely powerless over my need, but it was close. I knew the following day I'd wake with an uncomfortable stomach and a dark depression, but I'd fight that battle tomorrow. I needed relief right now.

This particular Safeway sold these generic fruit pies—Hostess knockoffs—that weren't half bad. Although Hostess pies cost forty-five cents apiece, these generics seemed to be on permanent special: six for a dollar. I had five minutes until I passed the market, until I had to commit. But who was I kidding?

I gave in. As I locked my bike outside the store, I felt a rush, started to salivate. Inside I went right to the bakery section. There was my display: two cherry, two apple, and two chocolate pudding pies. I counted my money. With change, I had two dollars and fifty-five cents. What the hell, why not get fifteen?

I wanted to go home and devour them in peace, but Mark was there so I couldn't. But I definitely didn't want to sit at a bus stop or in a park and eat fifteen pies. What if someone saw? No, I would just do like I normally did—ride around the neighborhood in my blue polyester uniform pedaling my bike with no hands as I ate my pies.

* * * * *

Initially, moving to Sacramento had the same impact on my crazy eating that Dad's leaving did: it scrambled my brains and helped me break my cycle of insanity.

Mark and I moved to Sacramento together to attend Cal State–Sacramento. Graduating from junior college to university scared me as much as going from high school to junior college did. But this time I didn't have a girl to drop. Dropping Kim in favor of studying seemed even stupider now than it had before. I should have kept trying—maybe after *two* bottles of cheap champagne, the eleventh shot at undoing her pants would've been the charm. Nobody likes a quitter.

Metropolitan Sacramento was huge—two million people, compared to Stockton's measly 119,000—and there was tons of stuff to do right nearby: the Sierra Mountains for hiking and fishing, South Lake Tahoe for gambling, and the American River for more hiking, biking, and floating in our inner tubes. And unlike San Joaquin Delta College, Cal State–Sacramento had a real campus, with big, old buildings, tall shade trees, and even a pub—if you were nervous about a test, you could have a couple of beers to steady your pencil.

Mark and I found a two-bedroom furnished apartment close to campus—vintage '70s furniture, a classic '50s building. We both worked at Orchid's Coffee Shop as dishwashers/busboys. The work was hot and required some hustle, but we had fun with it.

Although the move to Sacramento calmed much of my crazy eating, at the same time, food and eating remained intensely important to me—my consuming need to eat sometimes popping up in the weirdest of circumstances.

* * * * *

As we drove up a dirt road in the Sierras, Mark and I were both a little nervous, even though we were prepared for anything. Mark had an M1 Carbine with a thirty-round clip and a Smith & Wesson .357 Magnum, while I had a Dirty Harry .44 Magnum and an AKS—also with a thirty-round clip, basically a Chinese version of an AK-47. If the Russians came a-callin', we'd be ready. What made us nervous were the two guys from Orchid's we were with. They were a lot younger and crazier than we were. Tim owned the Jeep and saw himself as a ladies' man, Mr. Cool; Jack was a Tim wannabe.

However, it was a sunny day, and, as always, the mountains inspired me. No matter what the weather, I loved this area. Today Mother Nature was awakened by four guys with two weapons apiece firing at anything that moved. To increase our shooting options, Tim pushed the Jeep's front windshield forward—after all, if we got attacked by a band of renegade chipmunks, we wouldn't want to accidentally shoot out the front windshield.

Usually, Mark and I were responsible when it came to weapons. We knew it was both illegal and irresponsible to fire from a moving vehicle. Still, today when we saw something move in the bushes we'd swing around and start blazing—we knew better but we were caught up in the group stupidity.

"Mark, hold my pistol, I'm going to try and push over this stump," Tim said.

Tim was driving, Mark riding shotgun, with me and Jack in the back.

"Hey, Tim, is this safe? Maybe we should get out first."

"Don't be such a pussy, Ron."

Tim handed his pistol to Mark. Mark now had a pistol in each hand.

"What a minute, Tim. Let me put one of the pistols in my shoulder harness."

Tim didn't wait. Just as Tim bumped the log, a weapon discharged.

"Fuck, I think I shot myself."

It was Mark. I leaned forward. Blood was spilling over the seat and cascading to the floor. Nobody knew what to say or do.

"Where were you hit?"

Wincing in pain Mark pointed to where his thigh connected to his hip. A quick poll revealed that none of us knew much about first aid. All I knew was that if the blood kept flowing, we'd need a tourniquet.

"Get out of the Jeep, drop your drawers, and we'll see what we're up against."

I didn't know what else to do. At least it was something. Mark's face was white—he looked close to passing out.

"Mark, why don't you just lean over the Jeep."

I undid his pants and gently pulled them down. There were powder burns on the entrance wound and a hole in the back of his thigh—the bullet had gone clean through. "Good news, Mark—the bleeding's stopped."

He looked at me, "Really?"

"Yep, it's a great sign. All we need to do is get you to the hospital in Placerville and everything will be fine."

Of course I wasn't sure how fine everything would really be, I just knew Mark could use some good news—after all, we were currently two and a half hours from the nearest hospital.

Mark was a champ. Sure, each bump in the road obviously sent a jolt of pain shooting through his thigh, but as always, he was busy telling jokes and cracking us up. We were less than five miles from the hospital when I realized something very important.

"Mark, it's been over two and half hours since you were shot, right?"

"Yes."

"I mean, it doesn't seem like you're going to die or anything, right?"

"No."

"And when we roll up to Emergency it'll be all hands on deck—nurses, doctors, cops—they have to call the cops whenever there's been a shooting. For all they know we've just robbed a bank or were in a drug deal gone bad."

"So?"

"Well, I don't know about you guys, but I'm starving." I let that hang until I got a few yeahs in response. I continued, "We could go through a drive-thru. There's a Burger King right off the freeway. I'm just saying, who knows when we'll get a chance to eat again?"

Everyone laughed, Mark included. Before their laughter died, I sealed the deal:

"And, since none of us knows where the hospital is, we can ask the person working the drive-thru."

My logic was flawless. Tim waited until we were handed our Whoppers, fries, and chocolate shakes, then said politely, "Excuse me."

"I'm sorry, did I forget your straws?"

"No, we're good on straws. We just need directions to the hospital—this guy's been shot."

I couldn't fault Tim for his delivery. How often do you get to say a line like that? Eyes wide, the drive-thru girl gave us hurried directions in a panic. We fought to keep from cracking up until we'd gotten out of earshot.

We found the hospital easily enough. It was surrounded by pine trees and looked clean and new—a nice place to take your gunshot wound, I'm sure. Before heading in, we sat in the parking lot and finished our food. It felt good to eat. Not only was I hungry, I was feeling very anxious. I'd be able to handle the hospital and the cops better with a full belly.

Knowing a thing or two about firearms regulations, I told Mark, Tim, and Jack that we couldn't tell the cops the truth. It's against the law to fire from a moving vehicle or even just have a loaded gun within arm's reach of the driver. Under my guidance, we changed our story to unfit the crime.

When the last fry was eaten and all of our shakes had made that sad gurgling empty noise, Tim walked into the hospital. Shortly afterwards all hell broke loose.

Three nurses, a doctor, and a gurney charged the Jeep. Someone placed a call to the authorities. Within minutes a police siren was added to the mix. It was a slow news day—we were obviously providing the day's entertainment for greater Placerville.

In the end, everyone except me fucked up the story. After a police officer interviewed us one at a time, he came back to me and said, "You seem to be in charge of this group. Would you like to tell me why each of you seems to have a different version of the facts?"

My face got hot as it always did under stress. I stared at him, slack-jawed, trying to think. Before I could say a word he continued, "Let me put your mind at ease: Whatever you did, we're not worried about it. No one's going to jail here. You guys, and especially Mark, have suffered enough."

Just like Tim at the drive-thru, I couldn't resist. "Well, since you put it that way, the stories are different because the dipshits can't remember what I told them to say."

His eyes got wide. Another second passed, and then he started to laugh. A moment later, I joined him.

* * * * *

Stockton found me in Sacramento.

I was so burned out I couldn't stand it. I was working for months at a time without a day off, and if I wasn't working, I was attending class. Most days I did both. It had been two and a half years since I'd had my last date and almost twenty-one years since I'd gotten laid—and that's only if you believe in reincarnation. (I was hoping I'd had a lot of sex in a previous life to make up for this one.) I was tired of riding my bike everywhere, tired of being tired. Worst of all, I was bingeing and my weight was rising yet again—I was closing in on 250, for me a terrible milestone, one-eighth of a ton...

* * * * *

"Ron, what have you done?"

All I could do was stand there, my face red, and take it.

"This is the third time you've eaten all my food. What am I supposed to do?"

"I'm so sorry, man."

"I'm just thinking out loud. Should I hide my food? Keep it locked up? Maybe just not keep any food in the apartment?"

I hated it. Mark was such a good guy. What the fuck was wrong with me? I knew better. And yet... He'd baked a cake from an instant cake mix, and left two-thirds of it in a pan on the counter. I ate it all. Then, after also eating all of his Corn Pops, I opened his box of Frosted Flakes and finished them off, too. Of course, I then needed his milk to wash it down.

Once I've started I can't stop. After it's begun I can only watch helplessly. Because I know I'll be depressed soon after it's over, I usually start working on my excuse before I've even taken my first bite. "I deserve it, I need a break, I need an escape." Or my favorite: "I'll be perfect—starting tomorrow."

*   *   *   *   *

I dragged my bike and my grocery bag upstairs. Mark was away visiting his parents. I was so fucking excited—this binge was going to be great—my best ever!

With a knife I cut the cardboard off of my half-gallon tub of Häagen-Dazs peanut-butter-fudge ice cream and dumped it in a large mixing bowl. I microwaved a jar of Hershey's chocolate fudge sauce until it was warm and gooey, and poured it over the ice cream. Which left only my half-pound bag of plain M&M's and my half-pound bag of peanut M&M's; I poured them both on top. When I was done, I chased the monstrous sundae with four Snickers bars and two Reese's Peanut Butter Cups.

I couldn't believe I'd eaten all of it. A little over halfway through I'd had to stop and eat a bowl of cereal, just to break up all that sugar. And then depression came.

In the last few months my weight had shot from 228 to 260. My knee had given out on me a while back, making it hard to exercise. Not only that, recently I'd had to start buying Desitin again for my rash. My pants were so tight that I always kept my shirt untucked to hide my unbuttoned top button. I was so out of control, so full, so hopeless...

I looked over at the mixing bowl and put my hands on my painfully bursting belly. This was bullshit. I couldn't keep doing this. If I did, it would eventually kill me. Starting to get misty, I wiped away my tears and said aloud, "That's it, I quit. This time it's over for real—forever."

No sooner did the words leave my lips than my mind went back to work: "If I'm going to be good forever starting tomorrow, what's the harm in adding one more act to tonight's performance? McDonald's is open until 11:30. Why not add in a couple of Big Macs, a few cheeseburgers, two large orders of fries, maybe even an apple *and* a cherry pie..."

The thought excited me.

* * * * *

Even though the two darkest things in my life were now gone—Dad and the Church—I was acting crazier than I ever had. The disordered eating of my childhood had left me with a permanent scar: although bingeing devalued me in my own eyes, it was still my first line of defense in coping with any stressful situation, good or bad.

1982–1985

The Insanity

CHAPTER 8

Bookstore Body

Every hundred yards or so I burped up some food—my body's way of saying, "What the fuck are you doing? If you want to run in the morning, don't stay up the night before ramming 15,000 calories down your throat."

The previous night had been my very, very, *very* last hurrah. The following day, Mark was to return from his parents' house—and I planned to surprise him with an apartment full of food. That is, if I finished my run without a heart attack. Another burp. That one was sour.

In keeping with my new vow to eat perfectly and exercise constantly from now on, my overfilled stomach and I were going for a snail's-pace limp/jog. The good news was that it was November, a cool, comfortable month for wounded hippos to run. The bad news was that my stomach was currently sticking out so far I couldn't see my feet.

Due to a small cartilage tear, I was hobbling, in pain and keeping one leg straight at all times—I moved like I was wearing a cast. On top of that, my crotch sores were back in full bloom; every stride I took rubbed my skin rawer and rawer. At least the pain in my crotch was so loud I could barely hear the complaints from my lower back...

In spite of the pain, I couldn't have been more optimistic. I always was. It had happened now more than 200 times in the last four years: the morning after a night of wild eating, I'd awaken and immediately forgive myself, experiencing the strong sense of a new beginning. And when it came to exercise I didn't know anyone more hardworking and dedicated than I was. So why did I keep finding myself fat and out of shape? It wasn't fair.

I'd only gone about two miles, but man, was I tired. With all that food in my stomach I couldn't breathe as deeply as I wanted to. I decided to walk a bit. It was the strangest thing—I could taste what seemed like blood in the back of my throat, just like the first time I'd started running to lose weight four years earlier. The strange salty taste reminded me of being out of shape and starting over— something my parents did repeatedly and something I swore I'd never have to do again. Walking felt good—walking let me spread my legs and pull my sticky sweats away from my burning crotch.

Presently I weighed 268 pounds, a new fat-assed record. I'd be thrilled to get down to 200, or even 210. To get down to 200, I'd have to lose 68 pounds. If I ran an hour every day, I'd burn a total of 3,150 calories; if I took in 2,000, that'd mean a net loss of 1,150 calories a day—34,500 calories, or 10 pounds a month. Thus, if I were perfect, I'd be down to 200 pounds in seven months, by the end of June.

But wait, if I ate only 1,500 calories a day, I'd burn 1,650 calories every day—49,500 calories, or 15 pounds or so a month. Then I'd be at 200 pounds by the middle of April. Fuck, that'd be hot! What if I could eat just 1,250 calories a day? I'd be hungry as hell, and feel weak all the time, but who cared? I could lose 57,000 calories, or 17 pounds a month...

I decided to try to eat just 1,750 calories per day. If I could eat less, great. But this time I would make it. This time was different. By spring I'd be light enough to get a girl. Shit, by spring it would be three years since I'd had a date. Maybe I should take the money I'd spend on dinners, flowers, and movies and invest in a sure thing instead: Rick's favorite, Mustang Ranch. Sure it was cheating to hire a prostitute, but who wants to be a twenty-one-year-old virgin?

* * * * *

As I rounded the turn of the American River bike trail, I let myself bask in the glory of my accomplishment: It was the end of March and this morning I'd weighed in at 228 pounds and it *rocked*! My knee had healed, the fire in my crotch had been put out, my lower back felt fine, and I was even fitting into some of my old clothes again.

God, I loved where I was running. The trail, twenty-seven miles long, hugged the clear American River. It was a natural zoo; amidst the tall trees and sagebrush wandered squirrels, rabbits, dove, quail, pheasant, and the occasional turkey. Made me feel like I was somewhere else, some place far away.

I loved running now, too. Sitting on your ass doing nothing for an hour, you burn about 110 calories. Sleeping, only 80. But when you run, you burn 550. How perfect is that? Not to mention runner's high: I used to find joggers self-righteous—made me want to blast 'em with a fire hose; however, now that I was experiencing runner's highs myself, I was so damn positive I couldn't stand myself.

Best of all, it's physically impossible to go off your diet while you're actually running. So whenever I found myself yearning for sex *and* barbecue, I knew it was time to put on the running shoes.

Speaking of girls, running also reduced both my sexual tension and the shame-induced binges that followed masturbation. After masturbating, I was always torn between guilt and wanting more pleasure—both feelings drove me to the kitchen. If I were one of the fabled, lucky 7 percent who could just keep on choking the chicken until completely satisfied, would I stop at that? Nah, I'd still want to top it off by devouring a bucket of KFC.

Just one thing worried me: I realized now that when it came to eating, I wouldn't know normal if I saw it. All my life I'd either eaten too much, eaten way too much, or starved myself. And in the previous four years it had only intensified. For me, gaining or losing ten pounds in a month was no big deal; eating a normal amount of food seemed impossible.

Less than a mile to go. I ran through a quiet upscale neighborhood. The familiar finely manicured lawns and diverse architecture reminded me I was nearly home—time to do my daily math: if I ran twenty minutes more a day, I'd burn 2,900 calories a day (I was now burning calories at a lower rate than before because I was thinner and it was easier to run). If I ate less than 1,750 calories a day, that'd mean a net loss of 1,150 calories a day—or 8,050 or roughly two and a quarter pounds a week. Which meant that by the end of April I should weigh as little as 215. Excellent.

It was 1:20 in the afternoon; so far I'd consumed 875 calories. If I could stick to eating just one cup of sugar-free Jell-O and four rice cakes before dinner, I had a great shot at hitting my goal.

* * * * *

Not long after Mark and I proved ourselves as dishwashers/busboys at Orchid's, we were promoted to waiters. (A definite improvement: better money, a faster pace, and the chance to bullshit with the guests.) After a few months of waiting tables we heard there was speculation among the crew about our sexual orientation.

"Well, you live together, work together, and go to school together," one of the hotter waitresses said, "and neither one of you has a girlfriend—or even seems to want one."

Mark and I both laughed uneasily. We didn't have anything against homosexuality, we just didn't want any potential girlfriends saying, "Damn, I would've loved to ask him over for sex and beer, but I hear he's gay."

* * * * *

"Here's your check. Sorry to keep you ladies waiting. Did you need any more coffee?"

"No thank you, the coffee's fine. My friend and I have a bet. I said you're a model for sure, she said you might be."

"No I'm not a model. I'm actually Tom Selleck. I'm wearing a disguise and waiting tables because I want to see how the other half lives—been my fantasy for years. Now, don't forget to watch me in *Magnum, P.I.*"

"Seriously, are you a model?"

What the hell? The women looked to be in their early forties and they weren't laughing—they were either telling the truth as they saw it or they were extremely good actors.

"Seriously, no. Did my buddy Mark put you up to this? That guy right over there?"

"So, you're not a model?"

"No, but thank you. You're in my will, such as it is."

Well that was strange.

* * * * *

"Now don't take this as a come-on, but are you in the modeling business?"

It had to be the fifth customer who'd said it in the last month.

"No, but I'm beginning to think about it."

"You should look into it."

"And give up all this?"

"Seriously, you should."

"Maybe I will."

But if I looked so much like a model, why didn't I have a girl-friend? But maybe the no car, no money, and almost no practice with women explained that...

That day, after work Mark and I went to a bookstore. There, Mark persuaded me to at least check out some of the books about modeling. Searching the bookstore aisles, I felt a surge of sweaty-palmed excitement. There was no way modeling was really a possibility, but it was fun to dream.

After browsing a few minutes, I found what I was looking for: a big glossy book about America's top ten male models, filled with beefcake shots. There were large pictures of each guy and his income, followed by the numbers I was most interested in—height and weight.

Nervous in my excitement, I looked around the store like a shoplifter, then read eagerly about each model. Right away two things stood out: First and most important was their weight. They all weighed somewhere between 170 and 185 pounds. Factoring in height differences, that made me still between 20 and 25 pounds overweight. Second, all but one had blue or green eyes—mine are shit brown.

As Mark and I drove back to the apartment my mind was spinning. I hadn't weighed 185 pounds since seventh grade. I'd been trying to get from 205 to 200 for the last month and hadn't lost an ounce. Apparently I'd hit one of those weight-loss plateaus. So, me a model? No way! But what if... If those women weren't bullshitting me, they really thought I was model pretty when I weighed 205—imagine what they'd say if I weighed 185!

If I became a model that would solve everything. If a model couldn't get a girl nobody could—I'd go from no date to any date I wanted. And then I'd have such good cause to stay thin that I'd be thin for the rest of my life. And then I'd never do crazy things, things that embarrassed me, ever again. Modeling would be more powerful than my insanity.

* * * * *

My alarm clock read 10:00 a.m.—wonderful. My goal was to sleep as long as I could. Any hours spent sleeping were hours I didn't have to think about food, being hungry, or blowing my diet.

The coffeemaker was gurgling as I hoisted my leg onto the kitchen counter and stretched out my hamstring. For twelve days in a row I'd been perfect now—a record. I hadn't known I had it in me. I took my last sip of breakfast (two cups of black coffee) and jogged downstairs and out of my apartment building. It had been two weeks since I'd looked at the modeling book for the first time. The previous week I'd returned to the bookstore for a motivational visit.

School was out and it was a warm summer day. Now that I was thin, I liked it warm, even hot—heat felt better when I ran. I felt like I could run forever. I floated effortlessly over the asphalt trail that ran alongside the clear, fast American River now—it had never been so easy. Maybe it was because my weight was so much lower, or maybe it was because the vision of my fantasy future lifted me. I don't know, but I felt like I was special; the world just didn't know it yet.

After running five miles, I headed home for my between-meal snack: another cup of black coffee. It was 11:30 in the morning and I still hadn't eaten anything. Pretty good. Time to clatter back downstairs with my ten-speed slung over one shoulder. This time I'd ride the American River bike trail in the opposite direction.

After pedaling for forty-five minutes, I was dripping with sweat, weak, running on fumes. All I could think about was the emptiness gnawing at my belly. I tried to counter it with dreams of the fame, women, and money in my future; sometimes the dreams would drown out the hunger, sometimes they wouldn't.

12:35. I'd have a banana with my next cup of black coffee. I'd last eaten solid food the previous night at 10:30, which meant I'd now gone fourteen hours without food. Time to change into fresh workout clothes before heading across the street to the gym.

Getting a grip on a 100-pound barbell—light compared to what I was used to—I didn't even try to get in a quality lift. I couldn't. My tank was empty, bone dry. I barely had enough energy left to go through the motions—but that was still better than nothing.

1:28. I pulled on my swim trunks. I'd been swimming twenty lengths a day. Today I was going for twenty-five. Afterwards, I leaned against the wall in the shower, absolutely spent, trying to talk myself forward: "Come on Ron, mind-over-matter time. Stand up, finish your shower, put on your clothes, and get yourself over to Skinny Haven."

As I waited to be seated at Skinny Haven, I held my hand out in front of me: it shook. Not surprising really—it was now 3:30; in the last seventeen hours I'd run five miles, ridden twenty miles, done a full weight workout, and swum twenty-five lengths—all on only four cups of coffee and a banana.

"Right this way, Ron."

I had to concentrate to act normally, to keep from passing out or slurring my words. I made myself smile at the hostess even though I didn't want to spend the energy, did my best to follow her briskly—all the while thinking how much I'd rather collapse onto the floor, eating a Big Mac on the way down.

"Your waitress will be right with you."

"Can you tell her I'm ready to order?"

I knew I should wait patiently, but I was dying.

"Here's your water. I hear you're ready to order?"

"Yes, I'll have the Skinny Haven Banana Split." I ordered it because it was large and sweet. It was twelve ounces of low-cal soft-serve ice cream, sliced bananas, three kinds of low-cal syrup, and a sprinkling of finely ground nuts. It looked sinful, tasted sinful, and was good for you.

"It should be up in just a few minutes."

At 3:42 and three seconds the banana split arrived. My mind was focused entirely on the 335 calories in front of me. My goal was to keep my intake to 1,000 calories for the rest of the day.

After I'd devoured my Skinny Haven Banana Split, I was satisfied. But I knew it was only a temporary satisfaction: With the banana, I still had 565 calories and nine long hours to go before I could crawl under the covers to the safety of sleep—and then start the abuse all over again.

CHAPTER 9

The M Word

I groped for the alarm clock, hit the snooze button.

I loved waking up now. With my eyes still closed, I reached down and felt my stomach: no fat. In fact, if I tightened my muscles and ran my hands over my skin, I could even feel the separate cans of my six-pack. They'd always been there, just hidden under years of gluttonous eating. But now I was living perfectly, and my body felt thin and empty—wonderful.

Yesterday, before jumping into the pool for the twenty-five laps that would conclude my five-hour workout, I'd climbed on the scale. I always weighed myself *before* swimming because I didn't want the extra half-pound of water I sucked in doing laps and the few ounces my skin sponged up included in my total. But yesterday, standing on the scale, I'd done a double take.

Holy shit—179.

* * * * *

Brian, a cook at Orchid's, overheard me telling Mark that I needed a portfolio—a collection of photos of me to show to a modeling agency—something I'd learned while browsing through the male modeling manual on my third visit to the bookstore. Turned out, cooking was just Brian's day job. On weekends, Brian shot weddings and graduations; he even had his own darkroom. He offered to cut me a deal if he could use my pictures in his portfolio as well.

For our third shoot, we headed down to Old Sac, a tourist attraction meant to resemble Sacramento in the 1800s. Brian thought the old time saloons, train museum, and nearby Sacramento River would provide us with picturesque backdrops for our photos. But we had to hurry—this was the final day I'd have my rented white tux with its bright red bow tie.

Brian was a perfectly dressed stud with that smooth Billy Dee Williams charm that told you he was in control and it was all cool. "Ron, didn't I tell you I was going to take care of you?" he said, making a sweeping motion with his left arm. Two seconds later, a drop-dead gorgeous blonde walked around the corner. She was by far the most beautiful woman I'd ever seen in person, a cross between Bo Derek and Farrah Fawcett.

"Ron, I'd like you to meet Tammy. Tammy, Ron."

"Hey there, Ron!"

"Uh… yeah, hi."

I'd never seen such perfection, such flawlessness. I loved that she was so beautiful and so close, but I almost wished she weren't there—she scared the hell out of me. I was much more comfortable appreciating such beauty from a distance.

"Ron, can you help Tammy with her stuff?" Brian said. "You guys can change at the Firehouse Restaurant—they said it was cool."

I grabbed Tammy's extra set of clothes and shoes and followed her into the restaurant. As she walked into the restroom I marveled at her beauty, but I couldn't truly enjoy it: I knew in just a few minutes she'd emerge and I'd still be petrified.

"Sorry I took so long."

OK, now I was totally screwed: Tammy had changed into an elegant black dress that dipped low in the front and even lower in the back; every square inch of her visible body was bronze and intimidatingly beautiful.

Back outside, Brian explained what he had planned for us. I was so frazzled I only heard every other word. He was still talking when a vintage black Rolls Royce pulled up.

"Kerry, my man, thanks for showing."

Brian was amazing. He got Miss Heart Attack to appear by promising her some good photos of herself. He got the owner of the Rolls to show up by offering him professional pictures of his car. And through general bullshitting, he got the Firehouse Restaurant to let us use their courtyard for our garden backdrop, just because.

"Tammy, stand in front of Ron. Ron, pull her tight—make like you're whispering in her ear."

Oh shit, here we go. I felt Tammy's body against my crotch. Don't get a boner, Ron. Amazingly, so far I was doing fine—fear was my pink pill. Even Tammy's neck was a masterpiece. And as for her ear, it was perfect—if they ever published a magazine called *Play-Ear*, Tammy would be in it.

"Okay, Tammy, I want you to kiss him on the cheek and hold it."

My first kiss in three years. I could barely stand it.

"Now, Tammy, look into Ron's eyes."

I felt light-headed; my vision was becoming cloudy, a little dark. I'd been here before, during a few blood tests gone bad—the next step was flopping like a fool onto the ground. I shook my head. It cleared my head, but only for about ten seconds. The dizziness was coming back. This was *not* going to happen to me here—not in front of Tammy. I shook my head again.

"Brian, I need to go get something—I don't feel good."

Without waiting for a reply or looking at Tammy, I took off in the direction of a hot dog cart I'd seen on the way in. Don't collapse, you fucking dumbass. Don't even think about it. It's all just in your mind. Every few steps I shook my head, just to be safe.

I rounded the corner. The hot dog stand was still there; luckily there wasn't a line. My hand was shaking as I handed the vendor a five dollar bill. As soon as it was ready I snatched the hot dog out of his hand. Screw mustard and relish—I chomped into the hot dog, threw back some Coke, and chomped some more. As my vision started to clear, I realized the hot dog vendor was staring at me. With bread clinging to my teeth, the last bite still in my mouth, I forced a smile, "Hungry."

What must he have thought? In the middle of the day a guy in a white tux and a red bow tie, shaking like a leaf, charges his weenie cart and crams a hot dog down his throat in four ravenous bites. As I walked back toward my shoot, I realized it wasn't Tammy's beauty that had threatened to send me to the canvas. It was hunger. I hadn't eaten for eighteen hours.

✳ ✳ ✳ ✳ ✳

On my way to Brian's house—to decide which of the 500 photos we'd taken in the last three weeks I wanted for my portfolio—I found myself shaking my head. This was ridiculous, this couldn't be my life. My life was about struggling with my weight and its side effects, about insane nights of ramming thousands of calories down my throat—not wanting to, but powerless to stop—and years (three, but who's counting) without a date. I was way out of my league. But, here I was, pulling up to Brian's house in my new-to-me car. (I'd been able to purchase the twelve-year-old, spray-painted silver Toyota Corolla thanks to a loan from my brother Rick. It even had a hole in the floorboard so you could see the road pass underneath—very Fred Flintstone.)

We sat at Brian's kitchen table; he had a big smile on his face.

"I thought we'd look at your fat pictures first."

What kind of smart-ass crack was that? Still smiling wide, Brian spread out two dozen photos from the two-layers-of-clothing day. We'd been working near the capitol building that day and there'd been nowhere to change, so Brian had insisted that I wear my suit over my casual wear, in order to shoot both. Naturally, I'd protested. All my life I'd avoided sweaters because their bulk made me look like the Pillsbury Doughboy. Now I had to wear two sets of clothes at once? For my portfolio? No way—I'd look fat. We went back and forth on it, but in the end, Brian won. Miserable, feeling like a kid in a snowsuit, I let him snap his pictures, all the while knowing I'd look terrible in them.

"What'd I tell you, pretty boy?"

Oh my God, I looked thin. Damn, how thin was I?

* * * * *

My next step was to take advantage of a favor from a waitress at work named Katie. Her neighbor, an architect, who let her sun herself by his pool, was also a model on the side. Thanks to Katie, Andrew had agreed to meet with me and give me some free advice.

I was a few minutes early, so I just sat there, in my rusty Toyota. It was the most affluent part of town, and I was parked amidst Jags and Beamers; I definitely did not look like I belonged. Andrew's house, with its stonework and turret, reminded me of a castle. The fact that he was apparently rich as hell wasn't exactly helping my nerves. I squirmed uneasily. I was about to walk into some rich guy's house so he could look me up and down like a side of beef—and then what? If he said I wasn't cute enough, did I just quit? Commit model suicide by burning my gel and eyeliner?

It seemed every day I crossed another line, did something that freaked me out. I couldn't believe that despite all of my anxiety I was still holding it together—that I *wasn't* reaching for food and its stress-obliterating relief. I guess my hope for a miracle was just too powerful for my food urges.

A knock on the passenger side window: Katie. I took a deep breath, grabbed my portfolio. Here went nothing.

"Thanks, Katie."

"No problem, it's just fun to be a part of it. Don't worry about Andrew, he's cool."

We rang the bell, stood there. Finally, the huge oak door swung open to reveal Andrew. He was gorgeous. Even though he was in his early forties, he had to be the best looking man I'd ever seen. He was wearing a robe; a large white standard poodle stood at his side—how regal. This wasn't helping.

Good-looking people, male or female, scared the hell out of me. They seemed like members of some special club; I wouldn't be surprised if they had a secret handshake. Where they went, who they knew, what they talked about, and what they did were all completely foreign to me.

"Sorry, just finished a few laps in the pool. You must be Ron."

"Yes... uh, I mean I am. Ron. Sorry, I knew the answer to that question."

"Katie, can you take Ron into the conference room? I'll put on some clothes and be right with you."

"Ron, is he cute or what?"

"Very cute. Is he seeing anyone?"

A smile from Katie, then a serious look.

"Kidding. Just kidding."

We made our way through the house. Nothing was out of place. It reminded me of a Ralph Lauren ad with its many paintings and sculptures set against rich dark wood paneling. The conference room was more of the same. Katie and I sat at a large table. I opened my portfolio and waited.

A few nervous minutes later, "Sorry to keep you waiting."

Andrew now wore an untucked silk shirt over a pair of Bermuda shorts. He had salt and pepper hair, a square jaw, flawless skin, and those pretty blue eyes every model seemed to have, but I didn't. Pulling out the massive oak chair at the head of the table, he said, "Let me see what you've got."

I slid my portfolio his way. Katie and I studied his reactions as he turned each page. It was so surreal. "Hi, I'm Ron, nice to meet you. Would you like to look at a bunch of pictures of me? Let me know if you think I'm pretty."

"Very nice. I think you've got a good look. Take your shirt off."

All my life I'd done everything I could to keep my clothes on. Even as a kid I'd worn a T-shirt in the swimming pool. And I'd hated showering in high school—I was the kid who'd put "We should turn off the lights while we shower to save electricity" in the school suggestion box.

I unbuttoned my shirt and, without thinking, did what I'd done all my life: sucked in my stomach. I felt totally exposed, primed for ridicule.

"Okay, that's fine. Go ahead and put your shirt back on. I think you've got a great look, very athletic. That seems to be in right now. You need to watch your weight though—"

How could I still be overweight? I was half dead from dieting and exercise!

"...If I were you, I wouldn't lose any more. In fact, you could add three or four pounds."

Oh. My. God. Magic words I'd never ever expected to hear.

"...I'll call my agency and recommend they take a look at you."

I tried to focus.

"Now here's the deal," Andrew continued, "and you didn't hear it from me. They also own a school that's separate from their modeling and casting agency. Their agency is legit, they've got connections at Eileen Ford and Wilhelmina, and their models are in national magazine and TV ads. But the school's just another profit center. If they bring it up, tell them you're not going to spend any money—if they can't make money off of you, then you must not be worth their time. If they don't agree, just politely walk out."

He picked up the phone like it was nothing and got me an appointment at the agency for the following Friday.

A few minutes later I was in my car heading home, my head spinning with possibilities. It was the first day in ten years that I didn't believe I was overweight.

* * * * *

I didn't sleep much in the nights leading to my showdown with reality. Sitting in the waiting room of the modeling agency, tired and surrounded by pictures of pretty people, I felt like I'd made a huge mistake. What was I thinking? A couple of customers pop off about me looking good and suddenly I decide I'm a model?

As Sharon and Barbara looked me and my portfolio over, I kept waiting for them to stand up and say, "Hell no! And would you mind leaving through the back door? We wouldn't want anybody to get the idea you belong here." But that didn't seem to be happening —instead, I was signing a one-year contract with the agency. I couldn't fucking believe it. Was there a judge somewhere in the universe who kept score, deciding when people have suffered enough? Was it finally my turn for a better life? My hand was shaking so much, my signature was more of a scribble.

"Okay, before we let you go, we'll need to see you walk."

I followed Sharon and Barbara down the hall. Maybe they were taking me to a lab full of blinking lights where they'd implant a universal translator into my brain, just like on *Star Trek*—only this one would allow me to communicate with pretty people. A minute later, we entered a large room with mirrored walls and a two-foot-high runway down the center.

"Please walk back and forth down the runway for us—just be natural."

I climbed the stairs and started walking. They said to be natural, but shouldn't I be doing something?

"Good. Walk up and back one more time."

Seriously, this wasn't my life. It couldn't be. I felt like a liar. I knew, deep down inside, that if I told them that I'd been eighty-eight pounds heavier a mere nine months ago, they might not sign me—and I wouldn't blame them. If they knew my darkest secret—my insane eating—it would be over for sure.

"Ron," Barbara said, "do you know that when you walk, you lean forward and roll your shoulders forward? Straighten up and keep those shoulders back."

I adjusted myself, kept walking.

"Much better. Now take your shirt off."

Wow, here we go again—time to suck in my gut.

"Turn around please."

I tried, ever so slyly, to tighten my back and chest muscles.

"Great. Go ahead and put your shirt back on and step down, please."

Barbara started to say something—Sharon held up one finger, in warning. Barbara nodded. Sharon walked over and shut the door.

"What I'm about to tell you never leaves this room, okay?"

Not sure what the hell was going on, I said firmly, "Okay."

"You may not know this, but we also have a school. While our focus is on modeling and casting, we also make money from the school. It would be very helpful to us if you were to tell people that you went to school. Not here of course, but some school back east. You may never get approached but we need to have our stories straight. Do you understand?"

Oh my God. It amazed me how quickly they'd taken me into their confidence. Was the five-minute lesson, "Don't lean forward; roll your shoulders back," really all the instruction I needed to be a model?

"Yes, I understand."

"Excellent."

Sharon put her hand on my shoulder and motioned me toward the door.

"We'll see you in a couple weeks for the fashion show in San Francisco."

* * * * *

I sat in my car, with the windows rolled down, letting my new reality wash over me. In my head, I'd known all along that I was losing weight, shooting the portfolio, and meeting with Andrew for a reason. But I'd been dreaming for so long about being thin and good-looking that it felt like I'd suddenly jumped from fatso to model, in just one afternoon.

My life flashed before me: I was the ugly guy, the fat guy, the no-date-in-three-years guy. As if in a near-death experience, I saw the kids who'd teased me, looked down on me, and made me a wallflower—the ones who'd helped me create a self-image as a flawed, unworthy person.

Then I saw their futures: Nicole, who had dumped my ass after the senior prom, opening a magazine and seeing the new me—and is left stunned and yearning. The high school jock who verbally tore me apart in front of his buddies, watching me on TV as he rests a can of beer on his fat belly and yells at his litter of screaming rug rats. And finally, Tina, recipient of the anonymous love letters and stolen ring, thinking of me as she looks at her soft, unshaven husband snoring beside her and regrets her lost opportunity... Watching her face drop, I say, "Fuck, yeah!"

Shit, it was 2:47 now—I was late for work.

Not that I cared. Work sucked. I'd recently switched from Orchid's to The Barrier Reef, a promotion of sorts, from coffee shop to steak house. As a kid I'd dreamed of working at The Barrier Reef. The waiters in their assorted costumes seemed to be having a great time singing, doing magic tricks, and telling jokes. Then I got a job there. Talk about bait and switch! First, I was promised five shifts and only got three, and then I had to give more than half my tip money away. Most of it went to the cooks, busboys, and cocktail waitress, but some was demanded by the headwaiters who made out work schedules as extortion money. (The first time I forked over my shift protection money I'd been amazed by how frank the headwaiter was. He recorded my bribe in a ledger, making sure I could see the amount I gave compared to bribes from the rest of the servers, then said, "Are you sure this is all you want to give me, Ron? You know I'm making out the schedule tomorrow.")

After signing my modeling contract, I was two hours late for work and my brain was in overdrive trying to process my new identity. Thus, I was definitely in a take-this-job-and-shove-it mood as I walked into the shadowy restaurant where the waiters were setting up. Two of them looked up and shook their heads at me.

"You're in so much trouble, Ron."

I walked straight to the back and knocked on the door of the dining room manager's office.

"Mr. Nelson?"

"What happened, Ron?"

"I'm late."

"I can see that. And it's not acceptable. You know, Ron, there are a lot of people who'd love to have your job."

Boy, this guy was clueless as to how this place ran, how little money most of us actually took home. I kept waiting for the clerk at the grocery store to say, "Oh, you work at The Barrier Reef? You poor guy—your groceries are on the house." Nelson must have seen the utter lack of remorse on my face. This was not a good day to fuck with me.

"I think you need to talk to the general manager about your attitude. Then we'll decide if you work tonight."

I felt an energy spike that made my skin tingle.

Loud and clear, "Excellent."

He rocked back in his chair. Surprised, he told me to wait outside. Watching him through the glass as he picked up the phone, I smiled. My heart was racing.

"Mr. Adams wants you in his office right now."

To piss him off, I smiled and said graciously, "Thank you."

I'd initially been sure Adams was gay due to his overly stylish clothes, manicured hands, and the way he comported himself. Then I'd found out he was married and had two kids. So much for stereotypes.

Adams put out his hand for me to shake, "Nice to see you, Ron. Have a seat."

Instead of seating me in front of his desk, he motioned to a small table in the middle of his huge office.

"So, Ron, I know we've never really talked, but I'm still kind of surprised at what Mr. Nelson has to say. Why were you late?"

Still burning inside, I took a deep breath, searching for the most withering response I could imagine. It had to be professional, but also devastating.

"Because I chose to be."

Hah. Your turn, pussy boy. Jaw clenched, I stared into his eyes.

He looked straight back at me. His expression went blank, then shifted to a slight smile. Without dropping my eyes, I could make out his right arm moving. The next thing I knew, his hand was on mine.

"Ron, I like you and I'm sure whatever reason you had was a good one."

As he finished his sentence, his fingers slipped under my palm so that his hand clasped mine. I hadn't seen that coming. Now I was the one who was stunned.

He smiled, "As I said, I like you, Ron. Just let me know that we're fine and I'm willing to put this whole incident behind us."

He stared directly into my eyes, waited for my response. I stood up, which allowed me to pull away from his hand without it seeming purposeful.

"Should I get back to work then?"

He, too, stood up, stretched out his hand, "If you ever need anything or just want to talk, my door is always open."

Trying to maintain an air of normalcy, I put my hand back into his and gave him a firm handshake.

"Thank you."

As I walked back downstairs, I could feel myself being watched by a few of the waiters milling around. I grabbed a bunch of napkins and took them over to a table to fold.

Jeff, the funniest waiter besides me, said, "I'm surprised you've still got a job."

"I'm kind of surprised myself."

Folding napkins, I decided that this day would go down as the most bizarre of my life. I woke up an undercover fatty, but would go to bed a male model. On top of that, I was pretty sure my boss had just come on to me. I'd just gotten special treatment because of my *looks*. Okay, the come-on was from a gay guy, but didn't people say gay men were sticklers for good bodies? It was flattering—yet another stroke for my ego, on a day when it didn't seem like my ego could be stroked further.

CHAPTER 10

The Dream

I was on Interstate 80, headed toward San Francisco and my first fashion show. Music played on my radio but I didn't hear any of it. I was both euphoric and petrified. Signing the modeling contract three weeks earlier might have announced to the world I was a model, but today was the day I had to make it real.

* * * * *

Two days after Sharon and Barbara had anointed me pretty, I'd figured I now had what I needed to cross into the Promised Land, a.k.a. the land of female companionship. Since I was starting from zero, I decided to get scientific about the woman thing, treat it like a business. Love was my ultimate goal, but I also just needed to get laid.

Step one was to make a list of the ten women I'd most like to date, and then rank them from one—total goddess and scary—to ten—not so cute but not so scary. Since I was no longer going to church and kept to myself at school, the list was composed entirely of waitresses from Orchid's and The Barrier Reef.

Step two was to rank the top ten from most likely to say yes to most likely to file a restraining order—basically just the list in reverse order. Obviously the hotter ones were the most likely to say no, but it was fun just thinking about dating them. It gave me a sense of control, took some of my fear away.

With my battle plan folded up in my wallet, I went to work. I planned to utilize the Vietnam War tactic for approaching a hot LZ—a landing zone where you were likely to take enemy fire. First you locate the target. Then you swoop in with overwhelming firepower.

Since I was now working at The Barrier Reef, I engaged Mark, who still worked at Orchid's, to do reconnaissance. He took my top-secret top-ten list and wrote down each waitress's work schedule.

Monday, 5:00 p.m. According to intelligence reports, Michelle and Kathy worked this shift. I double-checked the encrypted list in my wallet to confirm their rank: Kathy, six, Michelle, two. From my car parked out front I could make out Six near the cash register up front. Two was nowhere to be seen.

Nervous as hell, I kept going over what to say. Although actually, that was probably just a waste of time. As kids Dad had made us write down our sales pitches and practice them before we hit the streets. I don't know if it was laziness or nerves, but in the end I'd always scrap "I'm representing the Knightsen Elementary School. We're trying to raise money…" and just blurt out, "Wanna buy a candy bar?"

I took a seat by the counter, near the kitchen.

"What're you doing here, Saxen? Come to get your job back?"

Earl was a cook I'd befriended who always gave me a double portion of roast beef on my French dip whether I asked for it or not.

"Just looking for a woman, Earl."

Talking to Earl helped loosen up my tongue, warm me up for combat. I decided that if need be, I was willing to go straight to nuclear: "Hi, did you know I just signed a modeling contract?"

Earl exited through the swinging door to the kitchen. I was alone again, rehearsing my cool, debonair approach when Michelle/Two ran in, late for work.

A few minutes later:

"Hi, Ron. What brings you here?"

"I came to see if you would go out with me."

She smiled wide, paused for two solid seconds, then said, "Really?"

Since "really" wasn't "yes," I immediately pulled the pin on the nuclear option: "Did Mark tell you I signed a modeling contract?"

I was shocked when she agreed to go out with me.

Even with a signed modeling contract, I found it hard to erase my self-image as unworthy and uncool. When the world suddenly decides you're good-looking, they don't give you an instruction manual to tell you how to act, how to think. My virginity, my long dry spell without a date, and my general lack of experience all increased my nervousness and lack of confidence. Part of me felt that, just like modeling, getting a girl and losing my virginity was crucial to putting the old Ron behind me, burying him forever.

＊ ＊ ＊ ＊ ＊

Michelle and I had been a couple for a few weeks and no sex. The plan was to give her two months and then move on. I refused to become the only thing worse than a twenty-one-year-old virgin—a twenty-two-year-old virgin. Virginity was driving me insane.

I entered the high-end mall for my fashion show and saw the long runway set up in the huge atrium. Just looking at it sent a wave of pure fear through every inch of my body. I walked over to a brisk, efficient-looking woman standing by a poster advertising the show.

"Excuse me, I'm a model. I'm supposed to go somewhere to get fitted?"

"Through that door on the left and then up the stairs—you'll see everybody."

I walked past Nordstrom and into the stairwell. I couldn't believe how overwhelming my fear was—my heart was pounding so hard I could hear it; my legs were about to collapse under me. I feared not just the show itself, but also the pretty people in it. What was I supposed to say to them? How should I act?

I reached the top of the stairs and walked over to the well-fed security guard standing in front of the door.

"I'm with the fashion show—one of the models."

Wow, I still couldn't believe it was true.

The security guard found me on his clipboard, checked me off, then opened the door. Behind it was a long shadowy hallway, with glass-walled rooms on either side. I didn't see anyone, so I started walking straight ahead.

Twenty steps later I stopped short. On my right, behind the glass, were a dozen women in their underwear. I quickly turned my head, frozen in my tracks. What the hell! Why had that guy let me in here? There was no other way I could've walked. I wasn't looking, but I knew they'd seen me—what the fuck was I supposed to do now?

"Are you lost?"

Mortified, I turned to face whoever had just caught me. What a way to start my modeling career—peeping Ron.

My mouth dropped. I was looking straight into the eyes of a gorgeous redhead in her underwear. She held her dress in one hand.

"If you're looking for the fitting room, it's this way."

Completely disarmed, trying like hell to look at anything but her, I followed her. A few steps later we entered a large, plain, uncarpeted room where I saw two more girls in their underwear, a well-dressed man and woman surrounded by racks of clothes, and a guy I was guessing was a model. He was.

"It's about time you got here, Ron. Hi, I'm Tom. It's just the two of us and all these women—my kind of show!"

We shook hands. Then Tom walked over to the guy with the clipboard. "The other male model's here. We can go ahead and get fitted now."

In all my life I'd never gotten a girl to so much as take off a blouse—and now I was surrounded by women in their underwear. I wasn't prepared for this. What if I got a boner? Any more excitement and I was going to experience spontaneous combustion—first there'd be an *I Dream of Jeannie* puff of smoke, then when the air cleared, all that would be left would be a pile of ashes shaped like a penis.

"So how long have you been modeling, Ron?"

"Counting today?"

Tom laughed. "Yes, counting today."

"One day."

"Oh my God, a virgin."

He didn't know how right he was. He threw an arm around my shoulder and said, "Stick with me, I'll walk you through it."

Tom was an inch or two taller than me with classic good looks, a beautiful smile, dark hair, and those annoying blue eyes. He took me over to a tailor with bleached white hair, rolled-up sleeves, and a tape measure hanging around his neck.

"Alright you guys," the tailor said, "there are going to be eight sets. You two are in six of them. We'll do the fitting for Ralph Lauren first."

"Do we just change in front of everybody, Tom?"

"What, are you shy? Oh, I get it, you're one of those guys with a really big dick—I hate show-offs."

All I could do was give one of those forced laughs that sounded like a cough.

Everyone was acting so natural. I was pretty sure my underwear was presentable, but there was no way I was stripping in front of all those people. All these women, Tom, the tailor with his clipboard— this was just too fast.

"Listen, Ron, it's no big deal: don't look hard and don't get hard."

I gave the tailor my measurements. He handed me a pair of black pants, a shirt, and a jacket.

"Try these on."

I couldn't. It was too much. "Excuse me, where's the bathroom?"

Numbed by the whole experience, I walked down the long hallway to the bathroom, tried the clothes on—all the while feeling like a fool for hiding in the boys' room.

"The pants are a little loose."

"Where'd you go, Ron? You *do* have a big dick, don't you?"

Fuck it. If I walked down that hallway again, I'd make a total ass of myself. Here went nothing.

As soon as my pants reached my ankles, Tom said, "Very nice, Ron. It was worth the wait."

I couldn't believe I was standing in a big crowded room in my underwear. Good thing I didn't know about this job requirement beforehand! I'd never liked my ass—now it was hanging out there for all to see.

In the next hour, as I was fitted, I discovered that Tom wasn't at all what I expected. Even though he'd been in the business for four years, Tom was just a regular guy, a big kid that didn't take himself too seriously.

Ten minutes before showtime. Tom and I shared the changing area—a large red canvas tent at the end of the runway—with twelve women. My space, with my six sets of clothes, was right next to our top model, Tiffany Michaels. A light-skinned African-American, she had looks and a figure that were striking. We were so close that we bumped each other twice while putting on our first set of clothes.

The music started. The women began to strut out. Tom and I waited for our cue. I felt like I was about to step off a cliff. For my first set I was wearing a suit by Perry Ellis, topped by an overcoat. To hold off utter panic, I tried to remember how to slide the overcoat off and drape it over my arm like Tom had shown me earlier.

"You're on guys."

I left the security of the tent—and finally entered the world of modeling. On the runway, I had to fight the urge to blink in the glaring white light. There was a sea of people out there looking up at me… Just keep moving. Tom had said to act like you own the place.

I made it to the end of the runway. Okay, time to stop, let the coat slide down… Shit, it was stuck. I hadn't practiced it with the sports coat on. Nothing I could do now though—I just had to pull. Damn, the arm of the coat was inside out, hanging down like an elephant trunk… I rolled it up in a ball, tried to act natural.

Jacket wadded under my arm, I sauntered back to the changing room, fighting the urge to quicken my pace to escape all the judging eyes. No time to cry, I had less than two minutes to get changed. Backstage of a fashion show runs like the Indy 500—you either move fast or get run over. While I unbuttoned my pants, a young female helper whisked off my shirt and tie.

The next two sets went fine. Then, just when I was starting to relax, I caught my toe on a seam in the runway carpet and stumbled. I didn't hit the deck, but I felt like an idiot.

My last set done, I stood in my imaginary cubicle, loosened my tie, and took a deep breath. Suddenly, Tiffany was back, to change for her last set. I needed to keep my face forward and not move my eyes to the left to sneak a peek... Still, it's not a foul if you don't get caught, right?

Damn, her caramel-colored skin was beautiful against her white bra and panties... I felt both wonderful and pathetic. I was twenty-one and this brush with Tiffany was the farthest I'd ever gone with a woman. Just one more peek...

Oh my God, she was topless—oh shit, I was staring. I hadn't known the last set was to be lingerie. Little did Tiffany know she was the first woman I'd ever seen even partially naked. And she was the first woman I'd actually gotten to touch while she was in her underwear (we'd accidentally bumped twice). After I had a smoke, I really ought to buy her some flowers and a thank-you card...

On the long ride home I listened to music and soaked in everything that had happened. The day made me feel like I was erasing the old Ron. Sure I'd had a few fuck-ups, but I was a model, and I'd just had what amounted to the best sex of my life.

* * * * *

Nine days after my first fashion show I was on my way to the fall fashion shoot for the newspaper's Sunday magazine. I was glad—every day that passed without more modeling work, my new self-image became a little more fragile.

I took the elevator to the photographer's studio on the sixth floor. My anxiety was back. Not as bad as it had been at the fashion show, but bad enough. I found the studio, walked inside. My adrenaline spiked.

The studio was a huge, high-ceilinged room, filled with cameras on tripods pointed at blue and white backdrops lit by what looked like open umbrellas with lights in their centers. I met the models I'd be working with, three women and one man. The male model was the opposite of Tom, arrogant and superior.

It felt like high school all over again. As soon as the camera stopped clicking, the other models huddled together, laughing and talking like the kids at the popular table, leaving me out. I was forced to get a soda or go to the bathroom, just so I'd have something to do beyond standing around looking pathetic.

My drive home from the shoot didn't feel anything like my drive home from the fashion show. I was a model, hand-picked for that shoot, and yet I still felt like shit. Negative voices chirped in my head, "You don't belong. You're a fraud. Your lies will be discovered."

* * * * *

I woke up; the second I realized it was *that* Sunday, I threw my pants on, hopped into the car, and drove to the local 7-11. The bell jingled as I entered. I could barely contain my excitement as I snatched up two copies of the Sunday paper and brought them to the counter. After I'd gotten my change, I actually ran to my car. I jumped inside, slammed the door, and began fumbling through the advertising crap. There it was—fall fashions.

My heart felt like it was going to jump out of my chest. Slowly, deliberately, I turned the pages. Shit, there I was. The picture was huge! A few more pages and there I was again with the two tall female models. Oh my God—a full page and it was just me. This was so unreal. I went back over all the pictures and did the math: I had two more pictures than the other male model, and my pictures were bigger. Screw that asshole.

Later that afternoon, Mark and I went to see *Ghostbusters*. As usual, I'd talked his ear off; now it was time to give it a rest.

"I'm buying, Mark."

"Yeah you are. It's the least you could do."

"Two for the 3:15 showing of *Ghostbusters*."

"$11.50. Oh my God, you're the guy in the paper, in the magazine."

I looked through the glass and there was the magazine, open to my picture—reading material for the slow times.

"Can I get your autograph?"

My face hot, I said, "Sure."

She pushed the magazine under the window and handed me a pen. I couldn't believe what I was doing. I signed the page she'd opened. As I was about to slide it back to her she said, "Can you sign one more picture for my girlfriend? She'll be so blown away."

As Mark and I entered the six-screen cineplex, we looked at each other and laughed. As we waited in the long line at concessions, I noticed a few employees looking our way. When Mark had finished placing our order, the cashier said to me, "You're the guy in the magazine, huh?"

Like normal, I turned beet red. "Yes."

The thrill of seeing the magazine and signing autographs bathed me in new Ron positiveness. But, as with a massive, mind-numbing food binge, I feared the feeling might only be temporary. After all, that seemed to be the pattern.

* * * * *

I looked down at the scale. 187. I'd gained 8 pounds since I'd signed the modeling contract. I knew it was because I'd eased up on my long workouts and let my meals get a little too big. I needed to get my shit together and get back on track. Today I'd work out for four hours and eat almost nothing.

A couple of perfect days and I'd be back where I needed to be.

* * * * *

Tom and I were on our way to a fitting at the most expensive clothing store in town. I'd signed my contract less than eight weeks previously and the following day I'd be doing live TV. We were to appear on a talk show featuring the famous Italian designer Ermenegildo Zegna. We'd be modeling his latest designs.

The minute we walked into the store, an elegant woman asked us if we'd like a beverage. A clothing store that served wine—I'd never known such places existed. It even had a grand piano.

"Ron, Tom," she said, "I'd like you to meet Filippo Lombardi, Mr. Zegna's chief tailor. His English isn't so good, but I speak enough Italian to get us by."

Filippo, a short, burly, dark-haired guy who appeared to be in his sixties, looked us over, took a few measurements, and then left to select the proper clothes. Neither Tom nor I had heard of Zegna, but apparently he was a big deal. When we'd been left alone, we checked out his clothing.

No way—ties were $110, sweaters $350. We walked over to the suit rack. The first one I pulled out was $1,850. It was like we'd just discovered the rock we'd been tossing around was shiny because it was actually something called a diamond. How could a suit cost twice as much as my car had?

At 9:15 the next morning, Tom and I arrived at the television studio. Tom had set his VCR to record our show so we could watch it later. The program, *Look Who's Talking*, started in forty-five minutes. I was scared—as always—and had no idea what to expect.

Filippo and his assistant helped us change into our first set of clothes, then sent us to the green room—the green room! I got a kick just from hearing the words. We were waiting for our cue in the fucking green room, just like guests on *The Tonight Show*. I felt like a kid going to Disneyland for the first time.

"You guys sit in here and we'll come get you when it's time to go on. You'll be right after the Amazing Kreskin. Help yourselves to coffee, sodas, and snacks."

Tom and I sat down at a large conference table surrounded by plush, comfortable, orange chairs. Seated with us were Filippo, Amazing, and a well-dressed man with dark hair, who looked to be around thirty. He glanced our way and said, "Hello, I'm Gildo Zegna."

A little intimidated, we both thanked him for choosing us to model his clothes. From the price of his clothes, I assumed he'd be one intimidating guy—turned out he was anything but. He was relaxed, charming, spoke excellent English, and didn't seem to take himself seriously. He was so easy to talk to, I couldn't help asking, "How come your stuff's so expensive?" Oh God, did I say that?

Saxen boys in 1966 at the Subic Bay Naval Base in the Philippines. I'm the cute bag on the left.

Saxen boys in 1967 playing the "Who has the straightest arms and the darkest socks" contest—obviously I won.

Fourth grade photo.
Age nine, 1972.

Me and my brothers in front of my grandparents' house
in Ute, Iowa, in 1975. Showing off a day's catch from
fishing—I'm apparently sleepy.

Looking
confident
and strong
while fearing
I'd pass out
and embar-
rass myself.
Portfolio
shoot, 1984.

From the Fall Fashions
edition of the Sunday
paper, 1984.

SPORTS FITNESS AND TRAINING

"I wish I'd had this book during my thirteen-year pro football career. Very precise and clear—it's something every athlete ought to have."
—Calvin Hill

■ Train for peak performance through specific workouts in 25 different sports

■ Prevent, diagnose, and treat injuries

■ Achieve top overall fitness

RICHARD MANGI, MD

PETER JOKL, MD

O. WILLIAM DAYTON, ATC

Cover of Random House's *Sports Fitness and Training*—published in 1987 and discovered by my sister's friend at a bookstore. This cover would go on to haunt me for the next decade to come.

Me in 1993 at my mom's house in Iowa, while trying to strike my thinnest pose at more than 100 pounds over my modeling weight.

Hiking in the Santa Cruz Mountains, 1998.

Me and the love of my life, Leslie, leaving for a cruise in 2002—
she's the short one.

Posing by the pool. New York, 2006.

Me showing 4' 11" Leslie what it feels like to be tall. Fire Island, New York, summer of 2006.

To my relief, he just laughed and said the Zegna family was known for producing the finest fabrics in all the world. They were the world's largest purchaser of high-grade silk and had six factories that provided material for most of the finest clothing designers. In fashion circles, Zegna was the pinnacle—everyone else followed them. I've heard that Armani actually used to work for Zegna.

When we'd stopped talking, I looked over at the Amazing Kreskin. He didn't look so amazing; he looked jumpy and disheveled.

A young production assistant named Jenny came first for Mr. Zegna and then for us. Jenny led us through a control room that looked like the bridge of the starship *Enterprise*, then parked us behind some curtains offstage. I was fighting panic. Tom offered to go first, but Zegna called my name.

Still, before I knew it, it was my turn to emerge from behind the curtains. I was so overwhelmed by the onslaught of bright lights, TV cameras, and studio audience, that I could barely make out the hosts and Mr. Zegna seated near the front of the stage. The next thing I knew Mr. Zegna, as calm as could be, said, "And Ron's wearing a design I'm particularly proud of..."

I walked to one end of the stage, then back again. Since Mr. Zegna was still discussing the designs of the clothes I wore, I headed back out across the floor, then back again. Then I just stood in the middle of the stage and waited for him to shut up so I could escape to the safety of the curtains.

Finally, it was over and I was flying high. The minute the show went off the air, the studio audience was allowed to get out of their seats and meet Mr. Kreskin, Mr. Zegna, and us. Suddenly Tom and I were surrounded by people—mostly women—who wanted to talk to us. I nearly burst out laughing when a woman said, loudly and slowly, "How do you like the United States? I'm sorry, do you speak English?"

I couldn't resist: "Yes. I learned my English living in a little town west of Rome called Sacramento."

After it was over, Tom and I rushed back to his place to watch ourselves on TV. Seeing myself on TV was both amazing and surreal.

Nine months ago, at 268 pounds, I'd hunched over a mixing bowl full of chocolate ice cream, hot fudge, and a one-pound sprinkling of M&M's, insanely gorging myself. It was an image I was still trying to separate myself from. By proving to myself that the wrong Ron was no longer valid, I hoped to make the right Ron real. Modeling on TV for Zegna helped.

* * * * *

That night Tom and I were to attend a huge benefit, a black-tie affair featuring Mr. Zegna. It was a big deal—the governor of California would be there, along with various sports heroes, and some local celebrities. Tickets cost up to $350.

After a fitting, there was a run-through of the fashion show to come. Throughout it, I felt weak from hunger, tired, and intimidated. Who knew there was choreography for a fashion show?

"Okay, guys—pick up the pace," the director said, I swear, looking right at me. "From the top, on a three-count beat…" A three-count what? I didn't know what I was doing and I was too embarrassed to ask. I was fucking clueless—once again I felt like I didn't belong.

During a break, I sat by myself on a set of bleachers about twenty yards from the outdoor stage. One of the female models headed my way. She was in the same league as Tiffany Michaels, but did more television than print work. I looked both ways. I was still alone on the bleachers and she was still coming.

"Hi, Ron. I saw you with Zegna on TV. You did great."

What was she doing talking to me? She was a little shorter than most models, around five foot seven, a brunette with dark eyes (about time I found someone else who didn't have blue eyes), olive skin, and an electric smile—way out of my league.

Surprised and shy, I said, "Thank you."

"I love your look, it's great."

Oh my God, my face must be cherry red. What the hell do I say to that?

"Thank you… again. I like your look, too."

Well that was brilliant.

"Are you doing anything after the show?"

Holy shit! Wait, that's right, Michelle... I've got a girlfriend.

"I've got a girlfriend. Ah... thank you though."

"Too bad. You know, you've got the best looking lips."

I didn't know what to say to that, so I just stared and smiled. The next thing I knew she'd put her hands on both sides of my cheeks, pulled my head toward hers, and kissed me right on the lips—a little hard and a little long.

"Sorry, I couldn't resist."

She smiled, turned, and walked away, leaving me in shock. A few seconds later I wondered if maybe she'd just been being kind—I must've looked pathetic sitting by myself, talking to no one. Or maybe my agent had put her up to it. She was around here somewhere.

* * * * *

An hour before showtime. Michelle and her friend Heather walked back to the changing area with me, past limousines, security guards—I'm guessing for the governor—guests in tuxes and ball gowns, and servers in tails pouring champagne. Friends and family were allowed backstage until forty-five minutes before the show. I was surprised: seeing all the female models made Michelle jealous. It made a certain amount of sense but at the same time it bothered me—for her, my success was a negative?

After Michelle and Heather said good-bye, I was left to myself. It had only been a couple months since I was signed, but already I was thinking about New York. On the one hand I knew I needed to be patient, but I also felt that I couldn't wait—I needed the bigger magic that only being in the center of the modeling universe could provide. At times, breathing in this new world I'd so desperately wanted seemed incredibly labored—not at all what I'd expected. But before I worried about New York, I had to get rid of the extra pounds I'd gained.

"Alright everybody, ten-minute warning."

CHAPTER 11

Shaky Ground

I was twenty-one years, eight months, one week, and two days old—and still a virgin. Oh I'd tried, but Michelle "wasn't ready." Blah blah blah. I wanted to get laid not just because I wanted to get laid, but also because I was hoping it would change me in some profound way—make the new Ron stronger.

Even not getting laid, I seemed to be spending most of my time at Michelle's in Davis, a bucolic college town near Sacramento. As a result, Mark was considering getting his own one-bedroom apartment. I felt bad but not that bad. I knew he understood—if I didn't get laid pretty soon the Catholic Church would automatically send out an application for the priesthood with my name on it...

The agency had called four days previously: Tom and I had been chosen for a free, day-long photo shoot with some kick-ass New York photographer. Every year this guy reviewed the talent books from modeling agencies around the country. After he'd chosen the models he thought were the hottest prospects, he traveled across America to shoot their pictures. The models got free photos for their portfolios and the photographer got stock photos he could use and sell any time he wanted.

It was 10:00 a.m. and I was waiting for the photographer in the agency's plush reception area, trying to forget how hungry I was. As soon as I'd heard about the shoot I kicked into high gear to lose the nine pounds I'd put on since signing my contract. It had been a punishing four days of nonstop workouts and no food. I'd dropped five pounds—and felt wobbly. All I'd eaten that morning were two cups of black coffee and an apple. I'd packed two lettuce and mustard sandwiches in case I got light-headed again.

The agency's heavy glass door opened.

"I'm Steven and this is my assistant, Sherry. You must be Ron. I recognize you from your pictures."

I gazed at them reverently. Whatever they did—the way they wore their clothes, the way they styled their hair, the way they talked—must be perfect, because they were from New York, mecca of the fashion world.

Steven, who looked to be in his midforties, was short and dressed in a preppy '50s style: long, untucked shirt and jeans finished off with leather Top-Siders, no socks. Sherry was a sexy brunette with olive skin and no makeup.

I loaded my pile of athletic, casual, and formal wear into their rental car and we were off. We spent the next five hours zooming around town, jumping out of the car just long enough to take pictures of me against different backdrops. Steven went through twenty rolls of film shooting me in every imaginable situation, from playing tennis to fishing. Thrilled to have a New York photographer captive for a day, I pummeled him with questions:

"So, do I have a look good enough for New York? Do you have connections at any of the top agencies?"

Yes and yes.

"What would you recommend I do next?"

"Build your portfolio, save your money, and go to New York. I'll give you at least five shots that'll look great in your portfolio."

This guy had no reason to lie to me, but I had my doubts. It was my nature—it came from years of wondering what hideous thing someone was thinking behind my back. Thus, whenever anything nice happened, I still asked why.

Two days later, I raced down to the agency to pick up the photos. I waited to open the package they were in until I could get home and could look at them alone—why I didn't know. Standing in my living room, I tore open the package.

Oh—it was sheets of slides. I guessed that made sense. That way I could print the ones I wanted. With my hands shaking, I pulled the shade off my desk lamp and held the two-inch squares of cardboard and plastic up to the naked lightbulb, one by one. I was so anxious about them—my first photos by a real New York photographer—that I could barely take them in.

In the first few shots I was smiling. I hated my smile. Let's see... damn it, my jaw wasn't clenched—I'd told him that was my best look. Damn, I looked dorky trying to play tennis. My arms looked soft... Of course, I'd been given the ones where I wasn't flexing. The slides were tiny, but I could tell—he'd fucking given me the ones he hadn't wanted and kept all the good shots for himself! What a waste. How were *these* going to help me get to New York? I couldn't believe I'd spent a whole day posing for him for nothing. And after I'd worked out so hard—son of a bitch.

Okay, I just had to put this behind me and move on. Time to get back into shape. On my way downstairs I flung all the slides over the railing, toward the dumpster. Shit, I missed. I retrieved them, and this time slammed them in at point blank range. They made a hollow metal thud as they hit the bottom of the dumpster.

"Two Big Macs, two cheeseburgers, one large order of fries, and a chocolate shake."

"Would you like a pie with that, sir?"

What the fuck. "Sure, make it a cherry."

* * * * *

My weight bounced back up to 193—14 pounds more than when I'd signed my contract ten weeks earlier. The constant backsliding shook me to the core. Every fuck-up felt like the old Ron fighting for air. Some days I believed in the new Ron, but most days I didn't—life was just too exhausting.

* * * * *

Through days of punishing diet restrictions and exercise I worked my way back down to 186 for a big event, a calendar shoot with Penina Meisels. Apparently she was a master photographer, arguably the best in California, and her work appeared everywhere. The agency said I was extremely lucky to be in front of her camera lens.

Her office was located in Sacramento's newly trendy warehouse district, surrounded by mature shade trees. Walking into an airy, unmanned lobby, I saw two black doors. The one on the left was marked Studio A. After double-checking the piece of paper in my hand, I knocked. No answer. I knocked again. Nothing. I let myself in.

It was just what I expected—huge and inspiring. Because I knew she was the best, the kind of photographer who could make your career, I instantly admired everything I saw.

The room was dark; everything that could have a color was black. The ceiling looked to be over thirty feet high and two metal staircases led up to a balcony. Hanging on the walls was everything from a Macy's swimwear ad to a photo of a juicy pot roast with all the fixings for the cover of *Gourmet* magazine. Photo gear was scattered across the room—cameras, lights, and backdrops.

"Ron?"

A guy with spiky green hair headed my way.

"Yes, I'm Ron."

"Great, we're just about ready for you."

Coming out of one of the small studios was a cute woman with short red hair. Striding up to me, she said, "I don't like the clothes they sent over for the shoot. With your jaw, the vision I have for you involves dark leather. Follow me. We're going to run downtown and do a little shopping."

The clothes screwup turned out to be the best thing that could've happened—even though Penina looked like a sweet little woman, she and her studio flat-out terrified me. The time we spent in her car driving from store to store gave me a chance to relax and discover what an amazing woman she was.

Once the ice was broken, she was more than willing to share what she knew about the modeling business, New York—where she used to work—and my chances of making it as a model. Talking about New York gave me energy, same as dreaming about being a model once had. If I could just find a way to hold on to my vision of new Ron, I was sure I could stabilize myself.

Unlike the New York photographer, Penina offered to shoot some pictures especially for me, something just for my portfolio. Of all the people I met on the other side of the camera she was by far the most revered—and the most generous. I was overwhelmed by her offer; there was nothing in it for her.

During the shoot it was obvious I was in the hands of a professional. Penina tried interesting poses and shots. She understood that my jaw was an asset and used it. When she left the room to get another lens I reached into the garbage can and pulled out some Polaroid test shots—even these looked good to me. If she didn't want them, I'd keep them. By the end of the shoot, I was flying.

"Give me your address and I'll mail you some pictures."

I scribbled down my address and thanked her, glowing with excitement. I was in awe of her kindness—she had single-handedly just restored my faith in people.

In my car heading home I was so revved up I couldn't stand it. I'd been working so hard, I felt I deserved a celebration. I'd earned it. I felt my adrenaline spiking—I knew what was about to happen. In less than a minute I went from visions of New York to visions of burritos.

Soon I sat in a parking lot, eating the first of three jumbo burritos with extra cheese. I didn't take them home for two reasons—first, I didn't want to be seen, and second, I wasn't sure that I didn't want to get something else, too. As I peeled back the wrapper of the third burrito, a sense of calm came over me. Today's session with Penina had been great—almost too great, too exciting. Filling my stomach with food quieted the loud voices in my head and relaxed me. I needed a day off to relieve the stress. Tomorrow, I'd be better than ever.

And Baskin-Robbins was on the way home.

* * * * *

I'd been running for just over an hour when I had to stop. I'd planned to run an hour and a half but I was out of gas. In the past ten days, I'd used every punishing weight-loss trick in the book to go from 191 to 184.

Tomorrow was a double tryout—winner got two shows. If I landed these two I'd be undefeated—and from then on I'd be perfect. No more gaining weight, no more Big Macs; I'd hit the weights hard and finally build some serious muscle mass.

* * * * *

Walking into the Civic Auditorium for tryouts, I had to concentrate to appear normal instead of how I truly felt—burnt, shaky, and in pain. The auditorium seated over three thousand people. Usually the sheer size of the room would give me an adrenaline rush. Not today—apparently I'd run out of adrenaline.

I'd gotten up at 4:30 in the morning in order to go for an eight-mile run and twenty-mile bike ride before tryouts. I'd drunk as little fluid as possible—dehydration made my muscles and jaw look more defined. Before my shower I weighed in at a thirsty 182.

My knees and back ached; all my muscles were sore. A few minutes previously I'd felt shaky to the point of collapse, but a mustard sandwich and a twenty-ounce coffee—my first food of the day—had helped. It was okay to drink coffee because it was a diuretic, it just made me pee—the liquid went, the jawline stayed. And I had to look good—I was competing against thirty-four models for one of just five slots.

"...and Ron Saxen, step forward. The rest of you can go home."

As soon as they'd announced that Tom and I were hired, I allowed myself to let go, to be who I was at that moment—one mentally and physically drained guy. Remembering I'd seen chairs set up backstage, I stumbled back and collapsed into one of them to catch my breath.

"Okay gentlemen, the first fashion show is in four weeks. We'll meet the day before for the fitting. The second show is in six weeks. There will be two underwear sets, so I want you guys lifting weights and getting your pretty little bodies looking as cut as possible. Oh, and Ron—I need to talk to you before you go."

This was interesting. Wonder what he wanted?

I forced myself to stand up and walk back down the long run-way, trying to walk as if I felt like a million bucks. Just had to hold it together a few more minutes… I stopped at the end and looked down at the judges' table.

"Listen, Ron. Now don't get me wrong—I pushed to get you on and you've definitely got the look. That's why we're talking. And if it weren't for the two underwear sets, I wouldn't be saying this, but I need you to lose five pounds. You can do that for me, right, Ron?"

I looked straight into the confident blue eyes of the man below me. "Ah… sure, not a problem."

"Good. I know you won't let me down. Look forward to seeing you in a few weeks."

I mustered up my last drops of physical and emotional courage and bounded off the stage with a bullshit zip in my hip.

"Nice job, Ron. You want to get something to eat?"

It was all I could do to say, "I've got to run, Tom, but thanks."

Not looking back, I limped in the direction of my car. Once inside I melted into the seat and let panic engulf me.

I was so weak, so burnt out on dieting and exercise, I felt like I was going to die. I had nothing left—and I needed to lose five more pounds? I knew why he'd said it: my body was soft. I was guessing from all the punishment. All I did was run and starve. I'd never had a good ass anyway… I was going to totally fucking embarrass myself modeling underwear. I'd lose my contract, everything.

"Large combination pizza please."

Tomorrow I'd be perfect.

CHAPTER 12

Critical Mass

The sunlight pried open my eyes. Fuck, what had I done? My hand went to my six-pack. It was still there, but not flat. It was now rounded and raised, full of yesterday's massive binge. I closed my eyes.

I raised my knees and they hurt, reminding me of yesterday's weight-loss attempt: a grueling twenty-seven-mile run/walk, which I'd topped off with thirteen donuts and six Taco Bell burrito supremes.

The day before yesterday I'd gotten the request to lose five pounds—and then eaten a large pizza, various candy bars and fruit pies, and a gallon of rocky road ice cream dressed with a pound of M&M's and sixteen ounces of hot fudge sauce.

In bed next to me, Michelle was still asleep. We were in the double-wide trailer she shared with an old friend from Southern California. We slept together a lot now, but were still both virgins. She was nineteen, I almost twenty-two, but like most women, Michelle was holding out for something more than lust.

I wasn't in the mood just now anyway. Not because Michelle knew what I'd done. She didn't have any idea—I'd hidden the evidence of my binge in a dumpster down the street before she'd returned home from work. But it's hard to get hard with a binge in your belly and self-loathing in your mind. I just wished I didn't have to face today—that I could get through the next twenty-four hours without having to actually live them. I'd like to go to sleep and wake up when it was over, food-free and perfect...

Who was I kidding? I couldn't do an underwear show no matter how much weight I lost. To be cut, I'd need to hit the weights hard. That took energy, and energy meant food. And right now I needed to starve, to punish myself.

Still, enough self-pity. Time to get my shit together. What was past was past. It wasn't where I'd been, but where I was going that was important and today I'd be fucking perfect. I'd run and I'd dig deeper than I'd ever had before to achieve a massive lift, even if I was weak. In the past I'd pushed myself until I'd almost passed out. I could do it again. When it came time to lift I'd just drink a twenty-ounce cup of coffee and down a handful of No-Doz. I was going to New York, whatever it took.

* * * * *

Whenever I mentioned New York, Michelle got upset:

"What about me? You'll go off to New York and you'll have girls crawling all over you. I'll never see you again."

"I have to go. It's the next step."

"You said you loved me. If you love me you won't leave."

That's right, in my attempts to move sex along, I'd played the love card. If your only girlfriend for three years is your hand, you should have your I-love-you license revoked. They should make you get a learner's permit and get it punched by three different girl-friends. On the third punch you'd get a free yogurt and the right to say the words.

* * * * *

I'd only been running for a few blocks, but already I could tell it was going to suck. It was still early, but the day was beginning to warm up. It was going to be hot. As a result of so much food in me, I'd lost some lung capacity—and the sour burping thing had returned.

Sometimes a burp would have just enough flavor to let me identify the food that had caused it.

After I finished running, I planned to drive into Sacramento for a killer lift. I had plenty of time—I'd taken the semester off from school to pursue modeling. Today was going to be awesome. I'd make it awesome.

Back from my run, I felt incredibly weak. I definitely *didn't* feel like lifting. Oh well, lifting didn't really matter, it was eating right that counted... I'd start lifting tomorrow. Everything would be fine. Although, I was supposed to go to work, and at work I sometimes got so weak that I had to eat just to keep going. If I could just chill all day, no work, it would be much easier to go without food...

"Thank you for calling Barrier Reef. How may I help you?"

"Hi Sandy, it's Ron. Can you let Mr. Nelson know I won't be coming in today? I feel like crap."

Excellent—now I could just kick back and spend some quality time with my other best friend, the TV. Old *Andy Griffith* reruns were on, followed by *I Love Lucy*. No pressure, no nothing, just a relaxing day.

* * * * *

1:00 p.m. Only 400 calories. I could keep it under 1,000 today easy.

* * * * *

2:00 p.m. No more good TV on until three when *Bewitched* and then *I Dream of Jeannie* came on. I was a little hungry. What did Michelle have that was low-cal and tasted good?

My search turned up frozen french fries. Well, they were potatoes, a vegetable, and I had to eat something. Let's see, "Bake in the oven at 375° for thirty-five minutes." I wasn't waiting no half-hour. I'd use the microwave. Where was the ketchup?

The smell of the french fries, the ding of the microwave, sent my saliva into motion.

Okay, a whole box of fries was 1,500 calories; this box had been two-thirds full at most. That meant I was currently at about

1,400 calories—not too bad. With my run, I had to have burned at least an extra 1,250 calories, anyway.

There were still twenty-five minutes until *Bewitched*. Did Michelle have bread and cooking oil? It had been a long time since I'd made fried bread...

As I filled a large pan with oil, I could see myself floating out of my control. There was a momentary pain as I separated into good Ron and bad Ron. There always was. From this moment on, good Ron would only be able to watch with sadness and despair as bad Ron began to tear me apart.

The oil was starting to crack and pop—time to drop in the bread.

Soon, I was removing crispy, oil-laden slices from the two-inch pond in the skillet. I ate the first piece quickly, burning my mouth. Three more pieces were soaking, waiting. For fun I squeezed one of the pieces of bread. A small puddle of grease formed on my plate.

After half a loaf of fried bread I headed out the door for the good stuff—cheeseburgers, ice cream, and candy bars. I knew that when the feast was over, I'd have to look myself in the mirror. But since stopping was impossible, I might as well enjoy my wickedness —and the quiet calm brought on by the absence of inner war.

* * * * *

Thursday morning, four days after I'd been asked to lose five pounds. I'd probably gained five. I tried my best to be cheerful, but it seemed like Michelle was beginning to sense something was wrong. I had to get my shit together. And since I didn't have to work today, there was no excuse not to run, lift weights, and get back on track. My next fashion show was in three and a half weeks.

But maybe all I really needed was to take the pressure off—no running, no lifting, just breathing and not eating, finding a way to make the hungry hours pass. In the morning, I was always empty, perfect. It was only at the end of the day—when I got shaky from not eating—that my plans went south. I knew: I'd have a movie orgy. Three movies would easily use up seven to eight hours. Then I could show up at work after the restaurant closed and hang with Michelle as she finished up her side work. That way I couldn't blow it.

* * * * *

The second movie was *Indiana Jones*. It was 2:15, and I hadn't eaten all day—my stomach was starting to hurt from hunger. I had to eat something. The movie was going to start in a few minutes. All I had to choose from was candy and hot dogs. One hot dog wouldn't be bad; I wouldn't even put any relish on it...

But soon afterwards, in the theater, my mouth started to water. It was beginning again. I hated to get up in the middle of the movie, but the voices in my head were so loud I couldn't enjoy what I was watching, even though it was an Indy movie. (Normally a picture had its predictable slow parts, but not an Indy movie: it's like a James Bond flick, nonstop action.) Instead all I heard was, "Just one more time and then I'll be good forever... I'll be the most successful model in the whole world... It'll taste so fucking good..."

My eyes slowly adjusted to the light of the empty, bright orange lobby. I walked up to the concessions booth; there was no one behind the counter. Finally an employee playing video games spotted me, came my way. He hadn't been expecting a customer; usually people only get up in the middle of a movie to pee, not to shovel two pounds of self-serve chocolate peanuts into a plastic bag. Just in case he watched me with judging eyes, I stared at the ground.

Once I'd returned to the dark theater, I let the large bag of candy rest on my lap. I didn't have to do this. I could stop. I was in control. But who was I kidding?

There was less pain this time. I didn't put up much of a fight. The darkness, Harrison Ford, and pretty Kate Capshaw sheltered us—good Ron and bad Ron—as the transgressions began.

I was insane.

* * * * *

7 a.m., Friday morning. This morning I felt no pain when I opened my eyes. There was no fight left in me—the two of me, evil and

weak and good and strong, were no longer battling. Bad Ron was going to have a long, uncontested weekend. But starting Monday, good Ron would be back in charge. Meantime I no longer cared if Michelle knew—I was tired of lying.

"Where are you going, sweetie?"

In sweatpants, with disheveled hair and a five o'clock shadow, I said, "Donut shop."

"I thought you had to lose weight."

"I do."

With a puzzled look and a half smile, "I don't get it."

"Here's the deal, ever since that guy told me I had to lose five pounds I've been pigging out. I'm sure I've gained over five pounds."

She just stared.

"And yesterday the modeling agency called and left a message about a possible job. They wanted me to call them back and I didn't—and I'm not going to. I've called in sick twice for work this week and I'm going to call in sick for the entire weekend."

Why the fuck was she smiling?

"I don't know what to say. Is there anything I can do?"

She was still smiling. Maybe it was just too big a shock, maybe smiling was just her instinctive reaction. Like when people smile at bad news, even though they don't mean to.

"Anyway, I'm off to the donut shop. Can I get you anything?"

A long pause and then, "No."

Before she could say anything else, I was out of the trailer, the spring-loaded door snapping shut behind me as I marched purpose-fully to my car. I was sad about my sins, but also at peace, because I knew that the entire weekend would be free of voices battling in my head.

* * * * *

Three weeks after the big audition, instead of losing 5 pounds, I'd gained 16. I now weighed 201. I'd been dodging the agency's increas-ingly frantic calls, but the first of the two fashion shows I'd been

selected for was now just six days away. The only thing I could do
was call in sick. To protect myself I called during lunch hour, upping
the odds that I wouldn't reach anyone.

"Excel Modeling, may I help you?"

"Is Barbara there?"

Come on Barbara, be at lunch.

"She's not here right now. Can anyone else help you?"

Perfect.

"No, I'll just leave a message. Tell her Ron Saxen called."

"Ron, they've been trying to get hold of you."

"I know. Just tell her I won't be able to make the next fashion
show. Something came up, and I've got to go out of town."

"Is there a number she can reach you at?"

"No. Goodbye."

I hung up quickly, before anything could go wrong.

It was so unfair that I was insane. I was a good person, but
here I was disintegrating, hiding, ducking phone calls from the
agency and Tom, and slowly killing myself with food. I knew this
wasn't God's punishment, because God didn't care about me. He'd
never helped when I was a church member and desperate for
help—why would He bother to fuck with me now? That would be
too cold blooded. I preferred to think of God as a nice person—not
like the God most people I knew believed in.

The irony was I was finally getting laid—and was too upset to
care. Sex was cool, but not as big a deal as I'd thought. Strangely, the
more miserable I got, the happier Michelle seemed. Apparently seeing me as flawed comforted her. The fact that my modeling career
was coming apart seemed to make her feel safer about us. It sucked
to think my girlfriend was actually rooting against me, pulling for the
wrong Ron.

* * * * *

The second gig, the dreaded underwear fashion show, was a week
later. I weighed 204 pounds, 19 more than I had at the tryout, 24
more than I'd promised the director I'd weigh. Again, I called in sick.

To make sure the agency and Tom wouldn't be able to reach me, I moved, changed my phone number, quit The Barrier Reef, and went to work at an Orchid's in a different part of town. Their hounding had made me feel even more ashamed—I was glad to put an end to the calls.

My relationship with Michelle was terrible. She seemed too controlling, and placed too much value on material things. After going to a car show I was shocked to find out that she felt sad because she didn't think she'd ever be able to afford a Mercedes or a Porsche.

We fought about the dumbest things. I was mad at her, but I was even madder at myself for not having the balls to end it, to get through her pain and anger, and then be free. After all, it was best for her, too—I was never going to be rich enough to make her happy, and there was my embarrassing dark side.

* * * * *

Three months after the underwear modeling tryouts, I weighed 227 pounds, 42 more than I had. In his sane moments, good Ron didn't know what to think. I'd never known or heard of anyone who acted this way. I must be crazy. Sane enough to live among normal people, but still crazy. Functionally nuts.

* * * * *

Six months after I'd vanished from the modeling world, I weighed 257 pounds, 78 pounds more than I had when I'd walked into the agency's waiting room. It must have seemed to the agency that I'd come from out of the blue and left the same way. I wanted to stop eating, but I couldn't, although I was trying.

Insanity wasn't my only problem.

Sprawled on a red beanbag chair in Mark's furnished apartment, I whined, "I swear, Mark, a few months ago I tried to break up with her. I even fucked around on her once, hoping to get caught and I did. Now we're engaged to be married."

Mark and I were on our third beer apiece. The alcohol was starting to liberate my mind and loosen my tongue.

"I was too scared to break up with her. If I wasn't such a pussy this would be over by now. But instead we bought a $5,000 ring with credit and money from my student loan. And now we live together and parents and family are involved."

"So?"

"What do you mean *so*? It's a fuckin' lot."

"Do you feel that you've done something so wrong, so bad that you don't deserve to choose your own happiness?"

"No, but she'd be so fucking pissed and hurt. I mean, when I tried breaking up with her before, it got crazy—I couldn't handle it."

"I repeat, do you deserve your own happiness?"

The conversation, the counseling, and the beer flowed for hours. By the end of the night, I'd decided to do the right thing.

At first I didn't want to leave a note like my old man did, but Mark convinced me that given my past experiences with Michelle it would be for the best. Doing it in person versus by note wasn't going to lessen her disgust and hate for me.

While Michelle was at work, Mark and I went over to the apartment she and I shared and gathered my things. Surprisingly, my things fit into one very large box. They say you can't take your things with you when you die; in my case I probably could.

* * * * *

Even though I knew the relationship was toxic and that I'd made the right decision—for both of us—I still felt guilty. I'd seen too much pain and fear in my life. I hated to think I was hurting someone else.

Michelle and I had our painful conversation; hard things were said. I guess that's the way it always is when only one side wants to say good-bye. She agreed to return the $5,000 engagement ring that was 50 percent paid for with the proceeds of my student loan. The store let us out of what we owed if we agreed to spend the $2,500 I'd already paid in the store. For my half, Mark and I bought ourselves cool watches—the least I could do for Mark after all he'd done for me.

That first night, as I drifted off to sleep on Mark's couch, I remembered the note Dad had left for us. Now I got it. It was just easier. My situation was nowhere near the same, but I felt the same way: dirty, but relieved.

And grateful. Saved again by Mark.

* * * * *

Heading home from work a few months later, I was hurt, disgusted, and a little bit happy. Happy that in only two weeks a television commercial I was in would air on TV. Hurt and disgusted because of how I'd learned about it.

While clearing tables after the lunch rush, I'd looked out the window and seen Peggy from the modeling agency walking across the restaurant parking lot. She'd hunted me down to get me to sign a release for the commercial. Must have been a shock for her to walk into the restaurant and find me, seventy pounds heavier, stuffed into my brown polyester uniform. I was surprised she even recognized me.

It killed me to think how much time she must have spent looking for me. Someone had had to do some serious detective work. And when Peggy got back to the agency it would be, "Oh my God, you should've seen him—he's fucking huge. The only magazine he could model for now is *GQ-Squared*. I'm not sure, but I think he ate my pen."

Peggy said the still pictures they were using in the commercial were from the shoot with Penina Meisels. I'd really liked Penina. She'd told me those pictures would get me work, help me get to New York. What would she think of me now?

What the fuck had happened to me?

Fighting back tears, I turned up "Sweet Emotion" by Aerosmith as loud as I could. Anything to drown out the noise in my head.

* * * * *

"Hey, Ron! What's up?"

"Tom?"

"That's right."

Oh shit, I'd given my phone number to Peggy in case she needed me to sign anything else. I did my best to be cheerful, but it was a struggle.

"Hey, man," he said, "our commercial's on tonight."

"I know—Peggy gave me the airtimes. I'm looking forward to checking it out."

Which was true, although I didn't know why: it was just going to hurt.

"You should see the agency—there's a huge picture of you in the lobby from your Penina Meisels photo session."

"What?"

"You heard me, dipshit. They're telling everyone that you're working the East Coast and Europe, and that's why you're gone."

"You know that's not true, right?"

"Yeah, I know."

That night, as I sat in front of the TV with a half-gallon of chocolate ice cream on my lap, waiting for the commercial to come on, I thought about what Tom had said. Other model wannabes now sat in the same lobby I had almost ten months ago and looked at my picture and dreamed, wishing they could be me.

I wished I could be that me, too.

1985–1996

The Road to Recovery

CHAPTER 13

The De La Fontaine Brothers

It was Sunday morning. I was sitting alone on the couch, eating donuts and watching a James Bond movie, when my commercial came on again. It had been two months and they were still running the damn thing. If I came forward with the truth—that Mr. GQ was an overweight, out of control glutton—I bet it would make the local news. Hell, it might even make the national news.

The ad made me both happy and sad. Happy to have touched a world most people only dream of, sad at being too insane to be able to hold onto it. Of all of my various self-inflicted wounds over the years, I can't think of a bigger one than modeling. Modeling encouraged me to continuously move the yardstick for what it took to be perfect Ron. Unless I ate only 1,000 calories a day or worked out for three hours or weighed 180 pounds, I was a total fuck-up. Modeling caused me to unwittingly amplify the negative voices inside of my head—creating an even unhealthier imbalance than the admittedly unhealthy one I started with.

Quitting modeling left me feeling even more hopeless than before: if the magic of modeling was powerless to heal my insanity, what could? I would spend the next twelve years switching from one venture to another, trying desperately to find something that worked.

* * * * *

Once again Mark and I worked at Orchid's Coffee Shop together and shared a two-bedroom apartment. My room was decorated with two posters—one of the Three Stooges, one of Laurel and Hardy—with orange crates for nightstands, candles for lamps, and a cardboard box for a dresser. I had just graduated from Sac State; Mark had a year left to go.

About three months after Peggy had tracked me down, the clouds over my life parted. They always did, but not until I was thoroughly broken—there was something about hitting bottom that sent me back up. I was perpetually afraid that one day I'd go down and stay down. But for now I had a new dream:

One Saturday night, after Mark and I had gotten home from work just in time to grab a beer and catch the last forty-five minutes of *Saturday Night Live*, a brilliant idea occurred to me.

"Mark, just look at this shit. How can they think it's funny? People watch this show and the show's not even funny *half* the time. We can write twice as good as that when we're drunk."

"What about school? And work?"

"What about it? I've got my degree, and I don't have to find a real job. I'll keep waiting tables, you keep going to school—until something huge happens, like *The Tonight Show*."

A few months later, Mark and I decided to go for it. For the following two weeks we had a blast writing our show. The freedom to write whatever we damn well pleased felt so good it should've been illegal. Nothing was sacred—I was finally going to find out if God was really into the lightning thing or if He was just all talk.

We called ourselves the De La Fontaine Brothers, the original name of Mark's ancestors who had come from France over a hundred years ago. They'd been running from something and changed their name to get a fresh start.

We rented a hall at the Red Lion Inn, hired a bartender, and printed up 150 tickets that we sold for $2.50 apiece. Personally, we'd have been happy to do the show for free, but we figured charging for it gave it value, made it more likely that people would show up. We were sold out a week in advance.

The day after we sold the last ticket, I booked three paying gigs for us over the phone—all before we had told our first joke. I pretended to be Bill Johnson, the De La Fontaine Brothers' agent. Apparently we were a successful act from Southern California working our way north.

* * * * *

Finally it was the big day. The night before we'd done two run-throughs and totally choked. Mark had even talked about pulling the plug. I'd told him fuck it. We couldn't give refunds—we had to just do the best we could. We practiced until two in the morning.

My sister Robin, who was sixteen and still in a cast from a recent foot surgery, had insisted on being our door person. She's a natural comedienne herself and wanted to help out.

Wearing matching white shirts, black pleated pants, and red suspenders, Mark and I waited in a vacant banquet room as across the hall the crowd gathered. People had drinks in their hands—excellent. Our first audience couldn't be too drunk.

Robin gave us our cue. With hearts pounding, we smeared the powdered sugar under our noses, around our mouths, and on our cheeks for our "we're on cocaine" opening.

"Let's get it on."

We sprinted across the hallway and jumped onto the stage. Mark looked a little freaked, but that worked well for our opening.

"Thank you all for coming! I mean it when I say it's fucking great to be here! Man, do I feel pumped or what!" I let out a scream and continued, "Shit, I even feel taller. Is it hot in here or is it me?"

Just then Mark stared at me with a panicked look. He pointed to the white powder on my face, I pointed at his, we both said "Shit!" and turned our backs to the audience to wipe it all off. And then we got what we'd come for: laughter.

After ten minutes my nervousness had all faded away and I was having the time of my life. Mark's nervousness was a little more persistent, but eventually he, too, joined the party on stage. It was definitely a learning experience: We were both surprised when the routine with Mr. Rogers as a hostage negotiator rocked—we'd thought about cutting it. The routine with Malibu surfers Biff and Tad being hired as astronauts because NASA could only pay minimum wage also did well, while the raunchy stuff made some laugh hysterically and others cringe.

An hour and ten minutes later the show was over and we were heroes. At times the laughter was solid, at times it was light, but it was always there. People came up to us afterwards to say, "When's your next show?" And, "Loved the Mr. Rogers skit."

We hung out for an hour or so afterwards, talking to everyone —and then stayed up late at home, talking about Reno, Tahoe, Vegas, a USO tour, and our debut on *The Tonight Show*.

Five days later—two days before our next show—Mark quit. He said it was to finish school but I think it was due to plain old stage fright. Maybe we were moving too fast. We'd already contacted the Department of Defense and were trying to figure out what it would take to get on the USO tour. We'd also put together some promotional packages and dropped them off at all the big casinos in South Lake Tahoe. We'd even managed to bullshit our way into a meeting with the entertainment manager at Harvey's Casino, across the street from Harrah's.

I had just two days to rewrite the act as a solo show, memorize it, and practice my delivery. I called Beal Air Force Base to confirm—but didn't mention the loss of the "s" in the De La Fontaine Brothers.

* * * * *

I drove Mark's car to Beal Air Force Base. My rust bucket had died and I couldn't afford to fix it so I'd sold it to a busboy for $100, which meant I was back to the ten-speed for work and Mark's car for comedy gigs.

I'd been told to arrive early because security was tight. Beal was a Strategic Air Command base, home of U-2 and SR-71 spy planes. I made it to the front gate with fifteen minutes to spare—and found out that the base was huge and the club was nearly ten miles away. Praying there were no MPs out, I squealed through the base until I found the officers' club sitting on top of a hill. It was old, white, and drab—very military. I grabbed my duffel bag, stuffed with the outfit I had worn for the show with Mark just seven days earlier, and ran up the stairs.

A band was already playing. I walked up to the bartender, "Excuse me, can you tell me where the club manager is?"

A minute later I ducked into the office of a forty-ish civilian wearing a dark pinstripe suit. He was going over the books at his desk.

"Hi, Michael, I'm Ron. Sorry I'm late."

"It's fine. Where's the other guy?"

"It's a long story. I promise you it'll be fine—where can I change?" I looked straight at him, a smile on my face. When he didn't say anything I added, nodding toward the hallway, "Is it that way?"

"Yes, down at the end of the hall, on the left."

Before he could say anything else I thanked him and disappeared.

I had a new twenty-minute routine put together, plus my old—as in 168 hours old—show in reserve. After getting dressed I hung out behind the band and spied on my audience. From where I was, all I could make out was a sea of dress blues, roughly 100 to 150 people. The place looked like a country club lounge, decorated in dark woods and pictures of officers and aircraft. There were a bunch of lieutenants, quite a few captains and majors, and even a few full-bird colonels. I didn't see many women. Finally the band took a break and Michael climbed on stage.

"We have a rare treat tonight—a comedian who's come all the way from Southern California. I'd like you all to give a warm welcome to Ron Allen."

On his way to the stage he'd asked what I wanted to be called—surely not the De La Fontaine Brothers. With only a second to decide, I'd chosen Ron Allen. Not only was it actually my first and middle name, it had an old time comedy ring to it.

I climbed on stage with my box of props and jumped into my routine:

"I know we've just met, but I've got to confess, I smoke thirteen packs a day. I smoke in my sleep, after sex, *during* sex, when I'm scuba diving… I even take a smoke break from smoking." I reached into my pocket, pulled out a pack of Camels. "I'm what you'd call a *chain* smoker."

I put the pack to my mouth. Instead of pulling out just a single cigarette with my teeth, I pulled out a long skinny chain.

Silence. No sound of any kind.

I skipped over a joke I thought might be weak and lobbed out two I'd written six hours previously. If anyone laughed I didn't hear them. Shit. I took a deep breath, and reached into my prop box for plan B: a wire mesh vegetable strainer tied to the end of a rope. I called it a military group-shower safety device—a.k.a. a dick restrainer.

Nothing. Holy fucking shit, I was dying. A few of the guys in the audience watched me with their hands on their hips; the rest had their arms folded. I could feel the sweat covering my forehead. I didn't wipe it away—wouldn't give them the satisfaction of kicking my ass.

"So, Taco Bell's coming out with a new low-cal menu. It's called "We're Closed.""

Zip. Zero. Fuck. Screw giving a twenty-minute show, how about fifteen?

"Any wine drinkers in the crowd? Wine in a box doesn't count! In your house—in mine it does."

A young lieutenant walked toward the stage, threw a dime at my feet, and headed for the door. It made a lonely clink in the silence.

"That's okay, lieutenant, I said you could keep the change—just watch the teeth next time." I grabbed my crotch, smiled in his direction, "Ouch!"

I then went for total shock—everyone likes the f-word, right? Nothing but stares. Mommy!

"Well, thank you very much. Sorry I can't stay longer but I've got to go join the search party—the one looking for your sense of humor."

A couple of boos. Fighting the impulse to run, I retreated to Michael's office to collect my duffel bag and get the fuck out of there.

"Ron, wait. Where are you going?"

"Listen, Michael, you don't have to pay me, just show me the back door so I can slither the hell out of here. I'm so sorry."

A few minutes later I was in Mark's car, headed toward the front gate. I was crushed. For a guy who wanted to be on *The Tonight Show* in one year, I was in trouble. Barely a single laugh. The farther I drove, the worse I felt. I had three more gigs booked and I didn't even have a show. I'd thought I knew what was funny—apparently not. What was I going to do?

Coming up on Yuba City, the urge started again. I knew what was happening but I didn't even try to fight it—I just didn't want to feel anymore.

After devouring two Double Whoppers with cheese, two regular cheeseburgers, a large fries, and a chocolate shake, I searched for a grocery store with a bagged candy section. I wanted M&M's—or maybe a box of chocolates and a large container of assorted donuts. Five minutes later I was anxiously waiting in line to purchase a carton of donuts and a one-pound Hershey Almond Bar.

I was stuffed, but I didn't want it to end—I wasn't ready to deal with reality yet. It took only a few minutes to find a Baskin-Robbins. Once there, I went in for the kill, coming out with a quart of chocolate-peanut-butter ice cream—big chunks of peanut butter, my favorite.

By the time I was deep in Central Valley farm country, surrounded by asparagus fields and halfway through the sixty-five-mile drive home, the passenger seat was littered with empty wrappers, I was depressed as hell, and I could barely keep my eyes open. A minute earlier I'd almost driven off the road. I pulled off to rest my eyes a few seconds...

Lights splashed on my face, a truck rumbled by. Where the hell was I? I glanced around, heart pounding. That's right, the show, the terrible show. And my stomach—Oh yeah. Shit, what time was it? I looked at my watch: 3:37 in the morning. God, I'd been lying there for almost five hours.

With my tires spitting out loose gravel, I pulled back onto the road. I hadn't gone off the deep end like that for months; it worried me. As always, it seemed my only way to cope with stress was to give in to the wrong Ron. I knew in a few minutes I'd be calling in sick to work again and searching for a 7-11—I had to take the edge off of my food hangover, dull my senses again.

*****

After a four-day food bender, I pulled myself together, scrapped my first show, and started all over again, writing a solid twenty-minute routine. For the next few months I did open mikes, more military bases, and opened for an Elvis impersonator. He asked me to go on the road with him, but I said no. I even managed to bullshit my way into an audition for the comedian/announcer spot in the Miss California pageant—way out of my league.

Tonight was my biggest night yet, though. I was the opening act at an A-list club, Laughs Unlimited. The show was sold out, 250 tickets at $8.50 apiece.

As usual, I was early. I looked at the stage, one of the top venues in Northern California, and thought about what it had taken to get here—the crappy shows, the writing, the rewriting. Shit, I was right where I wanted to be.

I was hanging out in the green room going over my notes when the headliner, Jazz Kainer, arrived. He was a good-looking blond guy who wore jeans, a Hawaiian shirt, and sneakers, and carried a guitar case. He seemed nice. The other guy, an older skinny black man named Peter Shark, shook my hand and instantly began to review his notes.

The green room was totally cool. Pictures of comedy's elite—Steve Martin, Bill Cosby, and Richard Pryor—hung above a couple of comfortably worn-out couches. There was a small refrigerator, a sink, and a coffeemaker.

The owner walked in. "Hey guys, the place is full. When it's over I'd appreciate it if you'd go to the upstairs bar and have a few drinks with the crowd—whatever you drink's on me. Ron, give me a couple of minutes to warm them up. Let's do it."

On the other side of the curtain the music stopped; the owner cracked a couple of jokes. I was ready to jump out of my skin.

"Let's give a warm welcome to a new talent. He hails all the way from here. Let's hear it for Ron Allen!"

With my entire body on fire I passed through the curtains. As the bright lights hit me in the face, I drank in the size of the crowd—it was huge; this was the real deal. With pretend confidence, I snatched the microphone from the stand, walked to the edge of the stage, and slowly looked left and then right.

"You buy into that pairing food with wine? Ya know what goes good with wine? Beer."

The place exploded in laughter.

"Now pairing food with marijuana would be interesting: 'Sir, the Colombian was an excellent choice. To go with that, I recommend you order the entire left side of the menu.'"

An even bigger laugh.

I couldn't believe how easy it was. The next few jokes did well, but not as well as the first two. As the end drew near I hit them with two I'd written just the day before:

"Did you hear? Cherokee tribes are trying to protect their dying language. I didn't know Keno *was* a language."

"Ya know, I drink a lot. I never had a chance—my parents gave us whiskey, honey, and hot water for colds, and brandy for sore throats. As a kid I thought Seagram's was a pharmaceutical company."

The crowd went nuts. Out of the corner of my eye I could see a red light: my time was up. I bowed and started to walk off the stage. As I headed toward the curtain—the crowd still clapping—the owner stopped me. "Not bad. You've got yourself an act."

After the show was over I went upstairs to bask in my glory. It was so cool. People walked up to me—a little nervously, like I was some sort of star.

"Hi, I'm Larry, this is my wife, Sandra... we just wanted to say you're really funny. So you live in the Sacramento area?" A minute later, two women, both way out of my league, bought me a drink.

* * * * *

Later that night, though, I started to unravel. What I'd learned that night, from the professional comedians, was that I'd really only risen to the bottom. The other comedians were better than me—one of them with sixteen years' experience—and they were still waiting their turn to get the call from Johnny Carson.

I'd seen comedy as a way to erase my embarrassing modeling career. I'd figured that as I became famous I'd somehow find the willpower to control my crazy eating. Then I'd get into acting, and become even more famous than if I were a top model—comedy and acting would give me even bigger magic than modeling. Now suddenly that, too, seemed unreachable.

After my modeling disaster, the thought of failing at comedy, too, was more than I could bear. To escape my thoughts I once again retreated to my favorite coping mechanism: wild one-person eating parties that didn't end until either I couldn't eat another bite or I passed out.

* * * * *

As I walked onto the stage for my next show, I knew it was over. I was already crumbling inside. It was only a matter of time before I totally gave in.

Throughout the entire show I felt like I was watching my own funeral. This time, at the end, I didn't bother to wait for the rest of the guys—as soon as I finished, I slipped out the back and into the darkness.

CHAPTER 14

Uncle Sam

It was just before midnight; the lights of Reno faded away as we flew over the great blackness that is the empty Nevada desert at night. The last time I'd crossed this wasteland had been a third of my life ago, when we'd driven to West Yellowstone to drop Rick off on his great adventure. Now, at over 30,000 feet up, I was on my way to mine: the Marine Corps Officer Candidacy School.

The red-eye to D.C. was almost empty; I had an entire row to myself. I wanted to sleep, but how could I? I felt like I was about to jump off a cliff. Everyone said the next ten weeks would be a shock to my system. It probably was for most people. But even the Marine Corps couldn't be as hard as life with Dad.

"Can I get you anything? Something to eat? Drink?"

"No, thank you, I'm fine."

Less than a week after quitting comedy, I'd decided to apply to the Marine Corps Officer Candidacy School. The military life had always appealed to me and I desperately needed something to grab on to, something that could whisk me away from all my failures. And to me that's what quitting comedy was: another failure, another chance to do something magical pissed away due to my own weakness. Because I had an insane relationship with food I'd walked away in shame from modeling. Because I was too impatient and started to develop stage fright I'd quit comedy after getting just the smallest taste of success. An image of myself was developing and it wasn't pretty: I was weak, partially insane, and a quitter, and no one likes a quitter—especially not me.

When I'd told Mark my plan, he was supportive as always. Before I left for OCS he'd received some good news of his own: he'd been accepted to the California Highway Patrol Academy. We were both overflowing with pride and patriotism as we shipped off to serve.

As with modeling and comedy, I was hoping that being a Marine would magically erase my past and all my sins. At the same time, in the back of my mind, gnawed a fear of failure—I was afraid it would be too hard, that I would lose control of my eating yet again and be kicked out—there's no such thing as a fat Marine.

* * * * *

Deciding to join the Marines had given me something to shoot for—just like when I'd tried to be a model. I trained like crazy, ate very little, and dropped 30 pounds, putting me back at a shaky but proud 208.

When I finally walked into the huge Marine recruiting station in Sacramento, I loved everything I saw—the posters of men in uniform, pictures of tanks and amphibious assault vehicles, and huge models of Marine Corps aircraft hanging from the ceiling. Within twenty seconds a staff sergeant approached me.

"Good afternoon, son. How can I help you?"

We talked for a few moments and he set up an appointment for me to meet with the officer-selection officer, Captain Ratcliff. By the time I walked out the door, I was floating. I spent the rest of the day looking at the brochures, imagining myself as the guy in the dress blues with a sword at his side.

The process of joining the Marines took five months, beginning with an FBI background check and an SAT-type test. They required college transcripts, letters of recommendation from college professors, a physical exam, and a fitness test. Based on the results of the physical fitness test, I would be rated first, second, or third class. To be accepted into OCS, I had to have a first-class rating. Once you've graduated from OCS, you're tested twice a year and expected to maintain your rating—the Marine Corps is big into fitness, and officers must lead by example.

Given my weight, Captain Ratcliff was surprised at my score on the physical fitness test. I finished first of the fourteen applicants, scoring 251—26 points more than I needed for a first-class rating.

Two weeks later in Captain Ratcliff's office, it was, "Sign here, and here." And then, "Repeat after me, 'I swear to defend...'" The words sent shivers down my spine.

I couldn't wait to climb into my dress uniform—white gloves, shiny shoes, and that sword. Women love a uniform. And there was all the travel, and of course, the money. I had the entire officers' pay scale memorized. My starting salary would be $27,500—way more than I'd ever made and enough to finally afford my first real car. And when I made officer it would kill Dad—he'd merely enlisted. Thus, if Dad had still been in the Navy, ten weeks from now, he'd have had to come to attention, throw me a salute, and call me sir—sweet.

I dozed off, only to be jarred awake by the plane touching down to pick up passengers at Chicago's O'Hare Airport. Through the darkness I could make out snow on the side of the runway.

Maybe this time I could keep my insanity under control. I had to try.

* * * * *

"All right candidates, you saw how I disassembled the M16A1 assault rifle," the gunnery sergeant said after taking a rifle apart—once. "When I say go you will begin the process. As soon as you finish you may take your seat. Are you ready?"

Four hundred men together, "Yes, Gunnery Sergeant."

"What did you say?"

Louder, "Yes, Gunnery Sergeant!"

"Begin."

The cavernous hall, filled with long rows of tables and chairs, was suddenly loud with the sounds of clacking and slapping as four hundred men moved like hell to break down their weapons and return to the safety of their seats—the longer you stood the greater the chances were that one of the twenty drill instructors would tear you apart.

Knowing what's going to happen to you definitely isn't the same as living it. I wasn't prepared for the total endless domination that was OCS. There was no break, no time for rest or relief—not even an opportunity to be insane.

There were two companies at OCS, Charlie and Alpha. The four platoons of Charlie Company all lived in one large four-story brick building only a stone's throw from the icy Potomac River. Each platoon had a platoon commander, two sergeants, and forty-eight candidates.

All forty-eight guys in our platoon slept in one large concrete-floored room called a squad bay on the third floor. It was lights out at 9:00 p.m., but most guys studied with flashlights in their bunks until way past 10:00. We got up every morning at 4:30 and had less than ten minutes to make our beds, use the head, change into our clothes, and be standing at attention in front of our bunks.

By the end of the first week, I knew it was all a game. If something took ten minutes to do, they gave us five and jumped all over us when we didn't make the deadline. One guy taught me a few tricks, like sleeping on top of your already made bunk and using your field jacket as a blanket. He knew what he was doing because a few years earlier he'd been an OCS platoon sergeant, but was now looking to move from being enlisted personnel to being an officer. He told me that if you really wanted to go for broke, you should sleep in your clothes. Then, when the instructor woke you up by screaming or throwing a metal garbage can against the wall, all you had to do was jump out of bed, put on your boots, throw on your field jacket, and stand at attention.

Once, I was ready in less than five minutes. The platoon sergeant glared at me; my buddy told me not to be such a show-off next time—drawing attention to yourself was bad.

Our heads were shaved regularly, bringing back memories of the time Dad cut all my hair off. Now I had to pay three dollars for the privilege. What a racket—we got our hair cut every Wednesday by two civilian barbers, all while being harassed by drill instructors: "Stand straight, move faster, keep the line tight, get your eyes off of me, get that look off your face." And of course it was the perfect time to question candidates on the little blue book of candidate regs: "What's the definition of a lawful order, Candidate Saxen?"

One time, when an overnight march was going to interfere with our weekly haircut, they brought us in on a Saturday for our buzz cut—a mere seventy-two hours after our last one.

"Now that I've shown you candidates how to reassemble your M16A1 assault rifle, you will put your weapon back together when I say begin. After you've completed the task, I want you to pull back the bolt, slam it forward, and pull the trigger. If it makes a clicking sound, you've done it correctly, and may sit down. Begin."

I hadn't done too badly when it came to breaking down the weapon. Generally if you keep tugging at something, you eventually find a way to get it apart—especially with the help of a little cheating out of the corner of your eye. Three guys had gotten caught looking at their neighbors during the breaking-down exercise and received integrity violations. If you got three violations—or failed two tests—you were dismissed from OCS.

"What's taking you so long, candidates? I thought you college boys were so smart!"

More than half the guys were seated and I was still standing. Reassembling the rifle was definitely not as easy as breaking it down. Keeping my face forward, I glanced to the left—no help. Shit. The last two fucking pieces just wouldn't fit.

"Are you cheating, you ignorant pieces of shit? Is that how your momma raised you?"

Two more guys got pulled off to the side. The drill instructors circled them like a pack of wolves converging on their prey.

It was now or never. I quickly turned my head to the right—perfect. I knew what I was doing wrong. About 75 percent of the guys were seated now. Okay, pull the bolt back, slam it forward, pull the trigger—nothing. Shit, it still didn't work. Two minutes later, less than forty of us were still standing. There was no way I was taking the weapon apart and starting over—I'd be skinned alive.

"Well Candidate, what the fuck are you waiting for? While you're playing with yourself the enemy just stuck a bayonet up your ass."

Even though I knew it was useless, I locked up at attention, pulled the bolt of the assault rifle back, slammed it forward, and squeezed the trigger. Without even thinking, smart-ass Ron took over and made a clicking sound with his mouth. Oh shit!

I held my breath.

"Sit down, Candidate."

Phew!

* * * * *

In chow hall, they wanted everyone to get plenty to eat as fast as possible. As soon as you finished eating, you had to line up outside and stand at attention. Usually, as soon as a quarter of the guys were done, the sergeants yelled, "Take your last bite!" Then everyone rushed like hell to line up outside.

A lot of the guys complained about the food; I loved it. Some guys claimed the cooks put drugs in our food to keep us from getting hard-ons in the shower. I say any guy who can get an erection with a sergeant yelling at his penis deserves a medal.

Today was what they called a black flag day, meaning it was damn cold and too dangerous to be outdoors for extended periods of time without proper gear—I heard the day's high would be only thirteen degrees. In chow hall, as usual, my plate was heaped with food.

"Move your mouths, you poor excuses for humanity."

Who would've thought my speed eating would be useful in the military?

"Keep moving your forks, you nasty undisciplined things."

Like a buzz saw I destroyed my plate of food at a ferocious rate of speed. As soon as I'd finished I looked up. My table mates, with two-thirds of their food yet to consume, looked at me, shocked. I immediately stood up and dropped off my tray. As I headed to the door, I could tell the drill instructors were giving me suspicious looks.

"Did you get enough food, Candidate?"

I came to attention and said, "Yes, Sergeant Instructor."

We were never allowed to look directly at anyone. But out of the corner of my eye, I saw him frown.

"Move then."

While 150 candidates still ate their food, I stood outside alone in the freezing cold. The sun was gone and the moon was full and I could see the light bouncing off the partially ice-covered Potomac. My ears and the back of my neck burned from the frigid temperature, but I finally had some time to think.

I had to start eating less. With the clothes they'd given me I couldn't tell how much weight I'd gained, but I must've put on a few pounds with all the food I'd been eating.

When I went on my first—and only—eighteen-hour liberty, three candidates and I stopped at the first convenience store we could find for beer to take to our motel. Along with my six-pack, I bought four Hostess fruit pies, two king-size Snickers, and a box of mini-donuts. Luckily, because we were all starved for anything that wasn't Marine, no one paid much attention, beyond, "Damn, you must be hungry!"

But I couldn't believe I'd devoured it all in front of three guys. I'd wanted to leave the motel to get more, but it would have been too embarrassing. To make myself feel better I told myself—yet again—that starting the following day I'd eat less, the following day I would be perfect.

* * * * *

I didn't feel well. I was so drained, I had almost no energy. At first I thought it was just the endless hours of hard work coupled with little or no sleep, but then I started coughing and couldn't seem to stop.

"Mr. Saxen, the doctor will see you now."

What a shock sick bay was in comparison with the rest of OCS—no yelling and screaming, no craziness. They actually treated you like a person. The day before they'd put me on bed rest; I felt much better now, but was growing concerned—if you miss more than three days of instruction for any reason, you're dismissed from OCS.

The doctor was a dark-haired Navy commander who looked to be in his late forties. "Have a seat, Mr. Saxen. How are they treating you?"

"I guess like they're supposed to, sir."

"Two things, son. First, just as we thought, you've got pneumonia. It's only in one lobe and with the right medication you'll be fine. Second, and I'm not going to bullshit you, there are some spots on your lungs. It may be cancer."

Oh my God. I stared at him. He had to be fucking kidding me—I'd just turned twenty-four and I didn't smoke—how in the fuck could I have gotten lung cancer?

"Now it may not be anything, but I think it's important to be honest with you. I've arranged for you to see a specialist. The best in the business is at the Bethesda Naval Hospital. We've got an appointment set up for you tomorrow. They'll pick you up at 0900 hours."

In an instant my life went to hell. All of the negative voices came rushing back: I might die and I was a fucking failure. I'd quit modeling, I'd quit comedy, and I was certainly going to be kicked out of OCS. The previous day plus today plus tomorrow was three days. I was finished.

A few days earlier I'd received a letter from Michelle. She'd called my mom's house in Stockton two weeks before I'd shipped out, and I'd given her my OCS address. I don't know why. Maybe I wanted the attention, maybe I wanted to show off about becoming an officer. Now, feeling so alone—like such a fucking zero—I figured I'd write her back. After all, I had nothing else to do today and I needed a distraction—I definitely didn't want to think about cancer.

* * * * *

It was a long lonely winter's drive from Quantico, Virginia, to Bethesda, Maryland. I did my best to make conversation with the minivan's driver, but it was hard—all I could think about was dying, being a failure, and my insanity. Eventually the driver dropped me in front of the hospital and told me he'd be back to pick me up in two hours.

The place was huge, full of officers from every branch of the military, with individual wings for various medical specialties. Bald and in my Marine camouflage, I searched for the pulmonary wing.

I found it, checked in with the nurse, then took a seat in the large waiting room. A few minutes later an old white-haired man with a cane and a portable oxygen tank sat down right beside me.

"What are you here for, son?"

I explained. He said, "Ah, well, I've had my share of lung problems—I'll tell you exactly what they're going to do. First, they'll give you this shot in the throat to numb you. Then they'll stick a tube down your throat, into your lungs. It doesn't hurt much, just feels really weird."

Well, thank you for the pep talk! This was definitely not the guy you'd want responsible for talking you out of jumping off a building. "Listen, it's okay not to jump—sure, all your friends and family will always think of you as some kind of suicidal nut case, but who really cares?"

"Mr. Saxen."

Scared as hell, I followed the nurse down a long hallway. She put me in a small room and asked me to sit on the table.

"The doctor will be right with you."

With every second my anxiety increased. What type of tests were they going to do? Was I about to be told I had cancer? How long did I have to live?

The next thing I knew the door had swung open and a full-bird colonel walked in. Instantly I jumped off the table and snapped to attention.

"Relax, son. There's no military in this room, just a doctor and a patient."

He put out his hand and I shook it. He said, "So, how are you?"

"Fine, I hope."

"Well, let's see what we've got."

He placed my X-rays onto the viewing screen. A few seconds passed, then he said, "So, how long did you live in the Midwest?"

Caught off guard, I said, "Ah... not very long, sir. When I was young I'd live with my grandparents in the Midwest for a bit whenever my dad got reassigned to a new duty station. But ever since my dad got out of the military in 1968 I've lived in California."

He dipped his head down so he could peer at me over his reading glasses. "Somewhere in your life you've been around chickens."

Surprised, I said, "Yes. I was the one in my family who was responsible for taking care of the chickens—scraping roosts, changing nests, feeding, and watering."

"Well, son, what you've got is spores from chicken manure in your lungs. Five percent of the time it'll kill you. The rest of the time, as in your case, the lungs form calcifications around the spores and you're just fine."

And just like that I went from dying to living. I wanted to give the doctor a big ol' wet one, but thought better of it.

Back in the waiting room, relieved as hell, I looked at my watch. I still had forty-five minutes before being picked up. I was hungry—I decided to have a moderate celebratory feast.

Having followed signs to one of the hospital's many cafeterias, I waited through its crowded line to collect a roast beef and gravy dinner with mashed potatoes and all the fixin's. I'd be good and skip dessert. I found a small table in the corner where I could be by myself to eat and think.

Even though the specter of death had left me, my euphoria was only momentary. Before I'd even finished my food, the voices of failure, self-doubt, and self-loathing had returned. What was I going to do with the rest of my life? My only relief was to get back into the food line.

* * * * *

I spent the next two weeks in Receiving and Separation—the place where OCS washouts, sick people, and fakers hang out while they wait to go home. I sat in my bunk hour after boring hour, staring at the cracked white ceiling and waiting for the doctor to clear me so I could go home—to what, I didn't know.

"Alright everyone, let's get ready to go to chow hall."

All of us losers climbed lazily out of our bunks—or flowed in from the TV room—and fell in behind Sergeant Stiles, our Receiving and Separation mother. I missed forming a nice neat line, I missed being part of an entire platoon bringing its heels down in marching perfection. We losers just shuffled off to chow hall through the cold and the fog, without discipline or pride.

They made us wait outside—we must have jumped the gun a little. They didn't like the winners and the losers seeing each other. I got it: we were the trash, the throwaways. It was fine with me—I didn't want to see them either. I didn't need the reminder.

There was my platoon, now down to only twenty guys or so. Twenty very tough guys, about to go off to a new beginning—while I still didn't know what the fuck I was doing. Mostly they kept their heads straight, but a few of the twenty couldn't help but steal a peek. Did they look down on us or did they wish they were free, too?

* * * * *

I hadn't accepted it yet as a final decision, but it was clear to me what I was going to do next. It was like the few minutes of sanity I had right before a binge—I hadn't yet committed the deed, but I knew it was coming and it was unstoppable. Deep down I suspected my plan was unwise—maybe even stupid—but my life was so unhinged I had nothing left to hold onto.

Michelle and I had definitely been bad for each other—too much tension, too much fighting, and too much difference in terms of our values, particularly concerning material things. But I'd changed; maybe she had too. If my short time with the Marines had taught me anything, it was how to maintain control under fire. I'd do my part—I'd refrain from doing the things that set her off. Hell, maybe it had been my fault we fought so much in the first place.

I just couldn't stand quitting and losing any more. I'd been a model and quit, engaged and broken it off, a comedian and quit, a Marine and failed, and to top it all off, I was a little insane. I doubted whether any woman other than Michelle would have me at this point—I was too fucked up. Oh sure, I might get another girl for a while, but as soon as she met the wrong Ron, I'd be screwed. I desperately needed something in my life, and I seemed to be running out of options. That was it then—it was decided.

* * * * *

I felt much better shuffling back to Receiving and Separation in the dank cold than I had when I'd left it, only forty-five minutes previously. Unlike most of these guys, I now knew what I was doing with the rest of my life.

* * * * *

I had a three-hour layover in the bustling Nashville airport to while away. After five more hours I'd land in Orange County and see Michelle for the first time in a long while. Maybe she'd be good for me this time. Maybe I could find a way to keep the wrong Ron at bay...

But where was I going to live? What kind of job could I get? What if I was just naturally a quitter and couldn't hold down a job? I'd quit everything else I'd tried...

It was getting noisy in my head again. I went to the newsstand and bought some candy. After all, my new life wouldn't begin until I got off the plane in California—this pile of candy didn't count toward my new life. After I got off the plane, I'd be good forever.

Clutching my purchases—two magazines, a plastic bag filled with four large candy bars, a one-pound bag of chocolate-covered peanuts, and a box of peanut brittle—I headed back to my gate. I figured I'd eat the peanut brittle first. It was the messiest.

As I put the first piece of candy in my mouth, I sat back and reflected on the decision I'd made. It would probably be nicer if I had a ring to give her, but it didn't really matter.

CHAPTER 15

Haunted

"So, they dumped you for being sick three days?" Michelle asked, digging into her green salad. "You know, your hair looks great short."

"You mean totally missing, right?" Reflexively, I rubbed my hand over my sandpaper scalp. "Thanks. Yeah, they said I could come back and start again from scratch as long as I do it before I turn twenty-seven, but who needs it?" My attitude, of course, was total bullshit: OCS had been much harder than I'd thought it would be; the possibility of going back and getting knocked out again would be a bigger failure than I could stand. I needed a victory in the worst way—a victory of any kind.

Michelle was definitely still cute—in fact, as her expensively-cut black hair grazed the creamy tan shoulders peeking out from her designer sundress, I lost my train of thought for a moment.

"Anyway, I uh... I have something to ask you. Don't stop me, I've put a lot of thought into this. I know we've had our tough times and all. And there's things we did that... Sorry, let me start over. Will you marry me?"

Her face lit up like a Christmas tree; she smiled from ear to ear.

"Oh my God, Ron! I had a feeling, but I didn't think you'd actually ask me. I thought you just wanted to get back together and—I'm sorry, you asked me a question. Yes! Yes, of course I'll marry you."

My three sick days had snatched away the military life I'd planned, but now, with a single stammered paragraph, I'd replaced that lost life with a new one. I had a new beginning now, a plan. I was relieved. I hoped it was love and not what it felt like: desperation. Maybe now I could relax, breathe again.

After we finished dinner, we drove along the Pacific Coast Highway. Looking out over the ocean, we talked about where we'd live, what we'd do, and how big the wedding would be. Then, against my advice, Michelle took me home to see her parents. It was awkward. I couldn't blame them for being cold; after all, I'd broken one engagement already. We didn't tell them the big news. They needed to get over hating me first.

* * * * *

While I looked for a job I could turn into a career, I worked at the Orchid's in Sacramento I'd worked at when I became a model. To save money, I stayed at my mom's house in Stockton and commuted. As soon as I could scrape enough money together, I was getting my own place. Michelle was staying in Southern California for six months to help build up our cash reserves so we could set up house in Stockton.

Which would be cool if marrying Michelle made any sense. Unfortunately, it didn't take long for me to remember why I'd broken off our first engagement. What the hell was I thinking? People didn't change. Michelle and I were still all wrong for each other—too much arguing and too much tension plus her materialism and her unresolved issues concerning her education.

Michelle had apparently been a straight-A student in high school, but when she'd gone to UC Davis she'd found she just couldn't cut it. She was smart enough, but had never developed good study habits. I guess after having everything come so easily for her all her life, she was shocked when she discovered she actually needed to study. Maybe if she'd graduated, she'd have been happier—I don't know. But either way it was tiring to always hear her complain about something she wasn't willing to do anything about. "You don't understand, I'm smarter than all the people I work with. I deserve better."

The familiar feeling of a big heavy chain tightening around my neck returned. I wished I had Mark to talk to. I'd left a message with his parents a while back but I hadn't heard anything. He was probably knee deep in training at the Academy. I was on my own. After a couple of glasses of wine, I got up my nerve and called her.

"Hi, Michelle, how are things going?"

"Great! I spent most of the day looking at wedding dresses. Just my luck, everything I like is expensive. That's what happens when you have great taste."

"Uh-huh."

The small talk went on for almost twenty minutes. To steel myself up, I refilled my glass yet again—all the way to the top.

"Listen, honey, I've been doing some thinking and I think we should probably slow things down a bit."

"What are you saying, Ron? You said..." Her voice headed up into dog-whistle range.

In the end, I guess I hadn't drunk enough wine. After I hung up the phone, I told myself I had good reasons for caving—after all, how could I put her through this twice? But the truth was, the only change between our last breakup and "Will you marry me?" was my desperation about the Marines not working out and my need to prove to myself that I wasn't a total failure.

* * * * *

I was sitting in the back room at Orchid's, eating dinner and reading the paper, when Cynthia, a waitress there, sat down across from me.

"So, have you set a date for the wedding yet? When's it going to be?"

"We don't know," I said, silently adding, "hopefully never."

But that wasn't likely. I'd had my chance to escape and I'd choked. In a few months Michelle would move up here and that would be that.

"Ron," said Cynthia, stirring her Coke nervously, "I need to ask you something."

Cynthia was an incredibly beautiful Latina who had a reputation for being a little bitchy—which either meant she actually was a little bitchy, or people were just jealous.

"It's a little embarrassing—I'm only asking you this because you're engaged and that means you're safe."

What the hell was she getting at?

"I've had my shots if that's what you mean."

"I'm serious. You're engaged, right?"

"Yes."

"Well, there's this huge wedding that I'm in—I'm one of the bridesmaids. Anyway, my ex-boyfriend, the one that just broke up with me three weeks ago, is also in the wedding party—and he's going to be there with his new girlfriend. I don't want to show up alone. And, since you're practically married, it's safe."

A little shocked I asked, "So... you want someone to go with so you don't have to stand around alone?"

"Actually—and I hate asking this—it would be great if you could pretend to be my boyfriend. That is, if you don't mind. Sorry, I know this is awkward—I just can't have him show me up in front of all my family and friends. He was my boyfriend for almost three years. He was like part of the family."

Unable to wipe the stunned look off my face I said, "When's the wedding?"

"It's a week from this Saturday. Sarah has already promised to take your Saturday shift. I'll even pay you the money you would've made so you don't lose anything."

To my surprise, I heard myself say, "You've got yourself a deal." After a little stretch of silence I added, "Okay, I guess we're on."

She put out her hand, I shook it, and she said, "Excellent." And then, just like that, she was gone.

I had to admit it: Cynthia was damn cute. Just shaking her soft, light brown hand was a turn-on. And I couldn't believe the request. It made me feel like some kind of gigolo—but in a good way. If she thought I could make her boyfriend jealous, that said something good about me, right? Or maybe just any guy was better than nothing?

I knew I shouldn't do it. If Michelle found out she'd be pissed—a fact which should probably have told me something. But like Cynthia had said, nothing was going to happen. Cynthia probably wasn't even interested and I'd be too scared anyway.

* * * * *

I showed up at Cynthia's at 11:00 a.m. Whoa, her work uniform didn't do her justice. I was definitely intimidated—with her beautiful long dark hair and strapless pink bridesmaid dress that showed every curve, she was by far the best looking woman I'd ever been on a date with—well, a pretend date anyway.

I hoped I was holding up my end of the bargain in the looks department. My hair was gelled up like it had been when I modeled, I was wearing a sports coat that looked pretty good on me, and I'd managed to keep my weight down to 203—only 18 pounds more than my modeling days.

When I returned from the Marines I discovered I'd actually lost weight at OCS—I was down to 196 again. I'd worked out steadily ever since I returned. Exercise was part of the reason why my weight never reached astronomical levels—it was my way of purging. Not only would I wake the day after a binge promising to be good, I'd run six miles—no matter my weight, no matter how painful.

While we drove to the wedding, I took a crash course on Cynthia. Turned out that even though she was beautiful, she had all the same issues, worries, wants, and dreams as everyone else I've ever met.

We arrived in the small town of Grass Valley and had no trouble locating its large, well-maintained Catholic church. The church parking lot was already filling up. Under the tall shade trees by the entrance to the church, well-dressed adults chatted while overdressed children tugged at their restrictive clothing.

Normally something like this would have scared the hell out of me—a beautiful girl way out of my league and a ton of people I didn't know—not to mention the lying part. But the long drive had relaxed me and I'd been through hell in Quantico and what could be tougher than that? Plus I was starting to see this as my last fling—a bizarre bachelor party thrown by a very creative best man. As a result, I felt calm and loose, ready to do my part and have a helluva time in the process. After all, who cared? I'd never see these people again anyway.

"So you want to make him jealous, right?"

"Of course, that's what I'm paying you for."

"Just so I'm clear, how are you with tongues down your throat?"

"Very funny."

"That's not a no."

As we got closer to the mass of people, I reached out and put my right arm around her waist and pulled her close. What a body! She looked up at me, smiled. "Hey!"

"Just doing my job."

We made our way through the crowd and got directions to where the wedding party was assembling.

I sized up the other bridesmaids. Yep, I had the best one.

"Sylvia, Beth, everyone—this is my boyfriend, Ron."

I enjoyed the mixture of smiles and surprised looks on their faces. Cynthia had told me that all her friends had heard about the breakup.

"Well, honey, I'll let you girls get ready for the wedding. I'll go introduce myself to some of the guests."

While everyone was still processing the moment, I closed the gap between Cynthia and me, put my hands on her hips, pulled her toward me, and before she had a chance to stop me, put my lips on hers. I manfully resisted the urge to thrust my tongue down her throat—maybe next time. I pulled back, knowing I'd just stolen some of her red lipstick. I looked down at Cynthia. She was smiling. She reached up with her thumb and wiped the lipstick off of me.

With our audience still drinking in the first act, I said, "Sorry about that. I know you told me not to." I gave her a kiss on the neck, and then, with a quick Cary Grant-ish "Carry on, ladies," headed into the crowd.

As the wedding proceeded I could feel my whole body coming alive with excitement. What a fucking rush. Pretending and lying, touching and kissing Cynthia... I knew I was getting dangerously close to crossing a line, but I didn't care—it felt just like it had when I'd had the affair to sabotage my first engagement to Michelle.

Cynthia's ex was named Miguel Sanchez. At the reception I looked up and caught him looking my way. I tipped my head up in acknowledgment and smiled. He clearly didn't know what to think. His new girlfriend was okay, but Cynthia was beautiful—why had he left her? I had to remind myself that looks didn't mean anything. Pretty could get ugly real fast. I knew about that! Still, on the drive over I definitely hadn't gotten any negative impressions of Cynthia.

I continued to kiss Cynthia at appropriate times throughout the afternoon and evening—I think we both knew that sparks were starting to fly. I knew I should stop, but I couldn't help myself. After all, it was my bachelor party.

"I think it's time to introduce myself to your ex."

"No, you don't. Everything's going fine, let's not mess it up." She kissed me.

But it was my bachelor party, too, so I decided what the hell—and walked up to Miguel. As soon as he noticed me, his expression changed. He was about five foot nine with a medium to small build—Cynthia could do much better. Without batting an eye, I stuck my hand out and said, "Hi, I'm Ron. I guess we've got Cynthia in common. No hard feelings, right?"

Looking stunned, he shook his head and said, "Hey man, we broke up."

Before we left I met her parents, her sister, a bunch of cousins, and various aunts and uncles. After the place started clearing out, I even entertained a few of the bridesmaids and groomsmen with excerpts from my old comedy routine.

On the way home we laughed about our trick. While we laughed, all I could think about was how good she made me feel. My happiness with her brought the stupidity of my relationship with Michelle clearly into focus and made me sad.

An hour later we arrived at her place. I turned off the car and just looked at her, too overwhelmed by my mixture of feelings to say anything.

"Time to go."

"At least let me walk you to your door." I didn't want the good feelings to end—there was only about thirty feet left to my evening. "How about one more kiss for the road?"

"Come on, Ron. You're getting married and I already feel bad about what we've done."

"It doesn't count. We were just acting."

Before she could say a word, I kissed her long and hard.

I left her place six days later.

* * * * *

Although I enjoyed my six-day bachelor party at the time, in the end it left me full of self-loathing. It was partially my betrayal of Michelle, partially Cynthia wanting more—and deserving better than a fuck-up like me—partially me wanting Cynthia, and partially just being engaged to Michelle and knowing it was wrong. What stopped me from doing what was right and ending it was pure fear—fear of Michelle's hatred and fear of quitting yet another thing.

In the month and a half after the affair ended I found it impossible to eat normally. My six-week food party netted me an additional eighteen pounds.

* * * * *

One Tuesday I was sitting in the family room of my mom's house watching TV when my sixteen-year-old sister Robin and her friend Rachel ran in.

"Hey, Ron, Rachel's got something to tell you. You're never going to believe it."

"What's that?"

"I saw your book at the bookstore downtown."

"What do you mean, my book?"

"There's this really huge book called *Sport Fitness* or something. It's you on the cover, I know it is."

At almost forty pounds more than when I'd modeled, the last thing I wanted to think about was thin Ron. I appreciated the compliment, but she was wrong.

"Listen, Rachel, I know what I've done and I was never on the cover of a book. If I were, I would know. Plus it's been almost three years since I modeled."

"You've got to check it out!"

"Come on, Ron, if she's wrong it'll be interesting to see someone who looks so much like you."

I pried myself from the couch and drove my sister and her friend to the large bookstore on Pacific Avenue. Rachel was so damn sure it was me—and so excited about it—that I was doing my best not to burst her I-know-a-celebrity bubble. No harm in playing along. It would be over soon enough.

We parked outside the large chain bookstore. I was glad my sister and Rachel ran in ahead of me. I was sure that before I got there my sister would have set Rachel straight.

I walked in the direction the two wishful thinkers had gone, and found them standing by a pyramid of books, motioning for me to hurry up. I closed the last few feet between me and the table. What the hell? This couldn't be real. There, displayed on a large table, was me. Speechless, I walked closer. I didn't get it. Why was I on the cover of a book? What the fuck was going on? I looked both ways like a shoplifter, like I was doing something wrong.

It was a large hardcover book called *Sports Fitness and Training*. I was in athletic wear that revealed well-muscled arms and shoulders, crouching down on starting blocks as if I were ready to sprint the minute the gun fired.

I stared at myself. It was coming back to me now. I remembered that picture. The photographer from New York had taken it—it must have been one of the stock photos he'd kept. He'd said I had what it took...

"It's you, Ron, isn't it?"

Slowly, "Yes."

I just kept staring.

Not knowing what else to do, I took the book from the display and walked to the counter to buy a picture of myself. I didn't know what to say or think. As the girl behind the register rang me up, I looked to see if she noticed. She hadn't. I couldn't blame her—I was wearing my forty-pounds-of-fat disguise.

As we drove home my sister and her friend giggled and laughed, thinking it was wonderful. But I knew better. I'd had it all—and pissed it all away. To me, that book, published by Random House, one of the most prestigious publishing houses in all the world, screamed, "Pure fuck-up." There was no way I could go back and start over again. Any agency that found out what had happened the last time I signed a contract wouldn't touch me with a ten-foot pole. I wouldn't either.

And then there was Michelle. Even if I could get back into shape and hold onto it, she'd been so insecure about my modeling the first time, there was no way she'd be able to accept it a second time. I felt sad: I really could've been somebody—if I weren't insane.

The voices in my head were getting louder now; I could feel the cold darkness engulfing me. I didn't care, not tonight anyway. But before I let go I had to get rid of my sister and her friend—I couldn't let them see me like this.

CHAPTER 16

White Wedding

After three months, I finally landed a job selling life insurance for a large insurance broker, Pippo and Sunset Financial. For once, being Dad's son had done me good—they'd heard of his legendary salesmanship and figured some of it must have rubbed off on me. Of course, I had to first convince them that I wouldn't sign on for the free training and then go to work for Dad, but that was easily done. When I told them exactly how well Pops and I didn't get along, the vitriol in my voice surprised even me.

I was one of eleven salespeople in the large, airy office in the good part of Stockton. I picked up a few pointers from the other guys in my office, including the three key steps to selling life insurance: one, get leads; two, get an appointment with the potential buyer any damn way you can; and three, close their ass. Pretty simple.

There are several ways to get leads after you've exhausted all of your family members and friends: You can scour publications listing marriages, births, and homes bought and sold. You can sell more insurance to existing customers. And you can cold-call names picked at random from the phone book. We had to make 100 cold calls every week.

Unlike most of the guys in the office, I loved making cold calls. All the prank calls I'd made as a kid left me fearless—my friend Ted and I had spent hours perfecting the art. We'd called the Peugeot plant in France and tried to order a dozen of their newest sedans. We'd had a towing service in Halifax, Nova Scotia, out picking up fictitious cars. We'd even had a conversation with the American Embassy in Moscow. But my favorite was when we'd set up a banquet for twenty lucky citizens with the governor of California. We'd taken care of everything from consulting them on their menu selection—how they wanted their steaks cooked, their choice of red or white wine—to asking them to "please have five questions ready for the governor." We'd gotten a 75 percent hang-up rate but the other 25 percent were fish on the line.

So I had no problem bullshitting. But out-and-out lying was something else. Apparently in this business, truth was only valuable if it helped you make a sale. Hiding the facts to close a deal wasn't considered lying—it was selling.

One day our tall and skinny office manager, Albert Stillwater, called me into his massive office. It was filled with trophies and plaques, his spoils of war.

"Ron, you're doing great. It's time I showed you a few tricks of the trade."

I pulled up a chair at the conference table.

"Do you know what this is?" He held up a newsletter from a local church. I shook my head.

"This is money. It's the Pleasant Valley Lutheran Church newsletter—it lists all the marriages, births, and deaths of more than a thousand church members. It's a gold mine—watch this."

He'd written phone numbers by all the names on the newsletter. He dialed one now, "Hello, Ed Mayfield! Ed, how are you?

"Yeah Ed, this is Albert Stillwater… from Pleasant Valley Lutheran? I'm calling about that talk we had a few months back about that new baby of yours. You remember—I'm with Pippo and Sunset Financial and we talked about making sure your family was well protected after your little girl came along… What? Well, I'm not surprised you don't remember, you were pretty busy. You said to contact you in a few months... Is Monday or Wednesday evening better for you? And do you want me there at six-thirty or eight o'clock? Excellent, I'll see you Wednesday at eight."

Albert hung up the phone. "And that's how it's done."

"Do you go to their church?"

"Hell no."

"Won't they notice that you're not in their congregation and they've never seen you before?"

"Trust me, they'll be so embarrassed that they can't remember me, they'll never ask. Once I get my foot in the door, my closing rate on these is 90 percent. It's as good as gold."

I went with Albert on Wednesday. I took the lead, we closed the deal, and I felt like shit. It wasn't stealing—we gave them something they could use and I made $850—but I hated the blatant lying.

The more I saw of this type of selling, the worse I felt. Sure it wasn't waiting tables, but who was I kidding, I was a bottom-feeder. Not that a college degree is the end all and be all—it isn't—but everyone I worked with had a high school diploma or even less. Either way, my college degree didn't mean shit and the people I hung out with weren't exactly impressive. One night while we were cold-calling, two of the reps got into a wrestling match—unfortunately I couldn't take part because apparently I'd skipped Business Wrestling 101 in college.

One night, I met with a couple that belonged to a church like the one I'd grown up in. To get through it, I told myself that this was a way of getting even with my old God—I even used church doctrine to do it.

"I see your policy with New York Life is a $200,000 whole life policy. It's a great program, don't get me wrong, but it's a permanent program. You get a better return if you hold onto the policy for thirty or forty years."

"That's right."

"Well, I'm familiar with your church and the Bible, and, based on their teachings, this policy is all wrong for you."

They were puzzled until we had a short discussion of Revelations; then they were mine. Their church, like my old church, believed the world was coming to an end very soon. No matter when you asked, they'd say the end was due somewhere between any minute and eight years from now.

On my advice, this couple canceled their $200,000 permanent program with New York Life and signed up for a $400,000 term program from me. The payment was two-thirds what they'd paid for their old policy. Oh, and I made $637 in the process. After I'd taken their check, they asked me to stick around for dessert. I sat in their modest kitchen enjoying ice cream and talking religion with their family of four.

It was after that sales call that I knew that this was yet another venture I'd one day quit. I tried to convince myself that what I'd done—switched this couple to a cheaper program that would save them money in the short run but continue to go up in price until they could no longer afford it—was okay, but I was a lying sack of shit, the kind of huckster who gave salesmen a bad name, and I knew it. And you can only know that kind of thing about yourself for so long until you either cave or make a change. As my sense of integrity plummeted—and thoughts of quitting yet another thing started to take hold—the negative voices in my head strengthened.

I started getting up late and spending my days staring at the TV. Most of our appointments and cold calls took place at night, so that was okay, but when I finally did leave the apartment, I'd pound the fast food pretty hard and then escape to a movie and a lap full of concessions. I was up to 237 pounds, 40 more than when I came back from the Marines.

Even though I was rarely at the office, Albert didn't give me any grief. What kept him off my back were my sales—I was a good closer and it saved my ass. Most guys had to take ten appointments to land two sales. I could do the same in four. Of course I didn't tell Albert that, but I figured as long as I was in the upper third of the pack he wouldn't care if I spent my days eating donuts and watching *The Price Is Right* and *Oprah*.

* * * * *

Even though I couldn't see what else I needed to learn, I still had to go to life insurance school. It was so fucking boring. I felt like I was back at church, forced to entertain myself by making up my own Bible stories.

The second day of school had just ended and I was waiting to pay at the Chevron station across the freeway, when I heard a voice that instantly grabbed me say:

"Yeah, I'll take two packs of Newport Box."

I leaned left to get a good look. Sure enough it was Wade Ashford, an old friend from church. Hard to miss him—he was six foot six, sandy-haired, and muscular. He'd been a wild one, smart as hell and always into something. When I'd last spoken with him he'd been a twenty-three-year-old district manager of six coffee shops. He had to be twenty-eight by now.

He made his purchase, and walked in my general direction.

"What's up, fuckhead?"

He stopped, looked at me, leaned his head closer as if that would help, then said, "Ron, is that you? How the hell are you, man?"

"Fine."

"Got a few minutes?"

"Sure."

We hopped into his new BMW—he always was successful—and caught up as we drove around the neighborhood, Luther Vandross playing softly in the background. Wade had left the restaurant business to become a realtor. At twenty-eight, he already had a nice place in upscale Danville and two kick-ass cars, the BMW and a Porsche Carrera.

He'd heard about the modeling—what had happened? I couldn't bullshit him; I told him it was a long sad story involving many Twinkies.

Suddenly I realized we'd left the housing tracts and driven into the deserted hills outside of town. He pulled onto the shoulder of the road and turned the car around so that it was facing the street.

"As a model you must have seen and done your share of drugs."

I stammered a little, "Of course."

Of course nothing—I was lying. I'd heard some of the women did stuff to lose weight, but had never done anything myself.

"Cool, man. I figured."

The next thing I knew he'd brought out a six-inch glass disc—a makeup mirror I was guessing—popped open the glove box, and pulled out a baggie of something white. A spike of fear went through me. I'd never done drugs, not even pot. I'd always been afraid of them. When I thought of drugs, I thought of a guy in tie-dyed clothes with a mane of wild shaggy hair, eyes rolling around in his head, and a needle in his arm. Not really me.

Wade poured a small pile of white powder onto the glass. He began chopping at it with a razor blade, forming it into two lines. Shit, what had I gotten myself into?

"My treat, you can go first."

To delay the inevitable, I said, "No, no—you first."

"That's cool, whatever."

He put the tip of the straw at the end of one of the two lines of white powder, covered one nostril, and then sniffed in while moving the straw down the line. After it disappeared, he sniffed hard, like he was sucking up a nose full of snot, and shook his head a little. "Nasty."

He motioned me forward and handed me the straw. There was no backing out now, I had to do it. I wondered if I'd get hooked and become an addict.

Telling myself just once couldn't hurt, I grabbed the straw, stuck it in my nose, and clumsily put it to the glass. Just as I was about to cover my other nostril the white powder scattered everywhere.

"You dumb fuck. What did you do?"

"I thought…"

He laughed. "You lying bitch. You've never done shit?"

Embarrassed, I said, "No."

"Here's how you do it."

And just like that I got a drug lesson—what a skill to add to my resumé. The stuff going down the back of my throat did taste pretty nasty.

"How long 'til I start to feel it?"

"A few minutes."

"So this is cocaine?"

"Fuck no, that shit's crap. You do a line of coke and it'll wear off twenty minutes later. This is methamphetamine—you know, crank, crystal. If it's good shit, you'll be amping for twelve hours."

Suddenly I realized that my brain and body had become perfection—fluid, pure, and energized. It felt as if I'd taken an increase-your-IQ-by-25-percent-and-have-more-energy-than-God pill. Wow!

Wade laughed. "The first time is always the wildest."

He said he used it to get a mental edge and boost the number of hours he could work—which for me pretty much dispelled the dark demonic nature I'd always believed drugs to have. I didn't suddenly believe drugs were a good thing, but it was pretty hard to link working more hours with Satan.

"And with this shit you're never hungry," Wade said. "It was great for losing weight. Hey, I can give you a to-go bag of your own. If you like it, I can score some for you whenever you need it."

I drove the thirty-eight miles home happier and more invigorated than I'd been in a while—maybe ever. For once the negative voices were quiet and life seemed easy.

* * * * *

It was Friday night and I was driving 474 miles to Southern California to surprise Michelle in Malibu. Since I'd decided to go through with the wedding, I figured I might as well make the best of it. I'd drive all night and show up in the morning with flowers in hand—she'd be so happy.

It was 9:30 p.m. If I continued driving until 11:00 and then got a hotel, I could leave early the next morning and arrive at her place in Malibu by noon at the latest.

For some reason, I'd brought Wade's little bag of white powder along. I hadn't touched the stuff since he'd given it to me two weeks ago. The experience had been both great and scary at the same time. What if I got hooked? What if I became a druggie?

Even though I'd had dinner at 7:00, I was getting hungry—and worried that I'd break my new diet. I'd promised myself I'd start it that weekend as I wanted to look good in our wedding pictures. But I sure could go for a nice decadent snack and a one-day diet delay... At the same time I sure as hell didn't want to show up on the beach of Malibu with a dozen roses in my hand and two dozen donuts in my belly.

Then I remembered what Wade had said about the powder and losing weight. When I'd used it that first time, I hadn't been hungry for hours—I didn't eat until just before falling asleep the next morning. I wouldn't be using it like an addict, it would be for a good cause—just like the way Wade used it.

I took the next exit that promised a convenience store. A few minutes later I'd gotten a cheap hand mirror, some razor blades, an extra straw for my fountain drink, and one seriously weird look from a clerk.

Fifteen minutes later, I pulled into a combination rest stop and scenic overlook. I did everything just the way Wade had, except in the dark, in case a highway patrolman was lurking nearby. The only light came from the almost-full moon and a distant streetlight.

After successfully snorting a mini-line, I hopped back onto the freeway. Twenty minutes later I wasn't feeling anything so I repeated the process, this time snorting a fatty. Twenty miles later my hair was on fire.

As the miles sped by I began to process my life. Okay, so I'd never be a fucking model. No big deal. The book cover was embarrassing, I admitted that. But what was the upside? It was so fucking simple: it would help me sell insurance. People liked hanging with famous people. I could look like the book cover if I got all the weight off. That wouldn't be hard, I just had to want to—and I did want to. Okay, so my insurance job was all about bullshit and lying, but so what? I'd work hard, get rich as hell, and spend my money doing good for others. Someone was going to do this job—why not me? And where was my calculator?

I turned on the overhead light and started driving with one eye on the road and the other on my calculator as I figured out exactly what I needed to do to conquer the world. I wished I had a third hand—I had to put down the calculator to write down my ideas, ideas flowing faster than my mind or pen could process.

We could make money, buy and sell lots of houses, and—speaking of making money, why shouldn't I sell Michelle's parents some life insurance? Let's see, her mom... What was that sound? Shit, the car.... Fuck. Come on you little bastard, just get me to the next exit... There were lights off in the distance. The car sputtered, lurched unhappily.

I pulled onto the shoulder of I-5 and screamed at the top of my lungs, "Son of a bitch!" I turned the key again and again; the engine refused to turn over. With the lights on and my calculator glued to my hand, I glanced at the dashboard. What? The gas gauge was on E. That didn't make sense. How could I have run out of gas? I looked at my digital watch: 4:37. 4:37?

Aloud, "It's 4:37 in the fucking morning? Where the fuck am I?"

After a four-mile walk to the lights in the distance (they looked much closer than they actually were), I learned where I was: just about to ascend the San Bernardino Mountains. Which meant I was about 150 minutes away from Malibu. Wow! I didn't even remember driving the last 300 miles. In shock, I refilled my tank and got on my way.

When I showed up in Malibu that morning, bright-eyed and bushy-tailed, with flowers in hand, Michelle was astonished. She was on her way to a wedding and brought me along. About 6:30 that night, I hit the wall and totally crashed. When I told her it was because I hadn't slept at all the night before, she thought it showed how much I loved her.

But the next day I had to drive back and I was now tired as hell. Obviously, I didn't have any choice—I *needed* the white stuff to get home safely. Only, this time I'd be much more observant. Keeping that in mind, I filled my gas tank before I took the meth. As the miles ticked away and the drug exploded in my veins, life became wonderful again. Being forced to quit modeling because I was insane, breaking off my engagement to Michelle, quitting comedy because I was impatient and had stage fright, being forced to leave OCS because I'd gotten sick—even making the cover of a Random House book and being too insane to seize the opportunity—all of that went from "you suck" to "who gives a fuck?" Until:

"Reno, 112 miles?"

A cold sweat broke out on my forehead. What the fuck was I doing? I'd overshot my exit by fifty-seven miles, cruising on past Stockton to the far side of Sacramento. I had to get a grip on myself. With both hands firmly on the wheel, I took the next exit and got back on the freeway heading in the opposite direction, pushing down hard on the accelerator.

＊ ＊ ＊ ＊ ＊

A few months later Michelle and I moved into a large two-bedroom apartment in a white stucco building overlooking artificial ponds. At first we got a kick out of just being in our new apartment and living together. But it didn't take long for things to slide downhill. It wasn't as bad as before our first breakup, but it wasn't good—definitely wasn't that oh-my-God-I-love-you-let's-get-married kind of feeling. Which you should definitely have if oh-my-God-let's-get-married is what's happening.

One night, when she was yammering on yet again about how her life was never going to amount to shit and she was so smart and deserved much better, I couldn't take it anymore and decided to take matters into my own hands:

"Honey, can I get you a Diet Coke?"

"Sure, with ice… It's so hard for a person who has as much potential as me—you don't understand…"

With her voice still droning on in the background, I poured some white powder into her drink. Enough? Nah, she could use a little more… I tapped the little plastic bag again. Whoa! I stirred it in vigorously, hoping she couldn't taste it.

"Here you go, sweetie."

"Thanks. Anyway, I should just…"

Twenty minutes later her eyes got wide, and she started talking faster, a big grin on her face.

"First, I'll just go back to school, then I'll…"

I felt a twinge of guilt.

"I don't know what came over me. I've never felt so great, so sure of myself. Starting tomorrow I'll…"

If I ever told her she'd be pissed—and she'd be right. But I had my defense ready: "Honey," I'd say, "I wasn't medicating *you*, I was medicating myself. I needed relief and believe me, I felt wonderful as soon as you quit being a pain in the ass."

* * * * *

Finally it was the big day, the day I actually finished something I'd started—even if it was something wrong. Michelle and I were to be married in a beautiful church in the old part of Sacramento. A few of my friends from Orchid's, where Cynthia still worked, were coming to the wedding. Not Cynthia, of course, although she knew today was the day I'd make my lie official.

And not Mark. I tried not to think about it. Ever since I'd called him to say Michelle and I were getting married, he'd refused to return my calls; he hadn't responded at all to the wedding invitation. My other friends thought this was bullshit, but I got it. He refused to be an accessory to the crime—I respected that and wished I'd done the same.

"Hey, Ron." It was Wade Ashford. He'd agreed to be one of the groomsmen, but was sure I'd bail. "So, you're really going through with this? You're such a pussy."

"Yep, that would be me."

It didn't even hurt to say it. I'd come to terms with my crime and my sentence—life. It's like the old AA saying: accept what you cannot change. Only in my case it's: accept what you will not change.

"Listen man, you don't have to do it. It's not too late to walk away."

"Fuck off—you know it's too late."

"Well, a good friend doesn't let a good friend walk off a cliff without a smile on his face. Follow me."

Wade led me to the inner sanctum of the church. A short plump lady who looked like a plainclothes nun caught us. "May I help you?"

"Boy can you ever!" Wade said. "This guy's got cold feet and I need a private place to settle him down or the whole thing's off."

Magic words. She pulled a set of keys out of her pocket. "Father Brogan's not in today. You can use his office." Unlocking the door, she patted my shoulder. "It's a big day, young man. Take your time. God will guide your heart."

The walls of the room were lined with bookshelves, crosses, degrees, awards—all of the external symbols of virtue. After a quick once-over, Wade found what he was looking for: conveniently, Father Brogan's huge oak desk had a glass cover. A few seconds later, Wade was chopping out two fat white lines of crank where moments before a Bible had sat.

I had to laugh. "Hey Wade, look—I'm having a white wedding."

* * * * *

After so many failures, I just couldn't stand to quit yet again. I had to regain some measure of control and prove to myself I could complete *something*—even though I knew that something was wrong.

So, with a chemically induced smile stretched across my face, I said, "I do."

CHAPTER 17

My Bed

After a three-day honeymoon in Mendocino, Michelle went back to work as a cocktail waitress at the Seville Steak House and I returned to my new job as an assistant manager at London's Palo Alto department store. Yep, I hadn't been able to take the lies at the insurance brokerage any longer and had, predictably, bailed. I fearlessly delivered my letter of resignation to Albert's desk in person—after he went to lunch.

Even though I was pretty sure quitting insurance was the right thing to do, it was still quitting—and I still felt like a loser. My life was like the nursery rhyme "Farmer in the Dell"; it went, "Hi-ho, the derry-o, Ron quits the modeling, Ron quits his first engagement, Ron quits the stand-up, Marines, and life insurance..." Sure, I'd followed through on my second engagement, but that was the biggest sin of all. My song kept getting longer and I was only twenty-four.

When I made the mistake of dwelling on the mass of garbage I called my life, I had to seek relief the only way I knew how: with a mountain of food and the promise to be perfect tomorrow.

* * * * *

For my first five months at London's, we stayed in Stockton and I commuted to Palo Alto every day, a round-trip commute of four hours. I had way too much time during my commute to think about where my life wasn't—and to discover that the freeway took me directly past over twenty-seven fast-food restaurants.

I tried them all. I wouldn't have been surprised if, when the new Burger King opened in Tracy, they'd asked me to cut the ribbon. "Ron, we'd like you to be our first ten customers. We killed a cow especially for you."

Sometimes I couldn't help myself and would stop off at a bookstore to look for my book, definitely a happy/sad experience. It had been almost two years since Robin and Rachel had discovered it, but it was still on the shelves. When I picked it up and held it, it was like holding a secret magical past. It felt like I was holding someone else's life, it seemed so far away.

After a year I was promoted to senior assistant manager and transferred to Hayward. We moved to Hayward to be closer to my job, and life with Michelle fell into a predictable pattern. Emotionally, we stayed in the shallow end of the pool to avoid confrontation. It wasn't all bad; occasionally we even had a good time.

＊ ＊ ＊ ＊ ＊

"Mr. Saxen, there's a guy downstairs trying to return a $249 stereo system that we're positive he just swiped off the counter."

"How positive, Tim?"

"Well, we had two on the counter, and now there's only one, and no one remembers selling it. What do you want to do about it?"

"I'll take care of it. Just stay close in case I need backup."

I hated this part of the job. I'd gone to college, come close to being an officer and a gentleman—if I'd stayed in the Marines, right now I'd be a first lieutenant looking to make captain—but here I was, tangling with low-life pieces of shit.

Once a gang of twenty-five kids had come through the store like a tornado, grabbing things, knocking displays over. I couldn't do anything but watch. Now we had undercover security. Tim had been a reserve police officer in Kansas; he was pretty good in confrontations.

The Hayward store was huge by London's standards—two floors and 50,000 square feet. The customer service and returns department was downstairs. Before I descended the stairs I peered down the stairway to size up the man I was about to confront. Looked like white trash to me.

To convict a shoplifter, you need to be able to prove a continuous chain of custody of the object in question. In this case there wasn't one—we couldn't know for sure the stereo from the counter was the one in his hand. However, we'd recently had quite a problem with shoplifters and I'd been ordered to crack down whenever possible, even bend the rules a little. Before I went to the customer service department I checked the electronics department. Tim was right, the stereo from the counter was gone.

From thirty feet away, the guy looked to be around forty. He was wearing worn jeans, a funky gray hooded sweatshirt, and a soiled A's baseball cap. Taking a deep breath, I closed the distance between us.

"I'm the manager. How can I help you?"

He turned to face me. Whoa, someone got beat with the ugly stick. He was sporting a shopworn face, with a few gaps in his grill and tattoos on both hands. He'd been around the horn a time or two.

"You can help me by giving my money back."

I added really bad breath to his resumé.

"No problem. Susie, where's his receipt? I'll sign it."

Susie was a tough, middle-aged lady who'd worked customer service for years. She'd seen it all, and knew what I had to do. She also knew that legally, I didn't have a leg to stand on.

"He doesn't have a receipt, Mr. Saxen."

I paused to let him see the fake confusion on my face and said, "You mean when you stole the stereo off the counter, you failed to get a receipt?"

There was a short pause while his expression went from a bullshit-innocent half-smile to so-you-want-to-play-hardball-huh?

"Fuck you, man. I know my rights. I didn't steal it. Give me my money. That's your policy."

Unfortunately, Mr. My-parents-were-related-before-they-got-married appeared to know the rules. We hadn't seen him take it and couldn't prove he had—besides, it was only stealing if you left the store without paying: he'd apparently swiped the stereo and then taken it straight to customer service without ever leaving the store.

I stood up straight, looked him in the eye. "No."

"Listen here you fat-ass-ten-sandwich-eating motherfucker, you owe me some money."

I was suddenly aware of every single one of the 271 pounds stuffed into my suit. I was the fattest I'd been in my entire life. As a model, I'd had a 32-inch waist; now I was wearing a baggy size 46. My face turned beet red. It was high school all over again.

My nostrils flared, my adrenaline spiked. I flashed back to the night I'd lost it with Mom's low-life boyfriend, Mr. Jennings. It was everything I could do not to snap. "No."

"I'm not leaving this store until I get my money, fat ass."

Keeping my eyes on him, I pushed the stereo in the direction of Susie, who quickly grabbed it and put it behind the counter.

"What stereo are you talking about? You seem confused. I suggest you leave."

"What if I fucking don't—you gonna eat me, fatso?"

The world went silent. I shoved him to the wall, grabbing his left hand, trying to force it behind his back—I couldn't, he fought me. Realizing that every second counted, I used my left leg to whip his legs out from under him, driving him hard to the ground. In an instant, Tim grabbed one of his flailing hands and slapped the cuffs on him. Before we picked him up, I leaned down, my mouth two inches from his ear. "Fuck you, asshole."

Tim and I took him—resisting and complaining—to the security room. With him in a chair, handcuffed and out of earshot, Tim asked me what I wanted to do next. After all, we didn't really have anything on him. The only thing we could do was run his record and hope like hell we came up with something. If not, we had to let him go. And legally he got to take the stereo with him. We pulled out his wallet and called the cops.

"I ain't fucking going to jail."

"It's not your decision, ass-wipe."

The adrenaline dropped and as Tim explained the situation to the cops I started to think maybe I'd gone too far. After all, we'd lost the chain of custody on the stereo. Then Tim told the police the guy's name—and their usually calm telephone manner vanished immediately.

"Do you have him under control? We'll move you to the top of the list."

Turned out he was a two-time loser with three outstanding warrants for his arrest, one for armed robbery.

* * * * *

Driving home from work that day, I couldn't stop thinking about the incident. I was glad the situation had worked out as it had, but devastated that I still had to take childish insults about my weight. What he'd said was hurtful, but hell, I'd handed him the ammunition—I really did have a fat ass. I pulled into a 7-11 for a bag of candy bars, the only thing I knew would make the pain go away—at least for a little while.

* * * * *

A week later, Wade Ashford showed up at work. I hadn't seen him for over a year. Since doing methamphetamine regularly was expensive, I'd quit cold turkey after the wedding. After that, I hadn't seen Wade at all. Until now. I told him I'd be off in an hour. Two hours later we sat on my sofa watching TV, two lines of white powder sitting on a mirror in front of us, waiting to join the two already up our noses.

Still raw from the fatso incident, I welcomed the drugs. I decided this time I'd use meth like medicine—I'd go on the new Ron Saxen Crystal Meth Diet. However, because money was still tight and Michelle was in complete control of our finances, I couldn't afford to pig out on the white powder. I learned to ration and I was pretty good at it.

Two months later, when Wade came over to play Nintendo, he showed me something new:

Taking a square-foot piece of aluminum foil from the kitchen, he folded it over, rubbing it smooth so that it didn't crease when he bent it, and then shaped it into a trough.

"This is a better way to use crank," he said. "It gets you high almost immediately, and there's no nasty taste in the back of your throat."

He poured the meth into the trough, stuck a straw in his mouth, then lit a fire underneath the foil and sucked in the smoke that rose as the drug cooked.

My turn. Wade stared at me.

"What are you looking at, goofball?"

"Nothing bitch, just wait."

A few seconds later a wave of euphoria drenched every square inch of my body. It seemed like I could actually feel the drugs encasing my brain—it was perfection. The transformation that usually took twenty minutes took less than one, and felt better, more pure.

From then on I didn't snort, I smoked. The only problem with smoking it was that, if I didn't watch myself, I went through a lot of product fast. But, since I was on the Ron Saxen Crystal Meth Diet, I rationed it carefully.

Money was a problem though, so I had to sell a few things. One day, Wade drove me to a pusher's house to hock an expensive watch I wasn't using. Outside his house were at least five guys dressed in maintenance uniforms, just standing around and pawing the ground with rakes, pretending to work. I pointed it out to Wade—didn't it seem a little suspicious?

"Don't worry—I'm a snitch. We're protected."

I didn't know what to say; it was too late to turn around. All I could do was follow him into the apartment.

In the dim light that crept through the closed curtains, I saw five or six guys sitting around a table, getting loaded. The dealer, who was short, blond, and muscle-bound, said hi without much expression, then opened a false panel in the wall near the kitchen and took out what looked like a two-pound bag of meth. The whole scene made me feel like a drug addict. I wasn't though; I was in control.

* * * * *

Every morning I got up before Michelle, hurried to the bathroom, pulled out my lighter, foil, the hollow barrel of an old pen—and, of course, some crank—and lit up. After that I'd put on my jogging clothes and go for a run. In just under five months, I'd lost forty pounds. My lighter weight plus the meth coursing through my veins made running feel effortless and being positive seem easy.

But then, one day, something felt different.

As I ran along, I suddenly realized that the world was a very strange place. It had been around for billions of years and there were Indians who must have lived right where I was running, Indians who had lived out their lives thousands of years ago, with their own worries and dreams—and now they were dead, forgotten. No one knew their names, no one cared. Someday that would happen to me, too. There would be a time when there were no memories of me, when I was only dust. If I would be dust and nothing I did mattered, what was the point? Why the fuck did I exist? Why?

I couldn't shake the darkness that had fallen over me. It was always dark outside when I ran in the early morning, but it had never caused an emotional problem before. It was so dark—the world was so dark. Why was I here?

My heart started to pound faster; tears streamed down my face. Why did I exist? Why did it matter? It didn't matter. So why did I exist? I shook my head and ran from the shaded darkness of the residential district toward the bright lights of the main streets. I ran right down the middle of the street—it was so early, there were hardly any cars. The light helped a little, but the tears still flowed. Nothing mattered.

Fifteen minutes into my panic and despair, a light switched on in my brain: I'd never felt like this before. What had changed? Oh yeah. The meth. With that realization I fought to shut out the terrifying thoughts, to wall them off—given meth's effects, I just needed to get through the next eight to ten hours and I'd be fine.

A few minutes later, I returned home—and flushed my last half-gram of meth down the toilet.

***** *

Soon after I quit drugs, Wade Ashford disappeared from the face of the earth. Not just from my life—he really vanished. Relatives and creditors started contacting me to find out what I knew, which wasn't much.

Turned out his drug use had fucked up his life. What started out as a way to work more hours and get an edge turned into total self-destruction. As a result, he lost his big house in Danville, both cars, his wife, and everything else he had. To escape the law, he ran. Because no one could think better on their feet than Wade, he managed to talk rental companies out of cars which he kept for months and never paid for.

That was how I kept track of him—car rental companies kept contacting me. I couldn't help them, but I appreciated the update on his itinerary. Rumor had it he lived on the beach in Costa Rica and was now involved in tourism.

***** *

Not long after the crank-induced challenge to my existence, I quit London's department store, just days after they offered to promote me to general manager of my own branch. They were shocked when I turned the promotion down, but it wasn't the life I wanted—at least that's what I told myself. I tried not to think about it, but the fact was, I'd just left my fifth career in five years and it was killing me.

For the next thirteen months I was a cigar salesman. Yep, I convinced store owners to sell my cancer-causing stogies, the dream of my childhood. The good thing about the job was it was easy as hell. The bad thing was it was easy as hell.

The job made me lose all remaining respect for myself. I could finish two days of work in one. I could work half a day and be in the Oakland Coliseum with my tie off and a hot dog in my hand in time to see the first pitch of an afternoon A's game. Where was my work ethic?

At one point I even asked if I could make more than the fifteen calls that were required every day. When I got a polite no, I understood. They didn't want me to ruin it for the rest of the guys. However, due to the decrease of self-respect—and increase of boredom brought on by too much free time—the frequency of my binges started to increase as well, as did how early I began a binge. Sometimes I'd fall asleep in my car as early as 1:00 p.m. as a result of a binge.

Having flushed the key ingredient in the Ron Saxen Crystal Meth Diet down the toilet, I tried losing weight the really old-fashioned way: throwing up. Apparently ancient Romans had used a feather to tickle the back of their throats and thus purge themselves after meals so they could go back for seconds. Maybe the Romans knew something I didn't—or maybe they had special feathers; after a week of moderate success, I gave it up: too much work and too disgusting.

* * * * *

A few months later, in an effort to regain my integrity, I gave my notice—thereby ripping myself from the malaise of my effortless cigar job, and throwing myself onto the sword of hard work and long hours. I was now a salesman for California's leading candy and tobacco distributor, the Sosnick Companies.

They'd previously been my largest cigar customer. I'd pushed my cigars at their Friday morning sales meetings and plied them with advertising money and catered breakfasts. As a sales rep, I often traveled with other salespeople, when their distributor allowed it. Of all the reps I'd ever met, Sosnick's were by far the happiest. They told me the hours were long but the opportunity for good commissions was excellent if you were willing to work. Even though it meant I was starting my seventh career in six years, I felt good about my switch to Sosnick—I'd finally made a move I was proud of.

Sosnick had four divisions. I applied to two of them, one in San Leandro, the other in Santa Clara, fifty miles south of San Francisco. I wanted to work in the San Leandro division—it was only six miles from our apartment in Hayward. However, when Sosnick offered me Santa Clara, I jumped at it.

Actually, I almost didn't get hired—some kiss-ass at Sosnick ratted me out to my boss at the cigar company and as a result the cigar company put on a full-court press to get me to stay. I even got a call from the vice president of sales, who turned out to be friends with the president of Sosnick. In the end, however, Sosnick's president let his sales manager make the decision and I was hired.

My territory was beautiful Santa Cruz, with its beaches and redwood forests. The town of Santa Cruz itself was a melting pot of college students, tie-dyed hippies, mountain rednecks, bikers carrying AARP cards, conservative executives, and old-timers who looked down on everyone else.

Luckily for me, my territory was weak when I got it. By working endless days, I built it into one of the strongest territories in the company within just a few years. Strangely, my sixty-hour workweeks were the easiest and most gratifying weeks of my life. I loved my job and got paid very well. In three years, my salary almost tripled and I was honored with both Sosnick's Most Improved Territory award and their Salesperson of the Year award.

For the first time in my life—sixteen years after my dad had left—I let myself erase the label he'd slapped on me as a child: lazy and never going to amount to anything. And for the first time since modeling, I was proud of myself and what I'd accomplished. Sure, my head still had its share of negative voices competing for airtime, but "You're not successful, you're a quitter" was, at long last, silenced.

* * * * *

Michelle and I now lived in Ben Lomond, a small town nestled amidst towering redwoods. The town was divided in half by the San Lorenzo River, a river so clean and clear it still got its annual salmon run. We rented a small house in town across from a little old church where I was sure long-winded ministers unwittingly forced bored-to-tears children to develop vivid imaginations.

We had two cats and two dogs, a black Lab and a Doberman. In a heated moment, Michelle said that if she had to choose between the pets and me, the choice would be easy. Good to know where I stood. I did like some things about Michelle, however. Our views on politics, religion, and nature meshed nicely. But our money issues caused big problems. And when you've got big problems, they tend to overshadow everything else.

I had no one to blame for my financial ignorance but myself, however. When we got back together and got married, I let her take care of the bills and write all the checks. She seemed to enjoy being in charge and I was glad to make her happy—until the day I woke up and realized I was a grown man who didn't have an ATM card, a checkbook, a credit card, or even the combination to his own post office box. I was a thirty-two-year-old man who couldn't pick up his own mail—and because I was so ignorant about our financial situation, I had no idea that a crisis was imminent.

* * * * *

"Ron, I've got some news and I don't want you to get pissed off."

"I won't get pissed off. What is it?"

"I know you're going to get pissed."

"Then why'd you bring it up?"

"I have to. There's no good way to tell you, but we can't take our trip to Hawaii in two weeks. Your wages just got attached."

"What?"

"It's some bullshit tax-screw-up thing. We owed some back taxes and things got messed up. I was working with them and then for some reason they attached your wages. They're taking a third of your check."

"*What?*"

And then all hell broke loose.

I was furious at myself for not taking charge of the situation sooner. Now I felt completely helpless.

One afternoon when I was home by myself, I found two unopened bank statements on the dresser, under a pile of laundry.

Realizing I hadn't seen a bank statement in over six years, I decided to take a peek. What I saw shocked me.

I soon realized that our credit was destroyed—and that it was unlikely this fact would ever change. Just like with bingeing, when you repeatedly cross into irrational financial behavior it just gets easier and easier to continue doing it. I coped with the situation the only way I knew how, the only way that seemed open to me: food.

※ ※ ※ ※ ※

One day, after I'd finished my sales calls early, I decided to drive into town and walk along the Santa Cruz Beach Boardwalk. It was the off-season, but there'd still be just enough people there that I wouldn't feel totally alone.

With a large cup of coffee in my hand and caffeine coursing through my veins, I drank in the cool salt air, the therapeutic sound of the surf, and took stock of my life. It was the perfect place and time for some hard truth-telling.

I was thirty-two years old and weighed 295 pounds, the most I'd ever weighed. At the time, a big six-foot-three football player named "Refrigerator" Perry played for the Chicago Bears. When I looked at him, I saw huge—he weighed 325 pounds; they wanted him to get down to 300. He looked massive and way overweight, and yet he weighed only 30 pounds more than I did—and was taller.

My pattern—as it had been now for years—was still to starve myself during the day, telling myself all good tasty foods were forbidden, only to lose control at night and binge, soothing myself with the promise of eternal perfection starting the following day. However, I now also found myself experiencing bouts of depression much more frequently than previously.

I couldn't believe I weighed 110 pounds more than I had when I'd modeled. And the book I was on the cover of, *Sports Fitness and Training*, simply refused to go away. I kept checking on it in bookstores. Why I tortured myself this way, I didn't know—maybe I just liked revisiting my brush with fame. By now the book was out in paperback, too. Wouldn't the publishers shit themselves if I showed up and said, "Hi, I'm the guy on the cover! This book worked so well for me, I fucking ate it!"

* * * * *

Sometimes I didn't find my picture, it found me. A few months earlier, Bucky, a customer big into bodybuilding, told me he was sure he'd seen me in *Muscle & Fitness* magazine. (I'd told Bucky about my brief modeling career previously, partly because it felt good to see someone's reaction to my momentary fame and partly because it felt good to confess.)

"No way, Bucky. It's been a ton of years, and I never did anything that would land me in *Muscle & Fitness*."

"I have it right here, check it out."

Bucky pulled out the January issue—Clint Eastwood was on the cover—and flipped through the pages. "There."

It *was* me—a younger, skinnier me. It was just like the first time I saw the book. Only this time, instead of being 40 pounds heavier than in the picture I was holding, I was 110.

Not long after that, I decided to try something different to lose weight—a cigarette diet. They said smokers lost weight for three reasons: smoking gave you something to put in your mouth, killed your taste buds, and provided you with an energy buzz. I was thinking that if I had to choose between being thin and dying of lung cancer or staying fat and dying of a heart attack, I'd choose thin.

Day one of the nicotine diet, I smoked an entire pack of menthols—I couldn't afford anything except the free samples I'd been carrying in my car. When I took my first drag, it seemed pretty cool. I saw why people smoked. Then I started to feel like shit, then turned green, then puked. As a weight-loss device, day one was a success, but not nearly as much fun as I'd hoped. Day two was almost as bad. Day three I quit, green turkey.

Just imagine if it actually worked—cigarette companies could market a low-fat, high-nicotine diet. "Sure there's the cancer thing," they could say, "but all we ever wanted was to keep America thin. And look at the thanks we get."

* * * * *

I'd reached the north end of the boardwalk. I decided I might as well stroll on the long pier. I could hear the barking of the sea lions hanging out on the pilings beneath the pier, waiting for free snacks from the tourists. The fresh air and the safety of open space without human interaction inspired me to be honest with myself; my mind drifted to my shameful binge after the previous week's sales meeting.

* * * * *

A large candy company had given each of us fifty of their new candy bars to give to customers as samples. I'd just begun the thirty-six-mile drive home and even though I'd told myself that I was starting a new diet that day—I had to, I was almost 300 pounds—I could hear the beginnings of the gentle whispering in my head that always led to shouting. To prevent an incident, I took action:

Just two blocks from the freeway, I stopped the car, grabbed the sack of candy bars from the seat beside me, and tossed them into the trunk. As I slammed it closed, I said aloud, "Now shut the fuck up."

I hopped onto Highway 17, a notoriously dangerous stretch of mountain road, and joined the traffic zooming around its winding curves. Proud of my decision, I cranked up the stereo just in case my friends in the trunk started screaming for help.

Michelle was away that weekend, visiting a friend in Santa Barbara—which meant I could get drunk and watch as much football as I wanted. She usually left me ten bucks and plenty of food.

What the hell, I should just let loose this weekend and start fresh on Monday. Maybe I should even start right now... No. Those candy bars were for my customers. But, well, they'd never fucking know. They didn't need samples anyway—they'd buy whatever I suggested...

Highway 17 was a killer—almost no shoulder and no place to turn off for a few miles. But I'd seen people pull off on the side when they got a flat... No, I should wait.

Screw it.

I pulled off onto the slender shoulder. My car shook with each vehicle that whizzed by. Because I was sure to get hit if I exited through the driver's side, I crawled uncomfortably across to the passenger's side, squeezed out the door, and walked back to the trunk. As I retrieved the bag of candy, a large truck zoomed by, blasting me with a gust of wind and dirty water.

Before I started the car I unwrapped six candy bars and lined them up in easy reach on the passenger's seat. After all, when it came to scarfing, it was safety first. The first four candy bars tasted great; I devoured the next fifteen simply to keep the party going and hold back the anxiety of reality.

* * * * *

On the boardwalk, listening to the sea lions, I shut my eyes against the memories that followed. Even though the sun was getting low in the sky and the temperature was dropping, I wasn't ready to go home yet. I still needed to come to terms with what had happened that very day during my sales call at Z's Liquors.

* * * * *

"Go easy on the order, Ron, okay? It's been slow."

"No problem. Did you see the Forty-Niners' game, Tom?"

"Of course."

"How about the..."

Everything suddenly got very dark. I looked left, right; the walls of my vision collapsed to black.

"Ron! Ron! What's wrong?"

And just like that, the lights came back on. I found myself sitting on the floor surrounded by cases of wine. My head started to clear.

"Ron, are you okay?"

Not quite all there yet, I said, "Sure, I'm... ah... fine."

"Your face looks flushed. What happened?"

"I think I started to black out."

"You should see a doctor."

Even though I was scared as hell, I not only did *not* see a doctor, I finished the last ten hours of my workday. I didn't want a doctor to see me because I knew the truth: I'd torched my body and now it was time to pay. You can't thrash yourself with weeks of starving and punishing exercise, followed by 20,000-calorie days that lead to fifty-pound weight gains in only four months, without paying a price.

* * * * *

Standing on the boardwalk, looking out at the Pacific Ocean, it was hard to believe there had been a time, however short, when most men would have wanted to look like me and most women would have been happy to date me.

I didn't want to die the wrong Ron.

CHAPTER 18

Another Man's Floor

Who the hell was calling at this time of night? I opened one eye and looked over at the clock. 10:48. I'd gone to bed over an hour ago. Groggy, I fumbled in the darkness and grabbed the phone.

"Hello?"

"Is this Ron Saxen?"

"Ah... yes... ah sure. Who's this? It's late, man."

"Mr. Saxen, we need to ask you some questions and we need you to focus."

I could hear road noise through the phone, cars whizzing by in the background.

"Your sister Robin has been in a serious car accident. I'm one of the paramedics treating her at the scene and we need to know a few things." A pause and then, "Are you still there, Mr. Saxen?"

"Yes... yes, I'm here."

"Is your sister allergic to any drugs we need to know about?"

Being so close to sleep made the whole situation seem surreal. "I don't think so. Although there was this one antinausea drug..."

* * * * *

One of Robin's coworkers picked Michelle and me up at the Burbank airport early the next morning. She didn't have much information, just that Robin had been taken to Northridge because they had a good trauma center and the most important fact of all—Robin was still alive.

On the way to the hospital, all I could think was that my sister couldn't die. Even though we'd come from a loveless family, there was something special between the two of us. It wasn't just that she was my baby sister—we shared the same wonderful weirdness, a truthful view of the universe through our own secret looking glass; we got it. Mark had, too, but he'd disappeared without a trace. Robin couldn't die. Without her, I would be alone.

Thirty minutes later we arrived. The hospital still showed signs of damage from the Northridge earthquake. While we waited for the doctor, a nurse brought us to see Robin. For the first time since I could remember, nothing about being in a hospital bothered me. I think it was because I saw this hospital as a big machine that's sole purpose was saving my sister's life. As I understood it, Robin had been driving her little white Honda Civic when a full-sized pickup truck going seventy miles an hour had rammed into her driver's side door.

On the way to the ICU, the nurse told us Robin was unconscious and had been since she came in. "We've got her floating on a nice bed of morphine. At times like this it's better if she doesn't know what's going on. It's not something you want to remember."

We walked through a sliding door and into a world of sterile machines, lights, tubes, and the chirping of hearts in peril. Looking at my sister I was struck by three things: how unmarked her face was, how unnatural she looked on life support, and how her chest rose and fell as the respirator forced air into her lungs. I'd never seen so many tubes and wires in all my life. More than anything, I was grateful for the science that was keeping my little sister alive.

* * * * *

A little over an hour later: "Ron Saxen?"

I looked up from the magazine I was not reading in the waiting room. A middle-aged man with gray hair and a white coat was standing a few feet away. I rose. "I'm Ron Saxen."

The doctor informed me that Robin had twenty-three fractures in her rib cage, a crushed pelvis, a broken collarbone, a fractured sternum, and a punctured lung. Additionally, they'd had to insert two tubes into her chest to drain the area between her lungs and chest cavity in order to prevent internal bleeding from recollapsing her lungs.

Then he added his final note: Robin had a head injury. There had been some swelling, and he had no idea how bad it was. To prepare us—and we wanted the truth—he explained that Robin might have to learn to read, speak, and eat all over again. She'd be like a child. I couldn't imagine my little sister, the brightest, funniest person I knew, reduced to that—just the possibility of it obliterated me, crushed my soul.

As the hours ticked away we began to fall into the rhythm of the ICU waiting room. Counting us, there were three families in there, plus various doctors coming and going, with relatives and loved ones hanging on their every word. Each time a doctor left there was a flurry of conversation that dwindled to silence as families either went to the pay phones to update absent relatives or settled in to wait for the next bit of news.

At first, Mom, Dad, and Michelle were all good team players. Dad curbed his I'm-in-charge-here-and-we'll-do-it-my-way mentality, Mom quietly coped with her disdain for Dad, and Michelle stayed by my side without complaint.

Then things started to change.

* * * * *

"Ron, we can't use up any more vacation days. If we do we'll have to give up our cruise next month and we need that trip. It's been four days and there's no telling how long Robin will be unconscious. You haven't called in sick for five years—call work and ask if they'll let you use your sick leave to stay here."

"What about unpaid leave?"

No way, she said. We needed the money bad. Rent was due in a few days, as well as some important bills; our finances were still a hopeless mess.

When work told me I couldn't use sick leave and I suggested unpaid leave again, Michelle said to me, "You don't understand. We have to get paid." Fed up with arguing about something that was so unimportant in the face of Robin's injuries, I bolted for the elevator.

As I walked down Roscoe Boulevard, alone in the Los Angeles heat, I couldn't hold back the tears. I shook my head and closed my eyes, trying to make it all just go away somehow. How could Michelle be thinking about something as meaningless as money when Robin might be dying?

Then there was the company—sure, they sprinkled me with atta-boys and named me salesman of the year—but apparently if the money train stopped for just one week, it was suddenly, what the fuck good are you?

When the chips are down you're alone in this shitty world; it's everyone for himself. All my life I'd been the funny one, the guy who tried to laugh, to cheer people up, to please others. If my sister died I didn't want to laugh again. Fuck the world and all the selfish bastards in it.

* * * * *

On my way back to the hospital I caught myself thinking, "So far I'm at 600 calories... If I eat just a bowl of soup at the cafeteria, I'll still only be at 900." Even in hell, I couldn't help counting calories and wondering whether this horror would be the shock therapy needed to dislodge my insanity. Of course, if I'd had the money I'd have loved to lose myself in a bucket of M&M's and the promise of future perfection.

* * * * *

A week later, Robin was still on the respirator, unconscious. It was decided—not by me—that Mom would stay by Robin's side and

Dad, Michelle, and I would go back to work, only returning if there was a change. According to Michelle, I didn't have a choice. We needed the money.

My first day back, I was a mess. Why was I working? I was just spinning in my hamster wheel, keeping all the assholes happy. I hated the world and I couldn't erase the image of my sister's chest, rising and falling as the machines pumped air into her broken body.

The door jingled as I entered Key Hong's coast-worn mini-mart not far from the Santa Cruz Boardwalk. Immediately he said, "Ron, your boss told me about your sister. How is she?"

Before he could finish his sentence, my eyes began to tear up. With all my pent-up emotions, I couldn't seem to hold it together for more than a few minutes. My retreat to two Big Macs, four cheese-burgers, a large order of fries, and a chocolate shake at 10:30 in the morning served only to thoroughly disgust me. I was so fucked up.

About halfway through the day I couldn't take it any longer. After calling my boss I called Michelle:

"I'm finishing today's calls and driving to Los Angeles to be with Robin. You can come if you want. I told Jim I don't give a shit about getting paid."

"What'd he say?"

"Nothing. It's not his call."

"I know she's your sister, but you can't just make a decision that affects both of us without talking it over with me first."

I didn't even answer, just hung up the phone. Fuck everyone.

※ ※ ※ ※ ※

Soon after Michelle and I went back to the hospital we got encouraging news: tests showed Robin's brain functions were normal. And then Michelle started up again:

"Ron, you have to do something about getting paid. We need the money."

"I really don't give a shit."

"Don't get mad at me, I'm just asking you to think about it. We have to deal with this."

Sure, I knew our finances had to be dealt with, but I didn't care. I'd sleep in my car to be by my sister's side. Maybe Michelle didn't understand because she'd never loved someone as much as I loved Robin.

Still Michelle had a point. I decided to call Sosnick again and explain the situation to the executive vice president. I'd never spoken to her and I wasn't sure she even knew who I was, but she'd seemed nice.

"Leslie Sosnick, please. It's Ron Saxen."

"One moment."

I gathered my thoughts, tried to hold back my emotion. I didn't want to come off like an idiot in front of someone so important, someone I hardly even knew. I couldn't believe I was reduced to begging.

"Hi, this is Leslie."

"Hello, Leslie. I don't know if you remember me. I'm the Santa Cruz sales rep, Ron Saxen."

"I'll be honest with you, ever since your branch merged into ours six months ago, I've been trying to put names to faces. I'm still trying, but what can I do for you?

A painful lump welled up in my throat. What can you do for me? How about waking me from this nightmare and telling me it was all a bad dream? I took a deep breath and blew off my whole logical explanation—I knew I didn't stand a chance of holding it together.

"My sister was in a terrible accident and may die." Saying that fractured the dam holding back my emotions. I proceeded slowly, no more than three or four words at a time. "And I need... to be with her... and... and I need... to get paid."

I pulled the receiver away from my face then, but she could probably hear my sniffling anyway.

"Take your time, Ron. It's okay, I'm here."

These caring words—words I so desperately needed to hear—from someone I didn't even know, let everything loose. "I called before... and they said... said no, it wouldn't be right. I ah... ah..."

"You don't have to say anything more. You take care of your sister—she needs you by her side. I'll take care of everything here."

A long pause. Finally I mustered up enough control to say, "Thank you"—and then I totally broke down and didn't care if she could hear me.

"Now you go to your sister. Call me if you need anything else."

I hung up the phone and let my emotions run free.

* * * * *

Robin came down with pneumonia and in the days that followed the doctors had to repeatedly vacuum blood and mucus out of her lungs to keep her oxygen levels up. Our spirits rose and fell on every bit of news.

And then one morning, fourteen days after the accident, Robin woke up.

We were all called into her room. Her eyes were open but she couldn't speak because she still had the ventilator tube in her throat. Her eyes blinked and we put a pen in the hand that was hooked up to the fewest machines and held a pad for her. Barely legibly, she wrote, "What happened to me?"

Fighting back emotion, I slapped a big ol' smile on my face, and said straight at her, "You drive like shit so you got into an accident. The good news is you're going to be fine. Can't say as much for your car, though. All in all, you've done wonderfully."

She just stared at me with bewildered eyes and started to write again. I picked up the paper. In the same barely legible scribble, "What happened to me?"

* * * * *

Shortly after Robin moved out of ICU we talked about the cruise she, Michelle, and I had planned for the summer. When I realized she was using it as a goal, a target to shoot for in her journey to recovery, I promised her she could still come along—everyone else said I was crazy.

Every day, inspired by the vision of her first cruise, Robin worked hard on her lung exercises, sat up in the chair beside her bed a little longer, shuffled a little farther in her walker, and tried to cut back on her pain medication. Watching her improve breathed life into my tattered soul.

A few days before the cruise, Michelle said, for the second time, "I don't think we should bring Robin with us—she's only been out of the hospital four days."

"There's no way I'm taking this away from her," I said. "She's earned it."

"What about me? I've been looking forward to this vacation for a long time, and I'm your wife."

And there it was, the selfish world rearing its ugly head again. My life was so shitty. Except for my sister, I was alone.

* * * * *

At first, the vacation was inspiring. We got a wheelchair so Robin could get around the ship more quickly and easily than she could with her walker. And then, after four sunny days, the seas got rough. Robin, her stomach weak from a constant onslaught of pain pills, became violently ill, her chills so bad she got the shakes. Oh God—had I fucked up in bringing her on this cruise? Had I really done it for her, or had I done it for me?

Michelle tore into me: "You shouldn't have brought her— you're risking her health. And what about me? You never gave a damn about how I felt about having your sister on our vacation."

I was so drained, I just let her go on. Maybe I did fuck up. But she had to know I'd meant well. Why pile it on?

While Robin rested, I slipped into the ship's twenty-four-hour snack bar to escape reality for a little while. Lying in bed that night, jammed full of food and disgusted with myself, I closed my eyes but left my mind open. For a guy who could be pretty perceptive at times, I was certainly a fucking idiot.

I was where I was simply because I hadn't had the balls to say "I don't" at my wedding eight years ago. If I'd had, it would have been a horrendous day—angry guests; returned bridesmaid dresses, tuxes, and wedding presents; Michelle and her parents wanting to string me up, with the police looking the other way, saying, "It's cool, I think he earned it"—but it would have been just one day, not eight years.

As if startled awake, my eyes suddenly opened wide: I was starting down a path that could only lead to one end—the end. I'd have loved to talk things over with Mark. Since he wasn't here, I was forced to play both parts:

"So Ron, do you deserve to be happy?"

"Yes."

"Are you happy?"

"No."

* * * * *

I wish I could say I followed through on my Mark-inspired decision the very next day. The truth is I wasn't that strong, and Mark wasn't there to back me up. My only chance would have been to wake Michelle up that night, say my piece, throw her a salute, and do a swan dive off the ship into the deep blue. The only flaw in that plan was the 200-mile swim to shore.

In the months following the cruise, Robin took great pride in graduating from wheelchair to walker to cane. When she first returned to work she was emotionally fragile and worried she wouldn't have the brainpower to continue in her fast-paced, high-pressure job. But as the days and weeks ticked by, she got stronger. Soon enough, she was showing the old Robin spirit, tastefully displaying her walker high on the wall behind her desk as "crash art."

I, too, returned to work. After my first sales meeting since Robin's accident, I spotted Leslie Sosnick in the hallway, heading toward me—she was a cute, petite, five-foot-zero blonde, the only person who had reached out to me in my time of need. I thought she probably didn't know who I was, however—she'd said on the phone she hadn't put names to faces yet.

"Ron?"

I stopped in my tracks, keeping a respectful distance.

"Yes?"

"I thought that was you."

Before I had time to think, she stepped forward and put her hand on my right arm, looking directly into my eyes. The gesture stunned me—reached into my heart and totally disarmed me.

"How's your sister doing?"

My composure disintegrated. Red-faced, I said, "Fine."

"And how are you doing? It's important that your sister's big brother is doing well, too, you know."

With that same lack of charisma, I said, slowly, "I'm great... doing great."

She squeezed my arm warmly.

"If you need anything let me know."

My eyes started to moisten. I couldn't speak, just nodded—yes. She let go of my arm and I escaped to the conference room.

When I'd first spoken to Leslie about Robin's accident and she'd been so helpful, I'd figured she might be handing out charity so she could say, "See how nice I am?" But not Leslie. Leslie was genuine. It was a wonderful thing to see such goodness. A month later, after a personnel shift put Leslie in charge of accounts receivable, she and I began talking about collections once a week.

*   *   *   *   *

After my revelation on the cruise, I had to face the fact that there wasn't a single good thing in my life except work—and even that was neutralized by our financial irresponsibility. It was easy to blame Michelle, but I knew I also had myself to blame—why had I married her? If I could go back eight years to the Marines' sick bay and talk to bald, scared Ron, I'd tell him to relax, take a deep breath, and be patient with life—and definitely not rush into anything.

But at this point there was little I could do about my life. First, I didn't have any money. Our finances were a mess, and Michelle controlled them. I didn't have a credit card, a checkbook, or an ATM card. If I couldn't even get twenty bucks without Michelle knowing about it, how could I leave?

Then there was the inevitable yelling and screaming and hating. Sometimes I was even afraid of what Michelle might do to herself—or me—if I decided to walk out. And then there was my lifetime conviction that I was a failure, that this was my fault—what could I have done to make the marriage better? Nope, I wasn't going anywhere.

I'd made my bed. Now I had to find a way to lie in it, to find happiness in the miserable world I'd created. In keeping with that philosophy, I decided to go back to school to get a master's in my first love, history. I planned to get my credential and then teach. Might as well work less—didn't matter how much money I made anyway: whether I made $20,000 or $120,000, we'd always be broke. Sadly, it was also my way of getting back at Michelle.

* * * * *

I took a class in women's history; we studied the diary of a Jewish widow who had lived in Germany in the sixteenth century. I got a kick out of learning something new, and it was fun talking to Leslie about Jewish traditions—or actually, about pretty much anything. Before I knew it, we went from talking once a week to one to three times a day. Talking to Leslie was what I looked forward to most in the day.

One night, a few months later, I realized that Leslie had also become the last thing I thought about before I fell asleep and the first thing I thought about when I woke. When I stared at Michelle across the living room and felt guilty, I knew what was happening was wrong.

Lying in bed that night, I finally admitted to myself how I felt about Leslie. Acknowledging my feelings was both scary and electrifying. Since she outranked me by a mile, we were both married, and in person she scared the hell out of me, it would have to be a secret crush. I didn't care though—it just felt good to feel good about something, even something impossible. After all, if I ever told her how I felt, her reply might well be, "Good for you—you're fired!"

* * * * *

My friendship with Leslie changed my firm belief that men and women couldn't be true friends. I was intrigued by Leslie. She fascinated me, not only because of her warm, true heart, but also because she didn't fit the typical mold of a powerful person. When she said something that exposed the difference in our backgrounds, I didn't feel inferior; we just had fun with it.

"The best part of my trip to Seattle was the restaurants the concierge set us up at."

"The concierge?"

"Yes."

"At the restaurant?"

"No. Do you know what a concierge is?"

"Of course I do. Who do you think you're talking to, honey?"

"I'm waiting."

"The concierge is the guy that hooked you up with the restaurants."

"So, who is a concierge, Ron?"

"Obviously he's a cierge that's served his time in prison. That's why they call him a con-cierge. If he'd ever broken out of jail, he'd be called an escaped con-cierge. I think it's great what they're doing now to rehabilitate convicts. Was it hard to look past all those tattoos?"

She laughed. "Do you give up?"

"No, but go ahead. What do *you* think a concierge is?""

"A concierge works at a hotel—he helps you make dinner plans, buy theater tickets, things like that."

"Oh, *that* kind of concierge. Why didn't you say so? I knew that. When I was a kid we called them by their Motel 6 name: the phone book."

* * * * *

It was curious. The destructive voices in my head had quieted and I'd begun to lose some weight. I hadn't noticed a specific moment when the noise decreased, it just had. I was cautious, though—been down that road before. When I searched for an explanation, all I could come up with was school, and of course, Leslie—two good things that hadn't been there before.

Whenever I fantasized about the impossible—life with Leslie—I'd be snatched from my daydream by the enemy, the wrong Ron. A woman so perfect deserved absolute perfection, not someone as flawed as I was. And the fact that, I'd only ever spent fifteen minutes in her presence, although we spoke five to seven hours a week on the phone, wasn't encouraging. For me the phone was safe—it hid me.

Still the goodness of Leslie and the fantasy of life with Leslie wrapped itself around me like a warm nurturing blanket, keeping me cozy and safe against the darkness. Oh how I wished I were normal!

As the months passed and our friendship strengthened, Leslie began referring to me as her special friend. I decided to risk telling her about my past, about the wrong Ron. Sure she might think I was weak and nuts, but I knew what I was doing: if I hoped to get to the other side, to Leslie's heart, I had to first walk through the minefield; risking it all was my only option. Even if going forward meant my own destruction—fired and divorced—I would not and could not let myself slide back into the abyss.

* * * * *

It was Friday, the day of our monthly sales meeting, and I'd arranged everything. I'd told Leslie I had something to tell her—and that it had to be said in person (yet another thing to be freaked out about). I went to work early, placed my copies of *Sports Fitness and Training* and *Muscle & Fitness* under some papers on her desk.

I wore black polyester pants because black is supposed to be slimming, and a baggy rust-colored shirt that hid the unflattering curves of my 265-pound body. If I'd been 85 pounds lighter, my old modeling weight, I was sure that the chances of this conversation going well would be that much higher. Still, I was proud of the 20 pounds I'd lost since I'd become Leslie's special friend.

Seeing her that morning sent me into a panic—it was all I could do not to pull the fire alarm and run. When she suggested I join her in her car so we could talk privately while she ran some company errands, I panicked even further. Walking out the front door with the executive VP, and climbing into her car while twenty sets of eyes watched was surreal—if the world and Leslie only knew how much this unfolding scene meant to me!

In the next hour I emptied my soul. Leslie listened and comforted—and then we cried together. At the end, when she saw the book and the magazine, I could see she was moved.

For me the experience was a dream come true. My only uncertain hope was that something positive, something more, had happened. Later that day, when I gave her a call and she said, "It's wonderful to hear your voice—every time the phone rang I hoped it was you," I thought maybe it had.

It had been almost a year since the cruise. Now, thanks to the fantasy of life with Leslie that burned inside me, the resolve I'd felt on the ship was finally back—and this time I didn't have 200 miles of ocean hindering my exit.

* * * * *

After I dropped the bomb, Michelle cried and said some hard things, but nothing surprising. I think she wanted to be meaner but—for the first time in our marriage—I was so calm and certain that she knew this wasn't a fight she could come back from. It was over.

Even though I was doing the right thing for both of us, I still felt like shit—I had taken up years of her life after all. I told her she could keep all the money in the 401(k)s and I'd take all the bills. I'd have thrown in a kidney for the chance to start over.

My offer to pay the bills seemed to calm her down. Or maybe she wasn't in love with me anymore either. I didn't see how she could be—we were very unhappy together.

After I'd said my piece and answered all her questions, she seemed cool and rational, but I didn't want to spend another night with her. People do strange things when they're wounded—and I had no reason to think Michelle would be an exception to that rule. With that in the back of my mind, I packed a few things and headed over to stay with my friends Jeff and Beth.

* * * * *

The next morning I woke up on Jeff and Beth's living room floor. My first thought, "Where am I?" was followed by, "Oh shit!" Not, "Oh shit, I made a mistake!" just, "Oh shit, I'm thirty-three and sleeping on someone else's floor."

It occurred to me that I'd played this scene once before, more than a decade ago—the first time I'd broken up with Michelle. That time I'd woken up on Mark's couch with nothing to my name but a box containing all my worldly goods. Ten years later I had the same box, plus a fist full of bills.

I drank in the magnitude of my sins—sins I'd committed against myself by making dumbfuck decisions and not having the balls to change course. In my thirty-three years, I'd already done so much and lost so much.

The day before, I'd woken up in my own place. I'd made my good-morning pot of coffee and taken my daily run through the tall redwoods. I'd had dogs and cats who set their clocks by me. Now I was lying on someone else's dark hardwood floor in a place that was totally foreign to me, a big-screen TV at my feet and Beth's artful photos on the wall. I still didn't have an ATM card, a credit card, or a checkbook. Just the forty bucks Robin had given me to get by on until my next paycheck.

I was only thirty-three but I felt old. To cheer myself up I said, aloud, "Better late than never." A cliché, but true.

At least, I hoped so.

* * * * *

"It's your turn, Ron—one more set and we're out of here."

"So, Jeff, burritos after our lift?"

Jeff, a tall, muscular Swede, and Beth, a spunky, cute, intelligent redhead, were my day-to-day support team. The two months I'd spent on their living room floor had been the best in recent memory.

Our evenings were filled with workouts and me spewing forth my life, with them offering advice and reassurance—plus, of course, the occasional evening group therapy we called getting drunk together. It reminded me of my days with Mark. Seems I've needed a lot of rescuing in my life.

In the time I'd spent with Jeff and Beth I'd lost another 25 pounds, putting me at 242, my lowest weight in seven years—very good for my confidence with Leslie. Leslie and I continued to inch our way to the edge of the precipice, our conversations often drifting in a direction we both knew wasn't normal for friends. One time I really crossed the line:

"So, Ron, if you're around the office this Friday, do you want to go to lunch?"

"I'm sorry, you said get a hotel where?"

"You're bad."

"I'm sorry, did you just say, 'The Holiday Inn isn't bad?'"

Happily my new days were so busy there wasn't much room for insanity. I couldn't remember the last time the voices had been this quiet. When I wasn't talking to Leslie, I was thinking about her. Other than that I was doing my job, working out with Jeff, having dinner with him and Beth, and repeatedly luring them into long counseling sessions.

However, what Jeff and Beth didn't know was that I had something planned that could change my life forever. If they'd known, I'm sure they would have tried to stop me.

* * * * *

"You've reached the voice mail of Leslie Sosnick. Please leave a message and I'll call you as soon as I can. *Beeeeep!*"

"Good morning, Leslie. Of course, it's Ron. I've been doing a lot of thinking… And well… so much has been said." I had to stop to clear my throat. "What I'm trying to say is… I love you. There it is, now I've said it."

My free hand was shaking. I sucked in a deep breath and—before I could change my mind—pushed the pound sign. Done. The voice mail was sent. At that point, the only ones who knew my secret were me and the computer storing the unretrieved message. In about sixty minutes, Leslie would join that list.

On the drive to the sales meeting my heart and my brain couldn't seem to stop racing. When I stopped at Starbuck's, I felt like saying to the guy behind the counter, "If, in the next forty-five minutes, the woman of my dreams doesn't spray me with mace or fire me, this'll be a really good day."

I'd had to say the L word. We'd gotten stuck, neither of us willing to take the next step. If one of us didn't push forward soon, we risked losing all of our momentum. Leaving a voice mail was a simple solution—no balls necessary.

I would've felt guilty about her husband, but they weren't happy. Leslie provided everything in their relationship, financially and emotionally; he was a taker. If I could give Leslie the happiness she deserved, I wasn't going to waste any time feeling bad about her leaving him.

I'd convinced myself that if Leslie loved me back then it was game, set, and match. I'd become the new Ron, determined to stand up for my own happiness. I was finally ready to stop watching myself do things I didn't want to do. If I wouldn't stand up for myself, who would?

Just before entering Sosnick headquarters, I looked toward Leslie's office. Was she looking out at me? Was she freaked good or freaked bad? This moment had been building between us for months.

Entering the large twenty-cubicle office, I walked directly and purposefully toward Leslie's corner. Pausing before I got too close, I took in a deep breath and transferred the moisture from my hands to my pants, then continued forward—shit, she wasn't there.

The only other place she could be was in the conference room where the sales meeting was just minutes away from starting. After another quick swipe of my hands on my pants—and another deep breath—I entered the boisterous conference room. There she was, wearing a short, black skirt and a holiday-colored sweater. I just stared. At that moment I had all the hope in the world—and the knowledge that sixty seconds later everything could change, horribly or wonderfully.

I closed the distance between us and placed myself right behind the two salespeople she was chatting with. Our eyes met and for a moment her expression became very serious; then she forced a smile to pretend normalcy in front of the two salespeople. To rescue her, I said, "What's up, guys?"

"Hey, Ron, how's it going?"

When their heads turned my way, Leslie looked directly at me and mouthed, "Me, too."

2002–2005

CHAPTER 19

The Good Eater

Flying home from Minneapolis, after attending a sales conference for the Tennant Company, the largest manufacturer of industrial cleaning equipment in the world, I found myself thinking about my luck. When Sosnick was sold to our biggest competitor, Core-Mark International, some years back, I hadn't been able to bear working for an old enemy that ran such a sloppy organization, so I'd decided to get out of the wholesale business completely. I still couldn't believe I was now lucky enough to be part of one of *Fortune* magazine's hundred best firms to work for.

In fact, I couldn't believe how lucky I was in all ways. Within the next sixty minutes I'd be met at baggage claim by that same cute, petite, five-foot-zero blonde who had once scared the hell out of me. If I hadn't happened to call Leslie after my sister's accident, we would never have shared these last six magical years. Just as my dad's departure when I was sixteen felt like the darkest kind of magic, Leslie's arrival felt like the brightest.

She'd taken me in, huge flaws and all. She'd proven her love right from the very beginning, offering words of encouragement when I blew out my knee and my weight climbed from 218 to 267 in the two years following my knee surgery.

Even during that weight gain, something changed for the better. For the first time in my life I gained weight like a normal person, not an insane one. I stopped exercising and kept eating and the weight piled on—as it does for anyone with a healthy appreciation for chocolate and pizza.

* * * * *

It took me a while to figure out the difference between the insanity of the wrong Ron and the normal process of eating too much dinner and refusing to wave off an extra dessert. Discerning the difference was difficult because both actions led to the same unhappy result—being overweight when I didn't want to be. I still had mornings when I was a little blue about my weight, but nothing like the past.

Don't get me wrong. In the past six years, I'd fallen off the wagon more than a few times, but the episodes hadn't been as big or as long as they were during those dark years before I met Leslie. She and I had debated why I no longer acted as crazily with food as I used to. The first, most obvious answer was that there were now far fewer reasons to be insane in my life—fewer negative voices and, consequently, fewer things I felt a need to escape from.

One important step to getting to this point was quieting the negative voices related to being a quitter and working a meaningless job. I worked for Sosnick for seven wonderful years, and was at this point starting my sixth year at the Tennant Company, a company recognized as the best at what they did in all the world, a company with the highest caliber of people, and one I was extremely proud to be a part of.

Another thing that helped was finally gaining control over my own finances—something I'd definitely lacked in my marriage to Michelle. It used to tear me up that no matter how much money I made it didn't seem to make any difference. Michelle and I would fight about it, I'd get nowhere, and then I'd escape by pigging out—or getting drunk and pigging out.

I was both amused and appreciative when Leslie guided me through the activation of my first ATM card. "Now write your secret code someplace safe—not your underwear." It was strange to realize I hadn't been inside a bank in over seven years.

I took great pride in paying off all the old bills. When a collection agency tracked me down and started in with their spiel, I shocked them by saying, "I believe you, I'm sure I owe you something—just send me a bill."

Abandoning extreme dieting and forbidden foods was also good for me. I learned to do both one day while I was in my car making sales calls. I flipped on the radio and heard Dr. Dean Edell say, "To lose weight properly, and in a lasting way, you need to make a life change. After restrictive dieting is over, people tend to go back to what got them there in the first place. The only lasting changes are those you can live with for the rest of your life."

At times it has been tempting to revert back to the old days of excessive exercise and restrictive dieting for the positive reinforcement of a quick but unhealthy weight loss. But I know now that not only is this type of weight loss bad for me, it also plain doesn't work.

The second thing Dr. Dean Edell mentioned that day was his philosophy of "Eat, drink, and be merry." Ever since I'd been a child, eating even just one candy bar made me feel like a complete failure. That one candy bar would trigger the negative voices: "You've blown it—you might as well eat the whole place now," and before I knew it, the wrong Ron would take over.

But the truth is, whether I eat a 500-calorie turkey sandwich or the 500 calories contained in a Snickers bar and a bag of M&M's, the number of calories is the same. The day I chose to skip the turkey sandwich in favor of two candy bars was one of the most important days of my life. Slapping the candy bars on the counter and smiling at the 7-11 clerk, saying, "That's my lunch," was more empowering than I could've imagined. I admit that sometimes two candy bars leads to four, but never twenty-four. I rarely have the Hershey lunch, but it's nice to know I can and there's nothing to be afraid of.

Since Leslie and I don't do much cooking and spend a lot of evenings out, I've also had to adjust to eating at restaurants more frequently—which I love. Initially I kept myself from eating too much by planning ahead, deciding exactly how to handle the meal before it arrived. First course would typically be a salad; if it was something more caloric, I just ate half; same philosophy with the main course and dessert.

Eventually, successful dining out got easier and my plan became simple: order whatever I damn well pleased—dessert included—and eat just enough to be satisfied. Didn't always work out, of course. Sometimes you're crazy hungry and the food is just too damn good. Still, just trying helped my "proper eating at restaurants" climb from a measly 5 percent to a smug 90. I used to despise people who finished only half of the dessert on their plates—now I was one of them.

Speaking of dessert, I used to love rewarding myself with a sweet treat when I'd get a new customer, close a deal, or max out a promotion—sometimes I still do. In the old days, a reward that started out as one king-size Snickers usually didn't end until I'd downed two pounds of candy, three Big Macs, large fries, a large shake, and, if my stomach would allow it, seconds of all of the above. Now I usually reward myself with a trip to the movies. I can always tell when business is good—I've seen everything playing in the theaters. And the few times when I do opt for sugar, it's been a king-size Snickers and a regular Reese's—and that's it.

* * * * *

After my plane from Minneapolis landed, I quickly splashed water on my face and checked my hair before making the long walk to baggage claim to hug the biggest reason for my reduced insanity, Leslie herself. Loving her has made me realize I've never been in love before.

I'm lucky as hell and I know it.

"Sweetie?"

There she was, my favorite half-pint. Because we both have a goofy side, we ran to each other with outstretched arms like a commercial on TV.

* * * * *

My father and I now have what for us is a good relationship; to my pleasant surprise, I believe it has the possibility of becoming even more. Twice in recent years, while enjoying ourselves over glasses of cabernet, he's suddenly stopped, gotten teary-eyed, and apologized for the past.

My grandmother has told me that if my father were to write about *his* childhood, part of his story would be very much like mine. It seems our story really began in the late 1920s with my great-grandfather, who had a head injury that left pieces of glass embedded in his skull. As a result, he'd fly into fits of rage so severe that my grandfather's life would be threatened. In turn, my grandfather then beat the hell out of my father—who in his turn was rough with me. I like to think the beatings diminished with each generation.

My dad has gone through a couple of failed marriages and finally settled down with the right woman—one with enough spunk to challenge him when he's over the top but also provide the spice he needs for a meaningful life.

Mom went on to marry a nice man with a kind heart whom she met through her church. After graduating from Fresno State University in agri-business, she worked as an administrator in the agricultural departments of several state and federal government agencies. A few years ago she retired from her position managing a U.S. Department of Agriculture office in northern Iowa.

Unfortunately, thanks to the church she's attended so faithfully for almost forty years, we've recently become estranged. When she made the choice to put her God first and our family second, I had no choice but to say good-bye—hopefully not forever.

Michelle remarried six weeks after our divorce was final. Over the years she sent me two letters; I read neither of them. Using Google, she tracked me down again in the winter of 2005 and wrote me a nice e-mail, saying that after two more divorces she was now in a good place emotionally and living successfully in the Pacific Northwest. She's now working with horses, a rewarding occupation for someone who all her life dreamed of becoming a veterinarian.

My sister Robin went on to work with George Lucas at Industrial Light and Magic. For a wonderful little while she lived just a mile and a half from me and Leslie. When she invited me over for lunch to tell me she was gay, I knew what I was about to hear. As she said, "I've got some big news," I fired back, "I know what you're going to say." We went back and forth until I told her she had to go first in case I'd guessed wrong. I was right; I can't think of anything more wonderful than her happiness and the courage she shows in being herself.

My brother Robert is the family member who's kicked the most ass financially. Of the three boys, he always seemed to get the worst of Dad's wrath and take it the hardest. His way of getting even was to become one of the best salesmen on earth, beating Dad at his own game. And after a couple of bad marriages, Robert has finally found the right woman for him. He has his own water purification business in Arizona and is doing extremely well.

After years of languishing in the restaurant business and selling insurance for my father, my oldest brother Rick discovered something amazing—he's damn good at what he does. He moved to Las Vegas and became one of the best insurance agents in the city. He has almost as much business as he can handle because people like him and trust him—as they should. He's happily married to his wife Georgia; they've recently adopted her three grandkids, a blessing for all five of them.

My sister Rebecca and I are also estranged because of her continued involvement in the church and her constant need to be rescued—and the fact that we just plain don't get along. While she's on my do-not-call list, I continue to hope that one day soon she will find her way.

The last time I saw Mark in person was in the fall of 1986 when we said our good-byes as I shipped out to the Marine Corps and he entered the Highway Patrol Academy. I say, "saw him in person" because seven years later I did see him on TV—he was arresting someone on *Stories of the Highway Patrol.* Roughly every five years I figure out where he's stationed and have someone leave a message in his box—so far to no avail. It's my hope that the very existence of this book will be powerful enough magic to get him to return my call and renew our friendship.

Wade Ashford finally quit running from the law, his family, and his creditors, about the same time he quit doing drugs. Through determination and bravery he's made amends to his family. Last I heard he'd moved to Vancouver, Canada, and was making a name for himself in the ecotourism business.

Leslie and I are doing wonderfully and are constantly thankful for the miracle that is our life and our love. We know how lucky we are and that's a good thing. Periodically we look back at how we came to be and are still amazed. Our luck is never more apparent than when we leave the theater after watching a beautiful love story. We don't quietly walk away, saying to ourselves, "Wouldn't it be great if...?" For us the movie fantasy is our reality.

I was twenty-one when I first sat in a modeling agency. Twenty-one years later, with a therapist on tap and a healthy diet and exercise plan carefully mapped out, I embarked on a journey to take me back to modeling. It was to be a challenging and surprising adventure. But that's another story.

* * * * *

I decided to write this book while Leslie and I were in New Zealand, visiting Robin and her partner Grace, who both worked in post production for *The Lord of the Rings*. We were waiting for my sister to get home with our tickets to the world premiere of *Lord of the Rings: The Return of the King*. Yes, we would be in the same theater as Liv Tyler, Elijah Wood, Viggo Mortensen, and the rest of the cast—apparently Robin's accident hadn't put a dent in her career.

A few years previously, for my own amusement, I'd gotten back into comedy, writing jokes for others—even sold a few. So when Robin had asked me the previous year to write some jokes to forward on to relax her overworked crew, I'd been thrilled by the opportunity and sent her a couple hundred jokes. When she asked for more for the most recent movie, I was tapped out of things to say that wouldn't piss off Frodo and jeopardize my sister's paycheck.

So instead I wrote a story about a guy who escaped from San Quentin and stowed away on ships, jumped on trains, stole cars, hijacked planes, and led a bloodless coup of Pitcairn Island, the island inhabited by the descendents of those who'd mutinied long ago on the *Bounty*. The story ended when the main character, Ron, reached his final destination, Wellington, New Zealand. I timed the story so the last one-thousand-word installment was sent just before I boarded the plane to New Zealand. When I arrived I was amazed at how much some of her crew loved what I had written.

As Leslie and I sat on my sister's couch, sipping New Zealand wine and gazing out a bay window at the cobalt blue of the Tasman Sea, I had a thought, "Sweetie, I've been doing some thinking. You know I'm totally blown away by the reaction of Robin's crew to my story. Maybe I should give the jokes a rest. Years ago I talked about writing a book about my life. Maybe I should give that a whirl."

"If that's what you want to do, you should do it."

"But do I really have enough material for a book?"

"Just start writing—something'll come to you."

"Maybe I can impart some advice in a very long list of dos and don'ts. Like don't number 187: never follow up an hour on the treadmill by eating a whale—bad math and Greenpeace'll be pissed..."

"Right."

A month later, back in California, I spent a full Saturday combing the aisles of a large bookstore, hoping something would jump out at me that would help me increase my project from a booklet to a book.

I browsed through dieting, fitness, successful selling, relationships, comedy writing, and travel, looking for angles to lengthen my book. While they were certainly all things I could write about, I wasn't much of an authority on any of them—except maybe selling. I wandered into the psychology/self-help area. Maybe there was something psychological about having two lives in school? I ran my eyes across the shelves.

Wait—*Binge No More*? Bingeing was a good name for what I'd done so frequently back in the dark days, but a whole book on it? To me bingeing, if that's what it was called, was nothing more than really, really blowing your diet.

I opened the book. A few minutes later my life was changed forever.

* * * * *

That day in the bookstore I discovered I wasn't alone in my darkness and that I sure as hell wasn't insane. I had—or still have, depending on which way you swing medically—binge eating disorder (BED). (People tend to associate eating disorders more frequently with women than with men; however, while men make up only 10 percent of the eleven million sufferers of anorexia nervosa and bulimia nervosa in the United States, they make up a full 40 percent of the six million sufferers of BED.)

This discovery has made an immeasurable impact on my life. Until this point, I'd known I'd gotten better but not how; it was like getting the answer to a geometry question right without knowing how you'd solved it—feels like you got it wrong anyway. My guess was that I'd gotten better because I was happier—which meant that if the happiness went then darkness would return. Not a pleasant thought.

Binge No More showed me how the wrong Ron had been created. And if I could understand how he was made, he could be unmade. With my new knowledge I reviewed the story of my life and discovered the mystery of my bingeing wasn't a mystery at all—it was actually highly predictable. What started out as a way to cope with my chaotic childhood evolved into my weapon of choice for any stressful situation—good or bad.

Reading *Binge No More* also showed me why I had improved. And knowing how I'd done it, I stood a better chance of staying that way. To aid in recovery, the book also offered ways to eliminate the eat-one-cookie-and-you-might-as-well-eat-the-whole-box mind-set of black-and-white thinking, ways to improve my coping skills, ways to challenge problem thinking, and ways to overcome backsliding—something we all face.

When it comes to recovery, I firmly believe I did it the wrong way. Getting lucky in love is nice if it happens, but you don't need to wait for love to save you. If I'd read a book like *Binge No More* by Dr. Joyce Nash or *The Eating Disorder Sourcebook* by Carolyn Costin—or gotten in touch with an organization like NEDA (National Eating Disorder Association)—I wouldn't have suffered as long as I did.

If my darkest days rated full tens on the misery scale, after I met Leslie my life began to consistently fall between wonderful threes and fives. Since I've discovered the truth, I've lived in the one to two universe—an amazing place I've never lived before.

I don't have the perfect peace. I don't think one exists for me—maybe it doesn't for anyone. What I do have is an imperfect peace—one that I will take with a smile.

Be well.